Cromwell's Convicts

Cromwell's Convicts

The Death March from Dunbar 1650

John Sadler and Rosie Serdiville

Pen & Sword
MILITARY

First published in Great Britain in 2020 by
Pen & Sword Military
An imprint of
Pen & Sword Books Ltd
Yorkshire – Philadelphia

ISBN 978 1 52673 820 2

A CIP catalogue record for this book is
available from the British Library.

Printed and bound in the UK by TJ International Ltd,
Padstow, Cornwall.

Pen & Sword Books Limited incorporates the imprints of Atlas,
Archaeology, Aviation, Discovery, Family History, Fiction, History,
Maritime, Military, Military Classics, Politics, Select, Transport,
True Crime, Air World, Frontline Publishing, Leo Cooper, Remember
When, Seaforth Publishing, The Praetorian Press, Wharncliffe
Local History, Wharncliffe Transport, Wharncliffe True Crime
and White Owl.

For a complete list of Pen & Sword titles please contact

PEN & SWORD BOOKS LIMITED
47 Church Street, Barnsley, South Yorkshire, S70 2AS, England
E-mail: enquiries@pen-and-sword.co.uk
Website: www.pen-and-sword.co.uk

Or

PEN AND SWORD BOOKS
1950 Lawrence Rd, Havertown, PA 19083, USA
E-mail: Uspen-and-sword@casematepublishers.com
Website: www.penandswordbooks.com

Contents

Dedicated to all those who have been forced to build a new life away from their own homes. Among them the men of Dunbar whose stories are only now being told.

Acknowledgements

The fatal field ... where the desperate few ... defeated and totally overthrew the great army of the other side ... to the surprise of the world ...

Daniel Defoe, A tour thro' the whole island of Great Britain *(1724–7)*

Many of us growing up in the 1960s first encountered the British Civil Wars through fiction. The BBC's *Gamble for a Throne* in the early 1960s, novelists G.A. Henty and Captain Marryat, the film *Cromwell* starring Richard Harris and Alec Guinness; they all ignited our interest: that led on to the great historians of the twentieth century – such as C.V. Wedgwood. Of course, then it was referred to as the English Civil War. Decades on, the nomenclature has changed but our debt to those early sources remains.

We would particularly like to thank John Malden who so generously shared his invaluable research, Stephen Lowdon of Berwick parish church, Carol-Ann Miller of the Scottish Assembly, Tobias Capwell of Glasgow Museums, Charlotte Chipchase of the Royal Armouries, Leeds, Helen Nicoll of the National Museum of Scotland, Ailsa Mactaggart of Historic Scotland, Alison Lindsay and staff from The National Records of Scotland, The National Archive at Kew, Newcastle City Libraries, Colm O'Brien and other colleagues at Explore, the Society of Antiquaries of Newcastle upon Tyne, the staff of the Great North Museum, the staff of the Literary and Philosophical Society of Newcastle upon Tyne, staff at Woodhorn County Museum and Archive, staff at East Lothian Library and Archives Service, staff and volunteers at the Civil War Centre in Newark, staff and volunteers at the Lost Lives Exhibition on Durham's Palace Green, staff and volunteers at Newcastle and Durham cathedrals, Tony Fox and Geoffrey Carter of UK Battlefields Trust, Dr David

Caldwell, Adam Goldwater, Charles Wesencraft, Arran Johnson, the staff at East Lothian Records Office, Adam Barr for the specialist photographs, Chloe Rodham for the maps and Rupert Harding and Alison Flowers at Pen & Sword for another successful collaboration.

The American descendants of the men of Dunbar have been incredibly helpful in the preparation of this book, sharing histories, information and insights with great generosity. We would particularly like to thank: Misty Scheidt, Scott Fair, Marlene Lemmer Beeson, Becky Richardson, Roger Spring, Doreen Gray Leahy, Teresa Hamilton Rust, Bob Guy, Lawrence Claflin, Alice Waters, Michelle Start, Michele Fuller, Phil Swan, Skip Myers, Donna Myers Davison, Jean Seeley, Eve Hiatt and Douglas Darling.

Chris Gerrard and Andrew Millard at Durham University have been open handed with their experience and ideas – offering highly useful insights and comments that have done much to shape our ideas. We are deeply grateful to them, though they cannot be held in any way responsible for the opinions given in this book.

The Durham Team have put together a free MOOC (Massive Open Online Course) which will be of particular interest to anyone interested in the battle. You can find details here: The Battle of Dunbar 1650 – Online Course, www.futurelearn.com.

For all errors and omissions, the authors remain, as ever, responsible.

Rosie Serdiville and John Sadler, summer 2019

List of Maps and Plates

Maps

1. Battle of Dunbar
2. The Prisoners' Progress
3. Durham City

Plates

1. The harbour, Dunbar
2. Dunbar from Doon Hill
3. The Trial of Charles I
4. David Leslie, by unknown
5. Oliver Cromwell, by Circle of Adriaen Hanneman
6. Sir Arthur Hesilrige, by unknown
7. Looking up Doon Hill
8. A typical Dunbar cottage
9. Dunbar churchyard
10. The other Dunbar war memorial
11. Dunbar remembers
12. The entrance to Dunbar harbour from the landward side
13. Dunbar harbour today
14. Looking out to sea from Dunbar harbour
15. The old harbour at Dunbar
16. The ruins of Dunbar Castle
17. The monument to the men of Dunbar
18. Inside the walls of Berwick
19. The churchyard at Berwick
20. The road from Berwick
21. The walled garden at Morpeth Castle today
22. The interior of St Nicholas' Cathedral, Newcastle upon Tyne

Timeline

1638

28 February   Signing of the Covenant

1639

19 June   Pacification of Berwick signed

1640

20 August   Leven crosses the border
28 August   Battle of Newburn
30 August   Newcastle falls
26 October   Treaty of Ripon

1641

25 August   Scots army stood down
23 October   Violence in Ireland begins

1642

22 August   Charles raises his standard at Nottingham, Civil War begins

1643

18 August   Scots begin to mobilise
25 September   Signing of the Solemn League and Covenant

1644

19 January   Leven crosses the Tweed
February–March   Campaign in North East England
2 July   Battle of Marston Moor
29 August   Montrose raises the Royal Standard at Blair Athol
September   Montrose wins victories at Tippermuir and Aberdeen

1645

2 February	Montrose wins Battle of Inverlochy
9 May	Montrose wins at Auldearn
14 June	Decisive Parliamentary victory at Naseby
15 August	Montrose wins again at Kilsyth
13 September	Montrose defeated at Philiphaugh by David Leslie, atrocities follow

1646

5 May	Charles surrenders to Leven at Newark

1647

February	Scots army is 're-modelled'
26 December	The Engagers swap sides and support Charles I

1648

23 March	2nd Civil War kicks off
4 May	Scots begin to mobilise
17 August	The Engagers at Preston are defeated by Lambert and Cromwell
19 August	Scottish survivors surrender at Warrington
1 October	General ceasefire

1649

30 January	Execution of Charles I

1650

27 April	Montrose defeated at Carbisdale
21 May	Montrose executed
24 June	Charles II signs the Covenant and arrives in Scotland
25 June	Scots begin mobilisation
22 July	Cromwell invades Scotland
28 August	Cromwell retreats to Dunbar
3 September	Battle of Dunbar
3/4 September	Badly wounded Scots and camp-followers released

4–11 September   POWs are marched from Dunbar via Berwick-upon-Tweed, Belford, Alnwick, Morpeth, Newcastle upon Tyne and Chester-le-Street to Durham

1651

1 January   Charles II crowned at Scone

3 September   Cromwell wins the Battle of Worcester

3 December   Earl of Balcarres surrenders Scots forces

2013

23 November   First archaeological traces of mass burials uncovered on Durham's Palace Green

Being Introductory

Trail all your pikes, dispirit every drum.
March in slow procession from afar.
Be silent ye dejected men of war!
Be still the haut boys and the flute be dumb!
Display no more in vain, the lofty banner;
For see! Where on the bier before ye lies
The pale, the fall'n, the unlikely sacrifice,
To your mistaken shrine, to your false idol honour

Anne, Countess of Winchelsea (1661–1720)

'I beseech you in the bowels of Christ think it possible you may be mistaken'. So Oliver Cromwell, not quite yet Lord Protector, implored the Scottish Parliament to abandon their shaky alliance with Charles II. He failed to persuade. The campaign which followed, desultory at the outset, ended with Cromwell's decisive victory at Dunbar on 3 September 1650. Many regarded this as his finest hour. What ensued was not.

That September, approximately 5,000 men began a forced march from the battlefield of Dunbar to Durham, destined for the southern ports. It took them seven days, without food or medical care and with little water. They were now property; the chattels of a ruthless regime determined to eradicate any possibility of further threat. Hundreds died while at least thirty were summarily executed on this English trail of tears. Of course, there were others who made their escape along the way.

Those who survived long enough to reach Durham found no respite, only disease and despair. Exhausted, starving and dreadfully weakened, perhaps another 1,700 died there – most probably from fever and dysentery. For those who survived hard labour awaited them. They faced forced exile as virtual slaves in a harsh new world across the Atlantic.

And what were the prospects for their families left behind to fend for themselves? It could reasonably be defined as a war crime, perhaps not on a par with execution on the battlefield but a devastating conclusion nonetheless.

Transportation to a life of indentured servitude (effectively a time-limited period of forced labour) was a feature of seventeeth-century life. Its use after the Monmouth rebellion in 1685 gave Rafael Sabatini the major plot line for his 1922 novel *Captain Blood* – memorably filmed a few years later with Errol Flynn in the title role.

Accounts suggest the full tally of Scottish prisoners after the battle was in the region of 10,000. Almost half of these were non-combatants, camp-followers, tradesmen and the like; they were released without sanction. The uniformed captives were in the region of 3,900 (according to contemporary figures), but a reliable exact number is difficult to arrive at.

The men of Dunbar embarked on a series of forced stages. The long convoy (easily 5 to 6 miles in length) was initially shepherded the 20 miles (32km) to Berwick-upon-Tweed guarded by a single troop of twenty-five cavalry/dragoons. Or so the record maintains. This assertion could stand challenge, it seems impossible that a single troop, even mounted, could control so large a contingent.

We know most of the captives were quite young, mostly between 18 and 25, with some even younger. While not mentioned directly, it is hard not to think that Cromwell saw a commercial opportunity here, as well as a way of preventing future trouble. Transportation as an indentured servant had long been a means of capitalising on the American colonies' need for semi-skilled and skilled labour.

Their initial ordeal ended on 11 September when they were marched over Framwellgate Bridge into Durham into the bare sanctuary of the great Norman cathedral. They had already spent a night in a church – that of St Nicholas in Newcastle, where their disordered bellies had resulted in such fouling the burgesses had been obliged to pay for a major clean-up operation.

By now many were so weakened that disease spread easily. Of the 3,500 counted through the cathedral's doors nearly half, 1,700, died within a short space of time. Their remains were buried in pits dug within the bounds of the castle. . Within a decade the graves were lost as the area was developed and built over. The surviving Scots presented their English captors with a significant problem.

Holding such a large number of prisoners was costly but releasing them would be dangerous. One week after the battle, the Council of State, now England's governing body, decided to turn the problem over to the powerful Committee of Safety. This informed veteran Parliamentarian Sir Arthur Hesilrige, Governor of Newcastle, that he could dispose of as many of the Scots as he deemed fit to the coal mines and other industries.

Armed with that authority, Hesilrige consigned forty men to work as 'indentured servants' (effectively forced labour) in the salt works at Shields. He then sold another forty off as general labourers and set up a trade in linen, twelve of his prisoners used as weavers. He may have been making use of existing skills. Dental analysis carried out on one of the recently rediscovered bodies showed damage to the teeth consistent with regularly using them to saw thread ends. Heselrige was clearly a strong believer in private enterprise and was not above using his position to build up his personal wealth and then flaunting it.

Alongside these developments, the Council of State received several applications from entrepreneurs in the American colonies hungry for cheap labour. On 16 September, negotiations began. The petitioners, John Becx and Joshua Foote, conferred with their partners, the ominously named 'Undertakers of the Iron Works' (although in this case the term referred to finance rather than burial). Three days later, Hesilrige was directed to transport 150 prisoners of war to New England. The brokers, informed of the Council of State's awareness that illness had broken out, insisted they should only receive strong, healthy specimens of the best quality.

The chosen men were sent down to London by ship where they stayed in limbo while Parliament made sure they could cause no further trouble in the Americas. It was not until 11 November that the Council finally issued sailing orders to the master of the *Unity*, Augustine Walker. He weighed anchor right away. The passage from London to Boston normally took six weeks and was dangerous as well as disagreeable. Becx and Foote acquired these Scottish assets purely as a commercial venture. They paid £5 a head and could anticipate selling each man's contract for five or six times that amount in the New World.

In November 2013, during construction of a new cafe for Durham University's Palace Green Library, on the city's UNESCO World Heritage Site, human remains were uncovered by university archaeologists. The jumbled skeletons of what would prove to be twenty-eight individuals were subsequently excavated from two burial pits. It was the start of five years of meticulous investigation. A team of experts from Archaeological Services, Durham University – the University's commercial archaeology consultancy unit – and academics from Durham's Archaeology Department worked together to excavate and analyse the bones.

From the outset, the Durham Team acknowledged the possibility that these might be some the Scots soldiers of 1650. There has long been folklore about these men and what they did in the cathedral where they were held. Indeed, one local woman who visited regularly as a child has difficulty remembering when she first heard the tale, so ingrained a part of her childhood had it been. The driver of the digger which unearthed the remains was also quick to suggest they must be that of one of the Scots prisoners.

In May 2018 the twenty-eight men were reburied in Elvet Hill Road Cemetery in Durham, less than a mile from the spot where they were discovered. There was huge interest in the event, particularly in Scotland where newspapers had covered the Durham discovery in some detail from day one. Handfuls of Scottish earth were thrown onto the coffins and great care was taken to reflect the traditions of worship of these seventeenth-century Presbyterians. The service was put together by Durham Cathedral, representatives from the Church of Scotland and the Scottish Episcopal Church. Metrical Psalms from the 1650 Scottish Psalter and a reading from the 1611 King James Version of the Bible were included in the service – an expression of the wish of all involved to honour the traditions of the dead.

There had been much debate before the re-internment with many in Scotland keen to see the bodies brought north of the border. Indeed a petition was raised to that effect. On the day before the ceremony the *Scotsman* ran a headline '17th Century Scots Soldiers reburied in England'. Despite that, most of the reporting focused on the efforts made to honour the men and to respect the circumstances of their death.

What is remarkable about Cromwell's Convicts is how a group, still largely anonymous, have become, nearly 400 years after their deaths, men whose lives and situations are familiar. We may not know their names but we can see their faces and read the story of their lives on their bones. Men who went on to build a nation and to leave generations behind them. In the words of the St James Bible, 'That in blessing I will bless thee, and in multiplying I will multiply thy seed as the stars of the heaven, and as the sand which is upon the sea shore; and thy seed shall possess the gate of his enemies'.

Chapter 1

Tides of War

The Forward Youth that would appear
Must now forsake his muses dear,
Nor in the shadows sing
His number languishing

Tis time to leave the books in dust,
And oil the unused armour's rust,
Removing from the wall
The corselet from the hall

An Horatian Ode upon Cromwell's
return from Ireland[1]

James VI of Scotland and I of England has generally not been presented in a positive light: slack-jawed and unprepossessing, clever but constrained in his thinking, his achievements have been largely overlooked. A proficient linguist who rode and hunted well, he managed to prevail against both the rampant anarchy of the nobility and the politicking of the Kirk while successfully merging the crowns, no mean task in itself. He was rightly regarded as a highly successful King of Scots.

A Stuart Monarchy

Nonetheless, his English subjects were disappointed. He appeared a poor successor to Elizabeth and his son Charles seemed even worse. While James, a wily tactician, readily exploited the differences between his opponents, Charles very early mastered the knack of uniting the opposition against him. Charles did have his virtues – he was tolerant in an age of creeping intolerance, cultured, pious and brave – yet he showed little interest in his northern kingdom and less understanding. His policy, such as it was, encouraged Laudian-style episcopacy (rule of the Church by bishops), an anathema to many Scots. He excluded the Lords of Session from the Privy Council and then terrified the nobles by threatening to seek recovery of all Church property taken over since the accession of his grandmother, Mary, in 1542.[2]

'The most worthy of the title of an honest man ... an excellent understanding but was not confident enough of it; which made him often times change his own opinion for a worse, and follow the advice of a man that did not judge so well as himself'.[3] Clarendon's judgement of the King is certainly a fair one and Charles' vacillation would spill more blood than any tyrant's ruthlessness. His reign did not begin in a positive way: under the sway of his late father's handsome if empty-headed favourite Buckingham, whose ill-conceived foreign policy in the late 1620s exacerbated acute cash shortages and alienated Parliament.[4]

Charles' attitude to relogous diversity seemed suspicious to many of his subjects. Marriage to the French Catholic Henrietta Maria, daughter of Henri IV, fuelled fears of a return to abhorrent popery. His faith, based on the tenets of the Arminian Sect and a revival of the Thirty-Nine Articles, further stoked Protestant fears of papist intentions.[5]

Bishops' Wars

Charles really blundered when he tried to introduce the Book of Canons (often referred to, incorrectly, as 'Laud's Liturgy'). The Book of Canons, published in 1636, outlined Church law to be enforced on the Church of Scotland, based on the hated Five Articles of Perth. There was no mention of presbyteries, sessions or general assemblies. The book set out excommunication (the highest discipline of the Church) as punishment for any who denied the the King complete power in Church matters. Ministers required a bishop's licence to preach outside their own area and spontaneous prayer was banned. Instead, the Book of Common Prayer which was to be published in 1637, became the new and definitive text.

The Book of Common Prayer (or 'Laud's liturgy') incensed the Kirk on two grounds. First, it was written by the Scottish bishops, Laud and the King. The exclusion of Scottish ministers from the process created an impression that it was being forced on Scotland by England. Secondly, it adopted what were seen as popish errors, with its section on Communion seeming to the people more like a description of the Catholic Mass.

Riots ensued and an outraged populace flocked to sign the National Covenant in 1638.[6] As opposition swelled, protestors demanded the withdrawal of the liturgy and the expulsion of bishops from the Privy Council. Anti-Episcopalian sentiment began to mount and the Covenanters, as the signatories to the Deed were known, sought a free Parliament. The General Assembly of the following year openly defied the King and attempted to abolish episcopacy.

Charles was persuaded to use force against his Scottish subjects (the First Bishops' War), but his attempts to raise a functioning army foundered. The rabble he managed to gather drank and pillaged their way north but this never amounted to a military expedition.[7] The following year saw Charles once again trying to recruit adequate forces to constitute an army and, to no one's surprise, other than perhaps his own, meeting with little success.

The Scots fared rather better, their regiments swelled and drilled while the tide of change gathered momentum. The clerical estate was abolished. The Covenant became an obligation rather than a choice. Executive power rested in a Committee of the Three Estates (another name for Parliament drawn from the three 'estates', clergy, nobility/gentry and burgesses) and the Kirk (the dominant reformed church in Scotland), ably championed by Archibald Campbell, 9th Earl of Argyll.[8] The latter, both mighty highland chief and canny politician, effectively took control.

The Road to Civil War

Earlier, in March 1629, parliamentary sensitivity had reached boiling point with the riotous passage of three resolutions which condemned MPs to eleven years in the wilderness.[9] With Parliament in exile, the groundswell of opposition to the King's perceived abuses of the royal prerogative came from town and shire. Gentry disliked poor administration and tradesmen groaned under the escalating burden of unfair taxation. While those of the 'middling sort' were frustrated by the hide-bound functioning of the economy which restrained economic development and trade. Men like Oliver Cromwell, initially of the gentry, saw their future in new industries. Yet, in a world in which profit and investment were limited by the Crown, they could not even obtain a return on their money without taking undue risks with overseas ventures.

The innocuously branded Ship Money was hated by gentleman and commoner, squire, yeoman, merchant and artisan.[10] Ship Money was not a tax and didn't have to be approved by Parliament. It was a service which the nation's subjects were obliged to contribute for the defence of the realm with counties required to provide either a physical warship or payment in lieu. Payment was made directly to the Treasurer of the Navy, not to the Exchequer.

Added to all these resentments, Presbyterians wished to see a Church of England re-modelled on anti-Episcopalian lines similar to the Scottish Kirk. Puritans, while remaining within the framework of the Church of England, were not noted for tolerance.[11]

Charles ruthlessly arrested and imprisoned nine MPs insisting that, as a free prince, he was accountable to God alone and that he was the fount of English liberties.[12] Divine Right was a useful tool both for those who did not actually believe in it and those who did. This included the King, blind to the realities of a changing society. Despite the haphazard and burdensome nature of these unconstitutional taxes, despite mutterings from town and county and despite the strictures of Charles' nominee Archbishop Laud, who antagonised low church sentiment by enforcing measures which to Puritan and Presbyterian alike smacked of Rome, the administration staggered though the early 1630s.[13]

However, in 1638 two events occurred which were to propel the English polity towards civil strife. John Hampden's refusal to pay the hated Ship Money and his lukewarm prosecution (with only a bare majority of those on the bench prepared to grit their teeth and bow to the King's right) opened the floodgates.[14] This detested and illegal imposition became progressively unenforceable. Charles might yet have ridden out this particular storm if the row with Scotland had not then blown up in his face.

Despite defeat and humiliation, Charles was obstinately determined to enforce his will on his northern kingdom. The King chose Viscount

Strafford as his political and military advisor.[15] To his credit, Strafford saw continued war with Scotland as pointless but, bowing to the sovereign's will, advised that only by recalling Parliament could Charles amass enough resources to recruit an army capable of taking the field.

The 'Short Parliament' proved to be anything but accommodating. John Pym was the leading opposition spokesman, heading up a growing faction of MPs demanding that Ship Money be debated/dispensed with and that Members' privileges must also be on the agenda.[16] Persuaded to compromise, Charles offered to abandon Ship Money (no grand gesture as the tax was largely un-collectable by this point) but MPs were not minded to cooperate. Having learnt nothing from previous blunders, the King now reasoned he could re-open hostilities without parliamentary support and consigned this new, short-lived house to early oblivion.

One important consequence of the Treaty of Ripon, sealed on 21 October, was to oblige Charles to recall Parliament in the next month (it would become known as the 'Long Parliament'). The fiasco of the Second Bishops' War (the renewed war with Scotland) had only served to swell the tide of opposition which now included most MPs. Many who would continue to serve the King and even die beneath his banner were, at this stage, opposed.[17] Strafford became the prime scapegoat – an easy target. Pym moved for his impeachment and the King, though while he did not wish to see so loyal a servant lose his head, was also in need of a sacrificial lamb.

Nobly, the Earl volunteered his own neck as the price of peace. Charles had neither the ruthlessness to throw his man to the wolves, nor the resolution to stand by him. Besides, Pym wanted more – he demanded that Parliament must, by statute, meet every five years. On 20 May 1641 Strafford paid the price of loyalty to the Stuart cause. He would not be the only one to find the gratitude of kings rather sparse.

Neither Pym himself nor the more vociferous members could, at this point, be described as revolutionaries. They wanted to limit the monarch's power, to force recognition of Parliament's role as principal advisory body. None, at this stage, thought of removing the King. With Strafford gone and Charles humiliated, the summer of 1641 witnessed a series of concessions, including the abolition of Ship Money and the passing of the Triennial Act.[18] Some moderates were persuaded that sufficient reforms had been introduced but this fragile semblance of harmony was de-railed by the outbreak of rebellion in Ireland.[19]

This fresh crisis seemed set to tilt the balance of control further in Parliament's favour. Pym began to suggest that royal appointees be subject to approval by the legislature and that homeland defence should be a matter for Parliament rather than remain within the royal prerogative. Pym and the reformers pressed their case with the 'Grand Remonstrance', essentially a complaint by Parliament against all the Crown's perceived injustices since Charles had come to the throne.

Charles, with an impeccable talent for mistiming, decided now was the time for action and a heavy hand. On 4 January 1642 he entered Parliament and demanded the arrest of five members. All had been warned and had slipped away before. Confounded, the King wondered what to do next. He had no effective strategy for dealing with the opposition but felt sufficiently isolated and threatened to abandon Whitehall for the safety of Hampton Court. This began the inexorable countdown to armed confrontation, more of a slide than an avalanche, but a process, once put in train, which neither faction appeared able to halt. Reason was being ousted by belligerence. The parties were squaring up to each other with no apparent understanding of the consequences. The Dogs of War, once loosed, are very difficult to recall.

Fighting had already broken out in Ulster a year earlier and the flames soon spread to Scotland and Wales. It was a very British Civil War and one that would result, in percentage terms, in as big a loss of life as the Great War.[20] And, just like that war, it would not be over by Christmas.

In fact, it would be many Christmases before it was ended. The First Civil War lasted from 1642–6, flared up again in 1647–8, shifted to Ireland for the next couple of years, then to Scotland and ended (as few could have expected) with an obscure East Anglian yeoman running the whole show, virtual dictator of all England, Wales, Scotland and Ireland. Having beaten the King in 1646 and cut off his head three years later, some Britons were happy to welcome his exiled son and heir back in 1660. Outwardly nothing had changed yet everything had – kings from now on would remember 'they had necks'.

The Dogs of War

At first nobody was ready; England had not seen a major domestic war since the ending of the Wars of the Roses on Stoke Field in 1487.[21] Some, more than a few, had learned new tricks in the endless Continental wars but essentially the nation was unprepared. Both sides blundered onto the battlefield at Edgehill in October 1642. Charles had the chance to seize London and win but lost his nerve and retreated to his wartime capital of Oxford which swapped dreaming spires for earthworks and gun-pits.

Parliament's New Model Army ('New Noddle' as the Royalists derided) faced the King's veteran Oxford Army at Naseby on 14 June 1645 and destroyed it. That should have been the end but the war spluttered on into the next year until the final Royalist force was crushed at Stow-on-the-Wold on 21 March. The last big battle fought in England was at Worcester on 3 September 1651, on the anniversary of Dunbar. It was perhaps Cromwell's greatest victory, won after nearly eleven years of sporadic, often intense fighting. There had by that time been around 85,000 battlefield casualties and many more civilian deaths – nearly 2 per cent of the total population (around 5,200,000 in 1650).[22]

At the outset, Scotland had not been anywhere near as affected. Charles was King of both countries though the Estates were all for curbing the royal prerogative. James Graham, 5th Earl, and later first Marquis, of Montrose was identified with opposition to the King's policies as early as November 1637. He was one of the four representatives of the nobility on the 'Tables', the ad hoc forerunner to the Committee of Estates and one of the very first to sign the Covenant.

Montrose was born in 1612 and succeeded to his inheritance at the early age of 14. His academic career as a student at St Andrews was distinguished more by sporting than scholastic achievement. He was a dominant figure of the conflict: chivalrous and quixotic, destined for glory, yet doomed to failure. Initially, though, there was no hint of the famous cavalier to come.

In 1639, the Estates had become concerned at the apparent intransigence of the Marquis of Huntly, 'Cock o' the North', whose holdings encompassed wide and prosperous lands in the north-east. Fearful of invasion from the south, a potential enemy in the rear seemed too great a threat. So Montrose received a colonel's commission and was soon raising levies in Forfar and Perthshire. By mid-February he was marching north with 200 recruits. For a while the northern kingdom was spared the full quakes of conflict, early tremors were crushed.

History had not done with Montrose, however; his time, 'the Year of Miracles', was yet to come. It came and went in the atrocity of Philiphaugh and the gleam in the north died out. Charles' hopes of any Scottish miracles travelling south died alongside (though it was to the Scots army besieging Newark he chose to surrender). In terms of capitulations, this was a clever move. The King was aware how paper thin the alliance between Scottish Estates and English Parliament actually was. He hoped he might just be able to insert a wedge that would spread the cracks.

It was a strategy that would cost him his head.

What to do with the King?

As the Scots army began the long march to the border, away from the ravaged walls of Newark (which had finally thrown in the towel by royal command), relations between the Scots and the English, much as Charles had foreseen, were becoming increasingly strained. The Scots had hoped to export their constitutional developments to protect their own position. But the English Parliament was now having to deal with a new problem which might undermine this strategy.

In creating the New Model Army, Parliament had fashioned a war-winning tool. But it was also a monster which increasingly threatened to devour its parent body. Riddled with radical sectaries, the army was becoming alarmingly vociferous and though Fairfax, its Commander-in-Chief, shunned political involvement, his cavalry commander, Oliver Cromwell, did not.

Like Richard III perhaps, Cromwell has his fans and his detractors. To historians he is something of an enigma. Even those who served with him in the wars, such as Sir William Waller or General Lord Fairfax, found him unfathomable. The latter became increasingly wary, refusing to have any hand in Charles' trial and subsequent execution. Had it not been for the Civil Wars, it is unlikely many of us would ever have heard of the Huntingdonshire farmer: Cromwell could have ended up as just a footnote in county and parliamentary records.

Rather scruffy and careless in appearance, the shabby backwoodsman nonetheless made an impression. John Hampden prophetically remarked: 'That sloven whom you see before you, hath no ornament in his speech, that sloven I say, if we should ever come to a breach with the King (which God forbid), in such case I say, that sloven will be the greatest man in England.'[23]

Cromwell was not a soldier until 1642 when he was commissioned as a captain into the Earl of Manchester's Army of the Eastern Association. He proved energetic and efficient; instrumental in strengthening Parliament's grip over the whole of East Anglia. Within a year he had been made up to a full colonel and then commanded Manchester's cavalry. Cromwell had a particular and idiosyncratic genius for war: he would be the architect of Parliament's great victories at Marston Moor in 1644 and at Naseby the year after. He was Lieutenant General of the New Model Army from 1645–9 and Lord General during the Irish Campaigns of 1649–50. The violence of his actions in Ireland – the massacres at Drogheda and Wexford – has haunted his reputation ever since. He understood the importance of logistics, the supply of both cash and materiel. He had a significant role in winning ten major fights and was never defeated, the most brilliant captain of his day.

In 1647 Cromwell had wrestled with an ungrateful Parliament happy to disband its successful but costly army; a force that was now populated by radical groups whose revolutionary manifestos went far beyond what MPs were ready for. Indeed, they went far beyond what Cromwell was ready for. He was no republican, at least not yet. What he wanted was order. To achieve this he was ready to be ruthless – the sectaries were dispersed in heavy-handed fashion. Ultimately, Cromwell was one of those who realised they could never deal with King Charles, that nobody could rely on the King's treaty pledges. A new order was the only way to end the fighting.

What to do with the King? Charles was a valuable piece on the board. In more ways than one: the Scots were only prepared to sell him back to his Parliament on condition they received the first £400,000 of the promised £2,000,000 that was owed. As usual the King was his own worst enemy, trying to play the Committee along but steadfastly refusing to sign the Covenant.

On the streets of Edinburgh and other Scottish cities the worth of that document was wearing thin. Popular enthusiasm had been dampened by the harshness with which it was applied: there were those who now muttered against the ministers' rants. But that could change. What still held firm was a sense of Scottish separateness. Not independence but a definite feeling that there were two kingdoms here – union was a long way off; there were too many vested interests on both sides for that. The Covenanters still pinned their hopes on the promise made by the Long Parliament that had been the basis of their support for that institution: recognition of the Scottish Church settlement and the promise of reform in England.

Now, as religious and political ferment gripped the New Model Army, Congregationalism began to take hold. Religious independents were exerting their influence both here and in Parliament, supported by men like Cromwell. The suggestion that local congregations would make their own decisions without resort to either ecclesiastical or political control represented a direct threat to the Three Estates and well as the Covenant itself.

While a prisoner of the New Model Army and ostensibly immured on the Isle of Wight, Charles, in the closing days of 1647, met with three Scots commissioners and came to a compromise or 'Engagement' (as the agreement came to be known).

In return for pushing Presbyterianism down English throats, Charles would be supported by a Scots army. It is doubtful if the King, clutching at straws, and conspiring more zealously than ever towards his own downfall, seriously intended to keep his side of the bargain but the pact gave credence to a resurgent Royalist party who became known as the 'Engagers'. The Duke of Hamilton blundered into north-west England in the summer of 1648. Having lost disastrously at Ribbleton Moor and Preston Bridge, he found himself condemned to the block.

King Charles' ham-fisted attempt to impose the prayer book on Scotland was resented on religious grounds but also seen as an attempt to continue his father King James' efforts at integrating the kingdoms under an autocratic head. The response of the Kirk – to reform itself and abolish the office of bishop – was echoed and endorsed by the Scottish

Parliament – the Estates. They became equally outspoken in establishing mechanisms for governance that reduced the Crown's influence.

Charles blundered further as he tried to re-impose his authority by force of arms twice, in 1639 and 1640, only to be defeated by the Scottish Covenanter Army. Charles was King of Scots but completely failed to understand the people involved. Worse, he had sought to mobilise the resources of his other three nations against them. His attempt to destroy support for the National Covenant among the Presbyterians of eastern Ulster resulted in ministers and flocks heading back to strengthen Covenanter resolve, leaving behind them an economic crisis and untilled fields. Worse, the suggestion he might use an Irish army terrified the other nations – a Roman Catholic vanguard was a terror to take seriously. The Gun Powder Plot of 1605 was within living memory for many, the Armada was an event spoken of by their grandparents. It was too raw and too recent to be forgivable.

Ironically, the sternly Protestant Parliamentarians also failed to spot Scots sensibilities regarding constitutional change garbed in religious sentiments. By the end of 1647 Scotland was gripped by fear of the army's religious sectaries. It seemed possible that the military Congregationalists (those who argued local congregations should control their own affairs) would overwhelm Presbyterian support in Parliament (as indeed they did) and then impose the same result in Scotland. The Scottish struggle became one to allow the Kirk and Scottish Parliament to remain in control.

The Covenanting Scots, having successfully abolished episcopacy in 1638, had to ensure that this could not be restored by constitutional means. And the process of doing that gave the new Scottish Parliament that emerged in June 1640 unprecedented powers.

Having refused to be prorogued, a Standing Committee with no Episcopalian representation prepared the way for the assembly of a new parliament in June 1640. It met without royal assent and within a few weeks had transformed itself.

A Triennial Act was passed requiring Parliament to meet at least once every three years. They took steps to enshrine power in their own hands. For example, it was agreed that each shire commissioner should vote individually (previously there had been a shared vote for each shire). This doubled the size of the shire vote. Foreigners were forbidden from sitting in parliament, preventing Englishmen with Scottish peerages providing the Crown (or the English Parliament in later years) with proxy votes. The 1640 parliament also instituted the Committee of Estates to govern in the intervals between parliamentary sessions – making it impossible for an English Privy Council or any effective 'Governor' to intervene in Scottish affairs.

They went further in 1641 when they had Charles over a barrel. He was required to attend the new session to confirm this new constitution and to concede that parliament would advise him on the appointment of officers of state, privy councillors and judges. What Charles I was forced to sign up to in the 1641 settlement was limited monarchy and a form of parliamentary government in which a complex system of session and interval committees was established.

The Committee of Estates that sat from June 1640 until 1651 effectively usurped the place of the Privy Council in the daily conduct of government and oversaw, for example, the regular business of foreign policy and the conduct of warfare. Those committees were dominated by the newly increased shire and burgh commissioners who, of course, had a vested interested in maintaining their own power.

That interest was about more than status or control. There were significant financial gains to be made as the parliamentary records of the time show. A piece of legislation passed in August 1641 retrospectively applied the King's consent to the lifting of income due to the Crown and its use for 'serving of the present necessities of public affairs of this kingdom by warrant of the late committee of public estates'. 'Intromission' is a Scottish legal term denoting assumption of ownership. It is interesting to note that at least some of the money was used to pay 'diverse of his majesty's pensioners and servants'. One wonders if these individuals would have received these sums had the King actually been in power at the time.

Act regarding the king's majesty's rents uplifted by warrant of the committee of estates for the public use.

Our sovereign lord and estates of parliament, considering that during the time of the late troubles of this kingdom there were some of his majesty's rents, customs and impost uplifted and intromitted with for serving of the present necessities of the public affairs of this kingdom by warrant of the late committee of estates and by other public orders, and that there were sundry bygone pensions and fees, due to diverse of his majesty's pensioners and servants, satisfied and paid to them, according to their rights and pensions by order of the late committee of estates residing at Edinburgh, and his majesty, being graciously pleased to approve and allow of the foresaid intromissions had and payment made in manner and for the causes above-written, therefore our said sovereign lord, with advice and consent of the said estates of parliament, ratifies, approves and dispenses with all such intromission with his majesty's rents, customs and impost as have been uplifted, paid and intromitted with preceding 29 June last for the uses and causes foresaid, together with the payment made of the same by public order as said is, and declares that the same payment made and intromission had by warrant from the said committee of estates or by other public orders preceding the said 29 June last are, and shall be, sufficient exoneration to the payers of the said rents, customs and impost and to the receivers of the same by virtue of the said public orders and to all others concerned therein.[24]

The actions of the Scottish Parliament had a direct impact on England, with a number of the measures taken by the Scots adopted by England: the Long Parliament was to produce its own Triennial Act and institute reforms which diminished personal rule by the monarch.

It must have been an uneasy time for the Scottish Parliament, lacking confidence that their religious revolution could ever be safe until expansionist Anglicanism had been either brought under control and certain that their constitutional revolution would only be lasting once it had been verified by an English parliament. What greater protection could be available than an English neighbour committed to the same policies?

To achieve that the personal union of 1603 had to be restated. Not undone or eliminated: this was not about overturning that agreement, but about maintaining Scots separate-ness with the union. And it would take a threat to that regional autonomy to produce the apparent volte-face of 1650.

David Seel quotes the work of David Stevenson who had identified six features of the federal union that the Covenanters sought:

> The continuation of the union of crowns; retention of separate parliaments in England and Scotland; that close consultation take place between the two kingdoms through regular meetings of commissioners and, after 1647, through representation of each nation on the privy council of the other and at court; joint control of action in foreign affairs and trade; the establishment of free trade between England and Scotland; uniformity in religion, with each kingdom retaining its separate church, although uniform in government.[25]

The Committee of Both Kingdoms had been set up in 1644 to manage the course of the war and any peace overtures, 'so that the two kingdoms should be "joined in their counsels as well as in their forces"'. The Scottish Commissioners would withdraw acrimoniously in 1647 but in fact the Committee had started to break down much earlier due to several factors.

Some members of the English Parliament did not like the influence the Committee gave to the Scots in Ireland. The Scots in turn resented the fact that although the Committee held ultimate responsibility for foreign policy, diplomats supposedly representing the confederation of the Solemn League and Covenant began to sign treaties in the name of England rather than in the name of the League. The first of these was with Denmark in 1645.

In January 1648, shortly after the 'Engagement' became known, Parliament dissolved the Committee of Both Kingdoms and conferred its powers on the English members of the Committee. That must have sounded warning bells.

This was something of a mistake for it ignored what had been clear all along. The Scottish Parliament was made up of realists, whose overriding aim seems to have been that there should be a unity in terms of religion, not a uniformity of church structure and practice and that their constitutional revolution be safeguarded.

The Engagement fulfilled most of the secular aims that the Scots had held since 1640. They at last seemed to have achieved their fundamental quest to protect their religious and constitutional revolutions by limiting royal power and adding to the union of the crowns ties of union at other levels. The death of Charles was a death knell for their hopes. The build-up to it and the way in which it was done inexorably led them to the conclusion that, paradoxically, their greatest security could be had by making an independent treaty with Charles' son.

The execution of a British king, who was Scottish, by the English, who had failed to consult the Scots, smashed the alliance of the Rump and the Covenanters, which was only based on a joint detestation of the Engagers. Scotland, riven with divisions and fearful of the future, reacted with horror to the news.

The terms in which they protested at Charles' trial are significant:

On this day the Commissioners from the Estates of the Parliament of Scotland, residing in London, having received no Answer to their Letter sent the 6th, to the Speaker of the house of commons, on occasion of the Act for erecting a High Court of Justice for the Trial of the King; they this day sent a second Letter in which was enclosed the following Protestation: 'By our Letter of the 6th instant, we re-presented unto you what endeavours have been used for taking away his majesty's life: for change of the fundamental government of this kingdom ...'.[26]

This young king proved a difficult negotiator, a lot cannier than his father. Though he needed Scottish swords to carry him to Westminster, he refused the Covenant, wisely perhaps, for too ready a submission would have alienated English Royalists. Cynical and ruthless, he was still prepared to allow his father's unfailing champion, Montrose, to mount a fresh expedition to win Scotland by force. That didn't work, the attempt led to debacle and rout and ultimately to the capture and death of the King's great champion. Charles II had discreetly and ruthlessly distanced himself from Montrose who was just disowned and discarded.

On 23 June Charles landed in Scotland. When the King rode into his Scottish capital, beneath the towers of the Tolbooth, the skull of his most faithful servant was still fixed above his head. He probably didn't look. With Montrose callously abandoned and speedily forgotten, Charles could concentrate upon more pressing matters. Particularly pressing was one Oliver Cromwell.

Chapter 2

A Wet Season in Canaan

Trust in God and keep your powder dry …
Maxim attributed to Oliver Cromwell

On the sultry morning of 22 July Oliver Cromwell invaded Scotland.[1] Over 16,000 troops followed him, horse, foot and guns, trailing a long, armoured serpent that crossed the bridge at Berwick built, ironically, to accommodate James VI on his peaceful progress south forty-seven years earlier.[2]

Crossing the Rubicon

Captain John Hodgson was a player in the campaign:

> 27th June 1650 we marched out of York with our regiment, northward; the train of artillery came in the night before … We came to Sunderland the 6th July … 11th July I quartered, with our company, at Sir William Fenwick's four miles beyond Morpeth … being the 17th July, we were within eighteen miles of Berwick.[3]

Cromwell had gathered his army into review order at Chillingham Castle, an ancient border fortress.[4] The broadsheet war had already begun, as he sought to exploit divided loyalties in Scotland. They had declared Charles II king but he did not much care for the Kirk; or they overmuch for him. Many Scots had fought alongside Parliament to curtail his father's powers: they could not be sure what would happen if the son prevailed now.

Crossing the Tweed was ever both sides' Rubicon: 'The general made a large discourse to the officers on the bounds, showing he spoke as a Christian and a soldier …'.[5] Four days march on the passable high summer roads brought the army to the small but all-weather port of Dunbar. This was good; resupply could come by sea, easier and safer than the roads. Already Scots guerrillas, those new mosstroopers (organised border brigands of the seventeenth century), were making an impression.[6] Any army is only as safe as its line of supply – if this vital umbilical was severed the invader would be in trouble. Supply and concentration are war-winners, so far Cromwell was doing well with both. The trick was in keeping the whole show moving so as to put the army within musket-shot of the enemy. Leven knew that too.

Then things began to unravel. Only a portion of the supply ships sailed in, not enough to feed such a multitude.[7] The weather (summers were often poor in the mid-seventeenth century) began to look more ominous, cold and wet, unseasonable even for Scotland. Cromwell pushed on. His plan was simple, find the Scots army, fight them, beat them and get the job done. That wily old fox Leven kept up his Fabian strategy, time was his ally not Cromwell's. He was fighting on interior lines, well dug in and equally well fed. Every day meant more training, more chances to improve his army.[8]

There is some disagreement as to who was actually in charge of the Scots army. Stuart Reid maintains it was Leven, with Leslie only taking over as delegated field commander before the battle. A contrary view is put by Peter Reese who argues that David Leslie was always in overall command, with the older man relegated to a kind of consultancy role. This seems unlikely, Leven was a superb strategist and Leslie lacked that same deftness of touch.

Both sides used propaganda. Leven had issued dire warnings from the pulpits that Cromwell's soldiery would behave with the same callous barbarism they had shown in Ireland 'putting all men to the sword and to thrust hot irons through the women's breasts'.[9] As Captain Hodgson, in his vivid memoir, drily observed, 'the clergy highly incensed against us represent us to the people as if we had been the monsters of the world'.[10] In fact, Cromwell was punctilious in issuing stern edicts against looting and took care to ensure there were no excesses. Though, as we shall see later, this did not always hold up. At this early stage POWs were simply paroled and sent home.

Cromwell took Haddington, his advance unchecked until outpost bickering began at Gladsmuir. So far so good, by using sea power he had avoided over reliance on land supply which would have exposed his lines of communication to guerrilla-style attack, just the mosstroopers' ticket. Steadily the Scots' vedettes fell back in good order, their cavalry keeping the dashing General Lambert's troopers at a safe distance. Lambert was the *beau sabreur* of Parliament's army, highly capable; his Hollywood looks a contrast to General Monck's heavy potato face (though the latter proved more durable and wily).[11]

By the time Lambert, leading the advance cavalry, came up to Musselburgh, he was a bare 3 miles (4.8km) from the main enemy lines. So it was not until 29 July that Cromwell realised what he was up against. It was impressive and could not be outflanked. Worse, Musselburgh was unsuitable as a forward operating base. It had long sandy beaches but little viable anchorage for a supply fleet. In Ireland the English had been stalked by dysentery. Now, with the miserable cold and wet, poor rations and no tents, this scourge returned. Cromwell was not losing many men to enemy action but disease began to take a steady toll.[12]

Sabres were rattled and lances broken, Campbell of Lawers' musketeers sniped from the steep sides of Arthur's Seat, the perfect outpost. This was taken, lost, retaken but what really was the point? It was not at all promising. Leven would not be tempted, though a quartet of English warships battered away at Leith. Safe on its rearing granite spur, Edinburgh was a very tough proposition, Cromwell did not have enough heavy guns to besiege the place. Even if he could break into the defences (and it would be costly) there was nothing to prevent Leven throwing up a series of stop lines, each one of which would have to be expensively assaulted.[13]

As if this wasn't enough, the dire weather turned decidedly in Leven's favour. Cromwell ordered the army to fall back on Musselburgh, cold, wet, hungry and chased by those annoying mosstroopers. Lambert's cavalry was roughly handled with the General himself pricked by lances, knocked off his horse and briefly a prisoner till rescued. As Hodgson relates, the Scots 'cut and hewed Major-General Lambert, took him prisoner and were carrying him away towards Edinburgh, but the valiant

Lieutenant Emson, one of Hacker's officers, pursued with five or six of our soldiers and hewed him out …'.[14]

The English retreat had prompted local miners to barricade Musselburgh and they had to be chased out leaving around thirty of them dead.[15] No rest for the hungry, wet and tired; that night Colonel Montgomerie staged a cavalry raid on the English lines cunningly using exiled Royalists as a stalking party – making Cromwell's picquets think this was their own patrol coming in.[16]

Two troops from Robert Lilburne's regiment (the solder/agitator 'Freeborn John's' older brother) were caught off-guard in the outpost line.[17] Here, an untidy hit-and-run type of running skirmish began. Nobody won but the raid inflicted casualties and frayed nerves: 'There were 1500 horse that were resolved to sacrifice us that morning; being headed by Strachan, Lockhart, Kerr and a company of remonstrators [cavaliers]; and before we left them, they were sadly mangled.'[18]

Cromwell put a gloss on the action but the plain fact was he had lost the initiative which now lay with the Scots. On 5 August the English fell back on Dunbar. Getting supplies into Musselburgh had been thwarted by the vile weather.[19] Cromwell had perhaps relied too heavily on his ships and lacked sufficient wagons for road haulage. He had not brought enough tents either – this was supposed to be a 'smash and grab' summer campaign. He had not lost sight of the propaganda war, making a show over treating Scottish wounded with care. Later, those unfed, brutalised survivors of the battle, stumbling southwards after Dunbar, might have reflected quite bitterly on this.

Leven, Leslie, the Kirk and everybody on the Scottish side had their own problems. Most obviously in the tall person of Charles II who had arrived in Leith, uninvited on 29 July to boost morale among the troops and stake his claim to authority. The men did at least cheer, less so their senior officers. Worse it galled the vehement elements in the Kirk party, like the firebrand Archibald Wariston, who wanted the army to march out and march on to hammer the invaders. Both were a headache for Leven. In retaliation, as Simpson commented, the Kirk purged the ranks once again, perhaps as many as 3,000 rank and file with 80 officers were weeded out. This was not helpful.[20]

Thwarted he might be but Cromwell remained convinced of the rightness of his cause, writing in high indignation to the Estates from Musselburgh on 3 August:

Your Answer to the Declaration of the Army we have seen. Some godly Ministers with us did, at Berwick, compose this Reply; which I thought fit to send you. That you or we, in these great Transactions, answer the will and mind of God, it is only from His grace and mercy to us. And therefore, having said as in our Papers, we commit the issue thereof to Him who disposeth all things, assuring you that we have light and comfort increasing upon us, day by day; and are persuaded that, before it be long, the Lord will manifest His good pleasure so that all shall see Him; and His People shall say, his is the Lord's work, and it is marvellous in our eyes: this is the day that the Lord hath made; we will be glad and rejoice therein. – Only give me leave to say, in a word, 'thus much': You take upon you to judge us in the things of our God, though you know us not, – though in the things we have said unto you, in that which is entitled the Army's Declaration, we have spoken our hearts as in the sight of the Lord who hath tried us. And by your hard and subtle words you have begotten prejudice in those who do too much, in matters of conscience, – wherein every soul is to answer for itself to God, – depend upon you. So that some have already followed you, to the breathing-out of their souls: 'and' others continue still in the way wherein they are led by you, – we fear, to their own ruin.[21]

This seemingly pious cant had a purpose. Both sides believed not just in the abstract ideal of an omnipotent God but in a deity who was an active participant in human affairs, and whoever could establish and keep the moral high ground, gave himself a significant edge.[22]

And no marvel if you deal thus with us, when indeed you can find in your hearts to conceal from your own people the Papers we have sent you; who might thereby see and understand the bowels of our affections to them, especially to such among them as fear the Lord.

Send as many of your Papers as you please amongst ours; they have a free passage. I fear them not.[23]

What is of God in them, would it might be embraced and received! – One of them lately sent, directed To the Under-officers and Soldiers in the English Army, hath begotten from them this enclosed Answer; which they desired me to send to you: not a crafty politic one, but a plain simple spiritual one; – what kind of one it is God knoweth, and God also will in due time make manifest. And do we multiply these things, as men; or do we them for the Lord Christ and His People's sake? Indeed we are not, through the grace of God, afraid of your numbers, nor confident in ourselves.[24]

What Cromwell did possess was the capacity to adopt a plan and see it through to the end, confident of God's endorsement. He truly believed that faith, the confidence it brings and radiates, matters particularly when you are in an impossible situation.

We could, – I pray God you do not think we boast, – meet your Army, or what you have to bring against us. We have given, – humbly we speak it before our God, in whom all our hope is – some proof that thoughts of that kind prevail not upon us. The Lord hath not hid His face from us since our approach so near unto you. Your own guilt is too much for you to bear: bring not therefore upon yourselves the blood of innocent men, – deceived with pretences of King and Covenant; from whose eyes you hid a better knowledge! I am persuaded that divers of you, who lead the People, have laboured to build yourselves in these things; wherein you have censured others, and established yourselves 'upon the Word of God'. Is it therefore infallibly agreeable to the Word of God, all that you say?

I beseech you, in the bowels of Christ, think it possible you may be mistaken. Precept may be upon precept, line may be upon line, and yet the Word of the Lord may be to some a Word of Judgment; that they may fall backward and be broken, and be snared and be taken! There may be a spiritual fullness, which the World may call drunkenness; as in the second Chapter of the Acts. There may be, as well, a carnal confidence upon misunderstood and misapplied precepts, which may be called spiritual drunkenness.[25]

He never wanted this war, cannot afford or sustain it and ideally wants an easy way out of it.

> There may be a Covenant made with Death and Hell! I will not say yours was so. But judge if such things have a politic aim: To avoid the overflowing scourge; or, To accomplish worldly interests? And if therein we have confederated with wicked and carnal men, and have respect for them, or otherwise have drawn them in to associate with us, whether this be a Covenant of God, and spiritual? Bethink yourselves; we hope we do.[26]

Cromwell is not simply ranting here, he is asserting moral and spiritual superiority. The blame for what happens will not be his; it is theirs, the Kirk and the Estates, who would have been all too aware of where Cromwell's moral certainty had led in Ireland, a salutary precedent.

He was not done with more physical persuasion though. On the 11th he launched a second attempt, aiming to outflank Leven's lines from the west, advancing along what is now the line of the city bypass. He intended the fleet to cruise up the Forth to rendezvous at Queensferry and maintain his supply lines. It was a neat idea and, if it had worked, would have isolated Leven by closing his links westward to Stirling. He might then have had to come out and fight. Cromwell also tried diplomacy; setting up a parley after writing to David Leslie. Plenty of Scots may have been none too keen on dying for Charles II but they were still not ready to defect.[27]

He found time on the 14th to write in reply to Leslie:

> I received yours of the 13th instant; with the Paper you mentioned therein, enclosed, – which I caused to be read in the presence of so many Officers as could well be gotten together; to which your Trumpet can witness. We return you this answer. By which I hope, in the Lord, it will appear that we continue the same we have professed ourselves to the Honest People in Scotland; wishing to

them as to our own souls; it being no part of our business to hinder any of them from worshipping God in that way they are satisfied in their consciences by the Word of God they ought, though different from us – but shall therein be ready to perform what obligation lies upon us by the Covenant.

But that under the pretence of the Covenant, mistaken, and wrested from the most native intent and equity thereof, a King should be taken in by you, to be imposed upon us; and this 'be' called 'the Cause of God and the Kingdom'; and this done upon 'the satisfaction of God's People in both Nations', as is alleged, – together with a disowning of Malignants; although he who is the head of them, in whom all their hope and comfort lies, be received; who, at this very instant, hath a Popish Army fighting for and under him in Ireland; hath Prince Rupert, a man who hath had his hand deep in the blood of many innocent men of England, now in the head of our Ships, stolen from us upon a Malignant account; hath the French and Irish ships daily making depredations on our coasts; and strong combinations by the Malignants in England, to raise Armies in our bowels, by virtue of his commissions, who hath of late issued out very many to that purpose: – How the 'Godly' Interest you pretend you have received him upon, and the Malignant Interest in their ends and consequences 'all' centring in this man, can be secured, we cannot discern![28]

It was good propaganda even if it failed to drive the wedge deep enough. The dichotomy facing Leven, Leslie and their fellow Scots was that they were fighting for a cause they had only recently fought against. This Charles was the son of the one who had tried to force Laud's Liturgy upon them: they had twice led armies over the Tweed to thwart him.

Cromwell was smart enough to try an appeal to the desire to hold on to their liberties:

And how we should believe that whilst known and notorious Malignants are fighting and plotting against us on the one hand, and you declaring for him on the other, it should not be an 'espousing of a Malignant-Party's Quarrel or Interest'; but be a mere 'fighting upon former grounds and principles, and in defence of the Cause of God and the Kingdoms, as hath been these twelve years last past', as you say: how this should be 'for the security and satisfaction of God's People in both Nations'; or 'how' the opposing of this should render us enemies to the Godly with you, we cannot well understand.[29]

While he certainly labours the point, there is no denying the sincerity of the sentiment. Cromwell did not want this war. Leven and Leslie were former comrades and allies: that is why he points out the apparent absurdity of a nation having entered into a national covenant to resist tyranny now seeking to re-impose that same tyranny on England. Cromwell also knew that many of the Scots officers were equally unhappy even if they were not yet ready to abandon Charles II. He failed to grasp that Scotland suspected him, like Charles before him, of entertaining a grand vision of a 'United Kingdom'. The Scots, duly alarmed at what they saw as, in modern parlance, imperialism, favoured pre-emptive action as the best form of defence.

Leven did come out but only as far as Corstophine Hill where he took up a strong defensive position. Cromwell pushed in some outposts but did not try conclusions. Front of the front as ever, Cromwell had a near miss when a Scots dragoon shot off a round in his direction.[30] The ball went wide and Oliver yelled that if the man was under his command he would expect better marksmanship. The Scot shouted back that he had served under Cromwell at Marston Moor.[31]

Now he tried to sidestep but was foiled again at Grogar where Leven formed another formidable block. Yes, he would fight but on his terms not Oliver's. Cromwell was stymied and running very short of most things. He fell back first to Musselburgh and then on 31 August slunk back to Dunbar. At his war council he put an impressive gloss on this by saying Dunbar was a good base for gathering strength and supplies and an adequate balcony for further operations. He did suggest that the retreat might finally tempt Leven out.[32]

It was not Leven who came forth but David Leslie: the Earl had decided he was too old for field operations and left these to his subordinate. David

Leslie had a good track record but, as events proved, lacked the older man's deft touch. Cromwell might be looking for a fight but most sources agree his army was in poor shape, hungry, wet, cold exhausted and demoralised, hurried on their way by Scottish lances. Worse, far worse potentially, Leslie had got a brigade moving east past Dunbar to block the narrow pass at Cockburnspath. The English were bottled up and no help could hope to get up the Berwick Road to break the blockade.[33]

On 30 August from Musselburgh, Cromwell had written to the Council giving them a carefully edited report of the situation:

> Since my last, we seeing the Enemy not willing to engage, – and yet very apt to take exceptions against speeches of that kind spoken in our Army; which occasioned some of them to come to parley with our Officers, To let them know that they would fight us, – they lying still in or near their fastnesses, on the west side of Edinburgh, we resolved, the Lord assisting, to draw near to them once more, to try if we could fight them. And indeed one hour's advantage gained might probably, we think, have given us an opportunity.[34]

This was highly selective. The stark reality was that his campaign was slowly and expensively going nowhere. He had gone north to provoke a confrontation and Leven's Fabian tactics had got the better of his plans.

No need for the Council to be aware of the realities, at least not yet:

> To which purpose, upon Tuesday the 27th instant we marched westward of Edinburgh towards Stirling; which the Enemy perceiving, marched with as great expedition as was possible to prevent us; and the vanguards of both the Armies came to skirmish, – upon a place where bogs and passes made the access of each Army to the other difficult. We, being ignorant of the place, drew up, hoping to have engaged; but found no way feasible, by reason of the bogs and other difficulties. We drew up our cannon, and did that day discharge two or three hundred great shot upon them; a considerable number they likewise returned to us: and this was all

that passed from each to other. Wherein we had near twenty killed
and wounded, but not one Commission Officer.[35]

Again, Cromwell was trying to make the best of what had been a fruitless
gambit; it had consumed much powder and shot but achieved nothing.
For every round fired another man fell sick. Battle casualties on both
sides had been negligible but the grim reaper was batting for the Scots
and Cromwell's strength was haemorrhaging at an alarming rate.

The Enemy, as we are informed, had about eighty killed, and some
considerable Officers. Seeing they would keep their ground, from
which we could not remove them, and our bread being spent, –
we were necessitated to go for a new supply: and so marched off
about ten or eleven o'clock on Wednesday morning. The Enemy
perceiving it, – and as we conceive, fearing we might interpose
between them and Edinburgh, though it was not our intention,
albeit it seemed so by our march, – retreated back again, with all
haste; having a bog and passes between them and us: and there
followed no considerable action, saving the skirmishing of the
van of our horse with theirs, near to Edinburgh, without any
considerable loss to either party, saving that we got two or three of
their horses.[36]

He makes quite a lot out of some indecisive scrapping in which the Scots
certainly gave as good as they got and it was he who was retreating.

That 'Tuesday' night we quartered within a mile of Edinburgh and
of the Enemy. It was a most tempestuous night and wet morning.
The Enemy marched in the night between Leith and Edinburgh,
to interpose between us and our victual, they knowing that it was
spent; – but the Lord in mercy prevented it; and we, perceiving in
the morning, got, time enough, through the goodness of the Lord, to
the sea-side, to re-victual; the Enemy being drawn up upon the Hill
near Arthur's Seat, looking upon us, but not attempting anything.
And thus you have an account of the present occurrences.[37]

It was not a happy army:

> a poor, shattered, hungry, discouraged army; and the Scots pursued us very close, that our rearguard had much ado to secure our poor weak foot that was not able to march up. We drew near Dunbar towards night, and the Scots ready to fall on our rear. Two guns played upon them, and so they drew off, and left us that night, having got us into a pound as they reckoned.[38]

Cromwell expected that cool, dank evening of 1 September to be attacked at any moment and drew up his men in battle formation on the fields west of the port. His cannon and wagons were leaguered in the churchyard to begin with, though he had the big guns dragged out and deployed in the line. And he waited. Leslie was not intending to attack; he had pulled his men up the slope of Doon Hill overlooking the coast and from there looked down. The story goes that he intended to remain on the hill but was forced to come down at the urging of the religious commissars. Stuart Reid casts considerable doubt on this, rightly so and we agree. What was happening was rather different.

> About nine o'clock at night we had a council of war called; and debating the case what to do, many of the colonels were for shipping the foot, and the horse to force their passage; but honest Lambert was against them in all that matter, he being active the day before in observing the disadvantage the Scots might meet with in the posture they were drawn up in, and gave us reasons, and great encouragements to fight; first we had great experience of the goodness of God to us, while we kept close together; and if we parted we lost all ... thirdly, we had great advantage of them in their drawing up; if we beat their right wing, we hazarded their whole army ...[39]

Leslie was about to hand Cromwell a once in a lifetime opportunity to convert a potential Dunkirk into an El Alamein.

Chapter 3

Stubble Unto their Swords

I never beheld a more terrible charge of foot than was given by our army.[1]

Cromwell's military secretary Rushworth

Seventeenth-century Dunbar was a prosperous farming and fishing settlement on the south-east Scottish coast, a dramatic cliff-bound strand, linking Berwick-upon-Tweed to the Scottish capital. At 28 miles (45km) it is equidistant from both. It was not a big place to house an army with its horses, guns and gear. The narrow lanes would have been bursting and plenty of the burghers were given cause to dislike their uninvited guests.

Doon Hill looks down over the town like Moses on Mount Sinai but it was too far from the town to allow Leslie to block any retreat Cromwell might have wanted to make.[2] Nor is it a comfortable base for the defender – it is totally exposed and windswept. It seems likely that that Leslie was ordered or decided to move down and close the gap, to block the road south and properly bottle Cromwell up. If this had worked as it should, the English would have been in real trouble. There just were not enough ships for an evacuation. If he wanted to get his army away, Cromwell had to break out south and head for Berwick.[3]

It took most of the morning and early afternoon on 2 September to get the Scots army down the steep hill and marshalled by Meikle Pinkerton Farm. Seeing this movement Cromwell shifted his line forward to front the course of the Broxburn. Leslie shuffled out to conform. This does not imply he intended to attack. The Burn ran through a deep-ish cleft between the two armies, banks rather higher on the northern or English side. Trying to get across under fire would have been inadvisable. It appeared to be a standoff.[4]

Opportunity beckoned only beyond Broxmouth House where the dip flattens out. Here was the main crossing and both generals were aware of its importance. During that afternoon there was some skirmishing as both sides contested a smaller crossing further up at Brand's Mill. Leslie had by now realised that his army was partly in the wrong place – his right was weak and hemmed in by the narrow ground between stream and slope. To make good, he shifted the bulk of his cavalry over from the left. There was no room for his infantry, though. Clearly, this did not escape Cromwell's attention. Indeed, this move probably gave him his cue, his big idea. Though whether he was looking for victory or just for escape is not clear. Stuart Reid maintains the English just wanted to blast a path clear; the conversion of escape to victory occurred on the field. Peter Reese, on the other hand, is convinced Cromwell intended a decisive blow from the start.[5]

Reese also thinks Leven was with the army, Reid is sure he was back in Edinburgh and we tend to agree with this. For Leslie his work was done for the day. But Cromwell, in the saddle, scanning the ground, called an urgent council of war in the town. This was not necessarily a happy gathering. Some officers were all for taking the infantry with their many sick off by ship and leaving the cavalry, to try to cut their way out to the south and Berwick. As Stuart Reid points out, many would remember the Earl of Essex's debacle at Lostwithiel two years before when, harried by the King's Army, he had tried to get off by sea.[6] The results had been catastrophic.[7]

General Lambert, the *beau sabreur* to a more ponderous Cromwell, sometimes gets credit for the bold plan to deliver a mighty blow against Leslie's right and pin his army against the hillside where they could be properly finished off. Cromwell, in his official account, naturally claims the credit for himself though it is probable both officers saw the same opportunity. Cromwell then goes on to say he spoke to Monck who agreed (Monck's biographer asserts it was in fact he who had the idea).[8]

If we study Fitzpayne Fisher's map of the fight (a contemporary document, compiled from eyewitness accounts), we see some conflicting evidence. When the English had straggled into Dunbar on the 1st they'd crowded their transport inside the churchyard. It is reasonable to assume they would have remained there, or even have been moved to a safer location, if Cromwell had intended to fight. But Fisher's map suggests a different story, it clearly shows (and his study was intended to form part of a full campaign narrative) the wagons drawn up in and around Broxmouth House, the English start line.

This implies, pretty loudly, that what Cromwell envisaged was not a battle of annihilation but a break-out. He just wanted to deliver his army from immediate danger. The prospect of greater success came later, a golden apple dangled in the heat of the fight. The great victory was perhaps more about opportunism than planning – and it is always the winner who writes the official history.[9] On the other hand, Cromwell would make good use of his artillery in the battle – they would have been of little benefit leaguered up.

After the event Cromwell was upbeat, he could afford to be:

In their presumption and arrogance they had disposed of us and of their business, insufficient revenge and wrath toward our persons; and had swallowed up the poor interest of England; believing that their army and their king would have marched to London without any interruption … We lay very near him, being sensible of our disadvantage, having some weakness of flesh, but yet consolation and support from the Lord himself to our poor weak faith. That because of their numbers, because of their confidence, because of our weakness, because of our strait, we were in the Mount and in the Mount of the Lord he would be seen; and that he would find a way of deliverance and salvation for us; and indeed we had our consolations and our hopes.[10]

Perhaps Cromwell was sure Leslie intended to attack him and Reese agrees, Reid does not and nor do we. Leslie, despite the urgings of those round him, had no need to attack: Cromwell was beaten and hemmed against the sea. His deployment offered no real prospects for the offensive. Writing to Sir Arthur Hesilrige, Governor of Newcastle, the day before the battle, he was rather more pragmatic:

We are upon an Engagement very difficult. The Enemy hath blocked up our way at the Pass at Copperspath [Cockburnspath], through which we cannot get without almost a miracle. He lieth so upon the Hills that we know not how to come that way without great difficulty; and our lying here daily consumeth our men, who fall sick beyond imagination. I perceive, your forces are not in a capacity for present release. Wherefore, whatever becomes of us, it will be well for you to get what forces you can together; and the South to help what they can. The business nearly concerneth all Good People.[11]

He had clearly thought about the blocking force at Cockburnspath:

If your forces had been in a readiness to have fallen upon the back of Copperspath [Cockburnspath], it might have occasioned supplies to have come to us. But the only wise God knows what is best. All shall work for Good. Our spirits are comfortable, praised be the Lord, – though our present condition be as it is. And indeed we have much hope in the Lord; of whose mercy we have had large experience. Indeed do you get together what forces you can against them. Send to friends in the South to help with more. Let H. Vane know what I write. I would not make it public, lest danger should accrue thereby. You know what use to make hereof. Let me hear from you.[12]

It was a black night and foul, more like deepest dankest autumn. At the end of the council, there had been no dissenters. Those officers present quietly briefed their subordinates as the army got ready for battle. It is doubtful there was much enthusiasm; even the simplest of soldiers would know this was a do or die situation, a last gamble in a losing campaign. The Scots were already way ahead on points. Men were tired, wet, hungry and demoralised; they'd not had much sleep and nor was there much prospect of any. But they did have Oliver Cromwell, Parliament's greatest paladin. The call to arms would still quicken his men's pulses. If Cromwell was going into action then things might just get better.

The drums beat in the viscous light of pre-dawn, men shuffling out from under canvas or from whatever billets they had found, marshalling by companies, flags and colours furled, the steady para-diddle of the beat matching raucous cries from legions of gulls wheeling over the port, nature as ever, oblivious, 'scarce heard amongst the guns below'. The army was like myriad streams feeding into a single vast river, as the companies welded into battalions and formed up in their marching columns.

Their woollen uniforms damp, heavy with dragging mud and filth from the march, many unwell, hauling on leather bandoliers, powder flasks and hangers, muskets weighty and cold; matches would not be lit yet. Most would be hefting matchlocks, less cumbersome than at the start of the war, no longer needing the barrel rest, but still as fickle in bad weather. Cavalry would be shrugging into heavy, saturated buff coats, most carrying wheel lock or flint carbines, easier of use and more reliable weapons. The horses, underfed, would be skittish, a mount often knows better than his trooper when trouble's brewing. Like some giant beast stirring, the army gathers coherence. They have done this all before. NCOs bellowing, something in the air even though it promised to be yet another dank, dismal day after a blustery wet night. Summer, such as it had been, must have seemed like a distant memory, England like some foreign paradise, far from this cold northern shore with its jagged coast and screaming gulls.

Cromwell was radically thinning out his right, leaving a screen to hold the north bank of the stream, pulling all his weight to the left flank, his cavalry and infantry racked up like taxis. Lambert's mounted brigade formed a front line, Lilburne's the second. Behind them Monck's, then Pride's and last Overton's infantry were stacked with just Cromwell's own regiment and a couple of companies of Okey's dragoons, ready to fight on horseback.

Those dragging hours before battle, as ancient as warfare:

> The hum of either army stilly sounds,
> That the fixed sentinels almost receive
> The secret whispers of each other's watch
> Fire answers fire, and through their paly flames
> Each battle sees the other's umbered face
> Steed threatens steed, in high and boastful neighs
> Piercing the night's dull ear; and from the tents
> The armourers, accomplishing the knights
> With busy hammers closing rivets up,
> Give dreadful note of preparation[13]

Across the line of the burn, the Scots were standing to. They were, to a degree, better fed than their opponents over the narrow stream but many of their officers were still off looking for a comforting dram and a more comforting billet.[14] There's some question as to where Leslie was, possibly not on or directly near the field. They probably, unlike the English, were not expecting to fight; most probably thought that, having tightened the vice, their enemies would just throw in the towel and give up. They were wet and cold as well; officers might find a warm bed, they would not and they'd be just as cold and wet if less hungry. Both sides would be grousing through the night.

If anything the Scots had it worse: a conscripted army, probably, further from their homes than many had ever been, with any enthusiasm they might have had long since dulled. Most just wished the English gone and saw no need to fight them, the least tactically aware would sense the advantage they now enjoyed. We must wonder how many if any saw the risk inherent in their position, probably not; clearly their commanders missed it too.

There is much debate concerning the numbers involved. Modern authors tend to scale down past claims. In the field seventeenth-century armies lost many men through sickness and desertion. Neither side had suffered significant battle casualties but the earlier skirmishing would have exacted a steady toll. The number of sick and wounded Scots Cromwell released after the battle is a fair indicator of the wastage that resulted from stiff campaigning. Stuart Reid gives Cromwell around 7,500 infantry and 3,000 cavalry. The Scots were very likely weaker in terms of mounted troopers but stronger in footsoldiers, say 2,500 of the former and as many as 9,500 of the latter, giving them a potentially significant edge.[15] Reese favours a far more numerous Scots army, putting their total strength at about 21,000.[16] Reid's totals fit the ground better and the flow of battle suggests two sides rather more evenly matched.

On his far right Leslie had a weak and lonely cavalry brigade minding that flank, though the ruggedness of the ravine as it snaked north meant he was pretty secure. This really does suggest he did not intend to attack – the ground there was unfavourable. You would have had to fight your way over and across the wet gap which, if not insurmountable, heavily favours the defender. Moving to the right, he had his trio of infantry brigades, each of three regiments, Innes', Pitscottie's and Campbell of Lawers', drawn up in line abreast facing what were now only outposts across the burn. Directly or obliquely in the line of Cromwell's attack stood Lumsden's Brigade and, to the right, two lines of cavalry, Montgomerie's in front with Colonel Strachan's behind.[17]

Cromwell we know had been very much in evidence, going around his troops, 'a touch of Oliver in the night'. These details matter, they matter very much. He was asking his cold, hungry, sick, wet and filthy soldiers to rouse themselves to a great effort and it must be a measure of his own greatness that they could still respond, feel that quickening before action. They would be ready and their enemies relatively speaking would not.

Hodgson again was an eyewitness:

Towards morning we were ordered to march down to Roxburgh [Broxburn] House, all the whole army, neither regarding tents nor baggage; and as our regiment was marching in the head of the horse, a cornet was at prayer in the night … I rid [rode] to hear him and he was exceedingly carried on in the duty. I met with so much of God in it, as I was satisfied deliverance was at hand and coming to my command, did encourage the poor weak soldiers, which did much affect them …[18]

To the Sword

It was around 04.00, just before the grey murk of dawn filtered through what promised to be another foul late summer morning, Fleetwood's leading units moved off from their start line. His first objective was to control the crossings over the Broxburn, Brand's Mill, the main road and the easier ground towards the sea. Lambert's cavalry pushed back the Scots' outposts but the line soon thickened and hardened. Musketeers and big guns on both sides blazed away, a storm of noise erupting, great sheets of flame and devil's reek of burnt powder lighting dawn, very impressive though there seem to have been few casualties. Black powder weapons, big guns particularly, belch out vast sulphurous clouds of residue. Both sides would be partly obscured each from the other.[19]

Their artillery was not standardised but both sides would be using field guns, rather than the weightier pieces intended for siege work; minions (4lb/1.8kg shot), sakers/drakes (5lb/2.4kg shot) or demi-culverins (9lb/4.1kg shot). They were still heavy items, served by two or three gunners and up to half a dozen matrosses (assistant gunners). They had to be dragged to the firing line by horses and then manhandled into place. After each shot, which produced a violent, leaping recoil, the gun had to be laboriously pushed back.

Dark was giving way, the moon, still up when the firefight began, slipped away, grey clouds bellied, parted for a while then closed in. Like a volcano flaring, the firing spluttered out. First light proper wasn't till 05.30 and this breather should have given Leslie, certainly by now on the field, time to bolster the right of his line. He had plenty of men but where were their officers? Later he would write: 'It was our own laziness; I take God to witness that we might have as easily beaten them as we did James Graham at Philiphaugh, if the officers had stayed by their troops and regiments.'[20] This might be overly optimistic. It was laziness that did for Montrose as it was now about to do for Leslie. Besides, somebody, probably Brigadier Holbourne, had ordered the men previously to extinguish their slow matches to make them last.

Most infantry on both sides was armed with matchlock muskets which, as the name implies, needed a lit slow match (slow-burning cord) held in the jaws of the lock mechanism. Once the pan was primed and the charge loaded, the weapon was fired by operating the trigger which lowered the burning end onto the priming powder in the pan. This then went off and 'flashed' through the touch-hole bored in the side of the breech to ignite the main charge and send the heavy lead ball, typically .75in (190mm), on its way.

An unlit match was clearly no use to anybody and the prudent musketeer would ensure both ends were glowing before he went into action. Now the Scots needed to relight theirs. Fumbling with flint strikers in the wet half light, passing a flickering flame from man to man could not be done quickly. Yet, it seems the Scots had plenty of guns working during the initial exchanges. Some we do know were better equipped with 'firelocks' (early flint or dog-lock guns), which were much easier to use.

Nonetheless, at full dawn, when Lambert's men came cantering over the stream they broke through Montgomerie's Scottish cavalry and were only checked by Strachan's second line. A cavalry charge was rarely as accomplished as those depicted in films. Cromwell's troopers were trained to use impact and cohesion, 'shock and awe', charging stirrup to stirrup, though the pace would rarely get above a fast trot.[21]

They would have used their swords rather than pistols to hack a path. Normally their opponents would not just stand and brace, they would move forward to engage, the two lines colliding like breakers on the shore. Often one side would give way straight away or there would be a sprawling melee. Even if, as here, Lambert's squadrons barrelled pretty much straight through, momentum and order would suffer and they would lack the weight and impetus to repeat the move.

We know the Scots cavalry was 'light' as opposed to 'heavy'. Their chosen weapon, the lance, was very effective in attack, less so in defence. Cromwell's men, like the British sword-carrying cavalry of 1914, were not frightened of lancers, no matter how formidable. The lancer will lunge forward to spit his opponent at a distance. The good swordsman, keeping his nerve, will parry the thrust then close in past the lance to get in a killing blow with the blade. Reese suggests the Scottish lancers only carried dirks as a back-up weapon but this seems unlikely.[22] Like their reiver forbears, the lancer/moss trooper would surely carry a single-edged backsword, pretty similar to the one hefted by his adversaries.

As the cavalry milled, Monck brought his infantry forward, those levelled masses of pikes like giant bristling hedgehogs. His brigade closed with Lumsden's three regiments; the General of the Artillery's, Douglas of Kirkness' and his own. By now the Scots must have lit their matches.[23] They'd been scrapping in the firefight. Possibly, as he suggests, being mainly raw they had blazed away with such enthusiasm that they had shot off all their rounds and not been re-supplied.[24] It's also possible Lumsden himself had been an absentee and only arrived in time to get cut up. As did the rest, Douglas was killed as was Lieutenant Colonel Wemyss commanding the Artillery Regiment. The brigade just fell apart and scattered.

Fear in battle is a plague, it spreads like wildfire. Men who have fought and held their ground just run, driven by the contagion of blind panic.

Once the rot kicks in there's no containment. It may have been the case that the brigade was short of officers or a fair number of them. It is the job of officers to hold everything together: that is the reason why they have status, get better rations and, in this instance, better billets. They are there to provide rallying points, inspiration, leadership and grit, if necessary to the death. Without officers an army can all too easily become a rabble.

Homer sums it up neatly when he describes the hero Sarpedon, getting ready to risk his life attacking the Greek camp, reminding his friend Glaucus of their role:

> We hold the most honoured seats in Lycia, Glaucus. Ours are the best cuts at the feast; ours the ever-flowing cups ... Now we must stand in the front rank and lead the fight, so that the mail–clad Lycians can say: 'No cowards, these our Lycian kings. Theirs are the fattest sheep and the finest wines, but theirs the greatest courage too, who fight in the vanguard.'[25]

That's what Lumsden lacked: nobody to steady and cajole, to joke and to shame, to stiffen the sinews. Any raw recruit will flinch when a comrade is spitted on a pike, when another's head splatters and sprays you with bloodied brains and bone, when the stink of men soiling themselves clogs your nostrils. And when one goes the rest will follow. So far so bad but Lumsden's men held on long enough for Campbell to swing his brigade around to take on Monck's battalions. Men from Lawers' own regiment, Preston of Valleyfield's and Haldane of Gleneagles', did not flinch. They held firm, charged their pikes and saw Monck off. Strachan had rallied the Scottish cavalry and chased Lambert back across the burn. The attack had stalled.[26]

Hodgson was to be in the thick of it:

> The day broke and we in disorder and the Major-General a wanting, being ordering the guns: the general was impatient, the Scots a preparing to make the attempt upon us, sounding a trumpet, but soon desisted. At last the Major-General came, and ordered Packer, major to the General's Regiment, Gough's and our two foot

regiments, to march about Roxburgh house, towards the sea, and so
to fall upon the enemy's flank …[27]

Now it was Pride's turn but his regiments may have got muddled with
Monck's as they seem to have come into action piecemeal; Lord General's
first, then Pride's own and lastly Lambert's. It seems the brigadier
echeloned Lambert's to the left, presumably intending to outflank
Lawers' but Lambert's got mixed up with the rout of Lumsden's and
scrapped fitfully without contributing much.[28]

Lambert himself was making amends in the cavalry fight by bringing
Lilburne's mounted brigade forward and smacking into Strachan's
Scottish cavalry. They might have held but Cromwell's own fine regiment,
led by a Captain Packer, had swung wide to the south and crossed the
burn almost by the shore. They blitzed the right flank of Strachan's.[29]
This was decisive, the combined weight of the new onslaught broke the
mounted Scots, some flooded down the road south, the rest scattered
along the foot of the hill to the north. Leslie had hardly anything left.

This was it then, the decisive moment. Now it was that Cromwell,
with Lambert, could feel the earth move. The break-out (if indeed this
was just an intended break-out) was successful but more, that success
opened the door to a complete victory. The cavalry, jubilant in their
saddles, their swords bloodied, sang the 113th Psalm; 'Oh give you praise
unto the Lord'.[30] They could sense the world had turned, hunger and
despair were behind them; their tormentors were hemmed in and at bay.
Strung out in a thin ribbon, choked between the slope and the stream,
the Scots regiments were lined up like ducks in a shooting gallery. If
Cromwell hesitated it wasn't for long.

Lawers' men died hard. The battle was as good as lost but they fought
on, veteran English in front and cut up by cavalry on the flanks. Sir
John Haldane, at the head of his fine battalion, with his 2/IC Robert
Melvill and Major John Cockburn all died at their posts. The regiment
was ruined though both of the others in his Brigade seemingly got off
without massive loss. Possibly as Reid suggests, Gleneagles formed a
rearguard screen to let the others get clear. If so, like Newcastle's White-
coats at Marston Moor, they paid a heavy price.[31] It was barely 06.00:

One of the Scots brigades of foot would not yield, though at push of pike and butt end of the musket, until a troop of our horse charged from one end to another of them, and so left them at the mercy of the foot. The General himself comes in the rear of our regiment, and commands to incline to the left; that was to take more ground, to be clear of all bodies. And we did so, and horse and foot were engaged all over the field; and the Scots all in confusion. And the sun appearing upon the sea, I heard Nol [Oliver] say 'Now let God arise, and his enemies shall be scattered'.[32]

What followed was not really a rout – Leslie tried to get his men off in good order. Stewart's cavalry could just canter over Doon Bridge at the northern end of the Scots' position, Holburne, Innes and Pitscottie would have to shepherd their men across without orderly withdrawal disintegrating into a doomed stampede. Wedderburn's composite border unit, like Gleneagles', drew the short straw and bought the others time with their blood. Wedderburn went down as did his son, Lieutenant Colonel Home and Lieutenant Colonel Kerr, commander of Greenhead's (the other half of the joint regiment).

Innes' Brigade got cut up as well as Cromwell's cavalry harried their retreat, pouncing like wolves, Forbes of Leslie's Regiment fell apart though most of the rank and file got away. Holburne lost most of his Edinburgh Regiment and Colonel Stewart died with them. This suggests a series of desperate last stands, buying time. Some units undoubtedly broke up and bolted. More were corralled and captured on the beach at Belhaven. This intense pursuit lasted as far as Haddington where the remains of Leslie's shattered army drew breath: 'And the General made a halt, and sung the one hundred and seventeenth psalm … and afterwards we returned to bless god in our tents'.[33]

Cromwell's Victory

The Battle of Dunbar was over. Cromwell had won a momentous victory, snatched from the very jaws of defeat. He claimed he had killed 3,000 Scots and captured 10,000 more. This was probably an exaggeration. It may be the dead numbered less than a thousand with perhaps six times as many military prisoners. Quite a significant number of rear echelon personnel, camp followers, sutlers, waggoners and the like would be swept up in the final rout.

The next day Cromwell penned his official dispatch to the Speaker, William Lenthall. This is a carefully pieced together account, avoiding any suggestion of incipient defeat:

> We having tried what we could to engage the Enemy, three or four miles West of Edinburgh; that proving ineffectual, and our victual failing, – we marched towards our ships for a recruit of our want. The Enemy did not at all trouble us in our rear; but marched the direct way towards Edinburgh, and partly in the night and morning slips-through his whole Army; and quarters himself in a posture easy to interpose between us and our victual. But the Lord made him to lose the opportunity. And the morning proving exceeding wet and dark, we recovered, by that time it was light, a ground where they could not hinder us from our victual: which was an high act of the Lord's Providence to us.
>
> We being come into the said ground, the Enemy marched into the ground we were last upon; having no mind either to strive to interpose between us and our victuals, or to fight; being indeed upon this aim of reducing us to a' lock, – hoping that the sickness of your Army would render their work more easy by the gaining of time.[34]

We have to bear in mind that his is a winner's account, written after the event; Cromwell presents the story as a carefully contrived strategy. It's a bit reminiscent of Montgomery's post-victory account of the Battle of Normandy. Some rather felt he had adapted the facts to suit his version but, in the end, he'd still won.

Cromwell describes the battle as a choreographed series of marches and maintained that he was driving the campaign, not the Scots:

> Whereupon we marched to Musselburgh, to victual, and to ship away our sick men; where we sent aboard near five-hundred sick and wounded soldiers and upon serious consideration, finding our weakness so to increase, and the Enemy lying upon his advantage, –

at a general council it was thought fit to march to Dunbar, and there to fortify the Town. Which (we thought), if anything, would provoke them to engage. As also, That the having of a Garrison there would furnish us with accommodation for our sick, men 'and' would be a good Magazine, – which we exceedingly wanted; being put to depend upon the uncertainty of weather for landing provisions, which many times cannot be done though the being of the whole Army lay upon it, all the coasts of Berwick to Leith having not one good harbour. As also, to lie more conveniently to receive our recruits of horse and foot for Berwick, having these considerations, – upon Saturday, the 30th of August, we marched from Musselburgh to Haddington.[35]

He neatly glosses over any suggestion that the enemy had been getting the better of him:

Where, by that time we had got the van brigade of our horse, and our foot and train, into their quarters, the Enemy had marched with that exceeding expedition that they fell upon the rear-forlorn of our horse, and put it in some disorder; and indeed had like to have engaged our rear-brigade of horse with their whole Army, – had not the Lord by his providence put a cloud over the Moon, thereby giving us opportunity to draw off those horse to the rest of our Army. Which accordingly was done without any loss, save of three or four of our aforementioned forlorn; wherein the Enemy, as we believe, received more loss.

The Army being put into a reasonable secure posture, – towards midnight the Enemy attempted our quarters, on the west end of Haddington: but through the goodness of God we repulsed them. The next morning we drew into an open field, on the south side of Haddington; we not judging it safe for us to draw to the Enemy upon his own ground, he being prepossessed thereof; – but rather drew back, to give him way to come to us, if he had so thought fit. And having waited about the space of four or five hours, to see if he would come to us; and not finding any inclination in the Enemy so to do, – we resolved to go, according to our first intendment, to Dunbar.[36]

All was going according to plan, with no hint of desperation. He does admit, however, there was a hint of Lostwithiel in his position at Dunbar – but then Cromwell was not Essex:

> By that time we had marched three or four miles, we saw some bodies of the Enemy's horse drawn out of their quarters; and by that time our carriages were gotten near Dunbar, their whole Army was upon their march after us. And indeed, our drawing back in this manner, with the addition of three new regiments added to them, did much heighten their confidence, if not presumption and arrogancy. – The Enemy, that night, we perceived, gathered towards the Hills; labouring to make a perfect interposition between us and Berwick. And having in this posture a great advantage, – through his better knowledge of the country, he effected it: by sending a considerable party to the strait Pass at Copperspath [Cockburnspath]; where ten men to hinder are better than forty to make their way. And truly this was an exigent to us, wherewith the Enemy reproached us; – 'as' with the condition the Parliament's Army was in when it made its hard conditions with the King in Cornwall ...[37]

Nor was he going to understate the enemy's superior strength (real or otherwise):

> Upon Monday evening, – the Enemy's whole numbers were very great; about Six-thousand horse, as we heard, and Sixteen-thousand foot at least; ours drawn down, as to sound men, to about Seven-thousand five-hundred foot, and Three-thousand five-hundred horse – 'upon Monday evening', the Enemy drew down to the right wing about two-thirds of their left wing of horse. To the right wing; shogging also their foot and train much to the right; causing their right wing of horse to edge down towards the sea. We could not well imagine but that the Enemy intended to attempt upon us, or to place themselves in a more exact condition of interposition.[38]

And now for the master-plan:

The Major-General and myself coming to the Earl Roxburgh's House, and observing this posture, I told him I thought it did give us an opportunity and advantage to attempt upon the Enemy. To which he immediately replied, That he had thought to have said the same thing to me. So that it pleased the Lord to set this apprehension upon both of our hearts, at the same instant. We called for Colonel Monk, and showed him the thing: and coming to our quarters at night, and demonstrating our apprehensions to some of the Colonels, they also cheerfully concurred. We resolved therefore to put our business into this posture: That six regiments of horse, and three regiments and a half of foot should march in the van; and that the Major-General, the Lieutenant-General of the horse, and the Commissary-General, and Colonel Monk to command the brigade of foot, should lead on the business; and that Colonel Pride's brigade, Colonel Overton's brigade, and the remaining two regiments of horse should bring up the cannon and rear.[39]

Cromwell gives no indication that he may merely have been attempting a break-out as opposed to a break-in and the reality is he might have had both in mind, allowing opportunity to decide:

The time of falling-on to be by break of day: – but through some delays it proved not to be so; 'not' till six o'clock in the morning. The Enemy's word was, The Covenant; which it had been for divers days. Ours, The Lord of Hosts. The Major-General, Lieutenant-General Fleetwood, and Commissary-General Whalley, and Colonel Twistleton, gave the onset; the Enemy being in a very good posture to receive them, having the advantage of their Cannon and foot against our horse. Before our foot could come up, the Enemy made a gallant resistance, and there was a very hot dispute of sword's point between our horse and theirs.

Our first foot, after they had discharged their duty (being overpowered with the Enemy), received some repulse, which they soon recovered, for my own regiment, under the command of Lieutenant-Colonel Goffe and my Major, White, did come seasonably in; and, at the push of pike, did repel the stoutest

believe we have lost twenty men. Not one Commission Offic
as I hear of, save one Cornet; and Major Rooksby, since dead
wounds; and not many mortally wounded: – Colonel Whalley o.
cut in the handwrist, and his horse (twice shot) killed under him
but he well recovered another horse, and went on in the chase.[42]

The story certainly would not play so well in Edinburgh:

a certain Mr Haig was haranguing a congregation at the daily service
that Tuesday, and painting in glowing colours the defeat of the
Sectaries which had already he rashly promised his people, taken
place, when the door of the church burst open and a soldier, fresh
from the scene of slaughter and reeling with fatigue, stood at the
portal as an actual witness of the actual truth.[43]

This was a pretty rude awakening even if the story is apocryphal. Such
scenes must have occurred all across the capital and then like the boulder
heaved into the lake spread its unhappy ripples over the nation. God, it
seemed, was cheering for the sectaries.

The Wounded

When you're wounded and left on Afghanistan's plains, and the women
come out to cut up what remains … Kipling's dire prediction held good
for most wars, particularly in the seventeenth century. Local civilian
populations were frequently if not invariably victims of the armies. That
they would then show no compunction and no remorse in stripping and
finishing off the wounded was no great surprise. No sooner was the
shooting, hacking and gouging done than the vultures would be out.
Those dead and wounded left on the field would swiftly be recycled
into stripped and stiffening carcasses. These sights would be worse
than our worst nightmares. Though, of course, this was a Scots army,
annihilated on a Scottish battlefield. The locals would likely view this
very differently from normal. Particularly because, as we will see later,
the citizens of Dunbar had themselves already been made victims by the
English army.

There are not many eyewitness accounts for those who fought as squaddies, generally we have to wait for later wars for survivors to tell us about the horrors of close-quarter combat, such as Sergeant McClain of the Durham Light Infantry at Kohima, Burma in 1944:

> He got me through the side of my face. It felt like being hit by a clenched fist but it didn't hurt as much as a really good punch in a fight. I spat out a handful of teeth, spun round and he was a few paces away, facing me. He had a rifle and bayonet. I pressed the trigger but I'd got no ammunition. As he came towards me I felt it was either him or me. I was an instructor in unarmed combat, so I let him come and threw the light machine-gun in his face ... Before he hit the ground I had my hand round his windpipe and I literally tried to tear it out.[44]

Dunbar would have witnessed plenty of nasty scenes like this. There would have been some there to deal with the aftermath but battles produced enormous surges in casualties, often swamping the available medical services. Triage (prioritising patients for treatment) was unknown and its earliest use would be in the armies of Napoleon. It would take the Great War to make it the norm. If a hopeless case was lucky his mates might feed him enough liquor to dull the pain as he waited for death.

Death was waiting for an awful lot of those Scottish prisoners shivering in the numbed shock and horror of defeat on the battlefield of Dunbar.

Chapter 4

The Vanquished

Necessity hath no law
Oliver Cromwell, speech to Parliament,
September 1654

Never think that war, no matter how necessary, nor how justified, is
not a crime. Ask the infantry and ask the dead ...
Ernest Hemingway

His triumph in the field complete, Cromwell could turn to the
business of his prisoners, writing to the Council in London on
4 September:

I have sent the Major-General, with six regiments of horse and
one of foot, towards Edinburgh; purposing (God willing) to follow
after, tomorrow, with what convenience I may. We are put to
exceeding trouble, though it be an effect of abundant mercy, with
the numerousness of our Prisoners; having so few hands, so many
of our men sick; – so little conveniency of disposing of them; and
not, by attendance thereupon, to comit the seasonableness of the
prosecution of this mercy as Providence shall direct.[1]

He does strike a humanitarian note, though it may also be a pragmatic
one. Wounded, damaged or otherwise useless prisoners were a burden:

We have been constrained, even out of Christianity, humanity,
and the forementioned necessity, to dismiss between four and
five thousand Prisoners, almost starved, sick and wounded; the
remainder, which are the like, or a greater number, I am fain to send
by a convoy of four troops of Colonel Hacker's, to Berwick, and so

on to Newcastle, southwards. I think fit to acquaint your Lordship with two or three observations.

A troop could consist of anywhere from 30 to 100 riders. Given the rigours of campaigning, we can safely assume that numbers were down so if we say 50 per troop, this gives an escort of 200, possibly with some additional 'walking/riding' wounded on their way back for treatment in Berwick. That is not many to police a column at least 5 miles long and may explain, if not excuse, the seemingly trigger happy nature of the guards.

Cromwell was well aware that many of the Scots had mixed views on the revival of the Stuart fortunes but shows no insight into the real reasons for the choice made by the Scots Estates:

Some of the honestest in the Army amongst the Scots did profess before the fight, That they did not believe their King in his Declaration; and it's most evident he did sign it with as much reluctancy, and so much against his heart as could be: and yet they venture their lives for him upon this account; and publish this 'Declaration' to the world to be believed as the act of a person converted, when in their hearts they know he abhorred the doing of it, and meant it not. I hear the Enemy marched last up to us, the Ministers pressed their Army to interpose between us and home; the chief Officers desiring rather that we might have way made, though it were by a golden bridge but the Clergy's counsel prevailed – to their no great comfort, through the goodness of God.[2]

Through their arrogance and presumption the Scots were seemingly asking for a beating. This was, of course, a victor's assessment; Cromwell was going to some lengths to claim the moral ascendancy:

The Enemy took a gentleman of Major Brown's troop prisoner, that night we came to Haddington; and he had quarter through Lieutenant-General David Leslie's means; who, finding him a man of courage and parts, laboured with him to take up arms. But the man

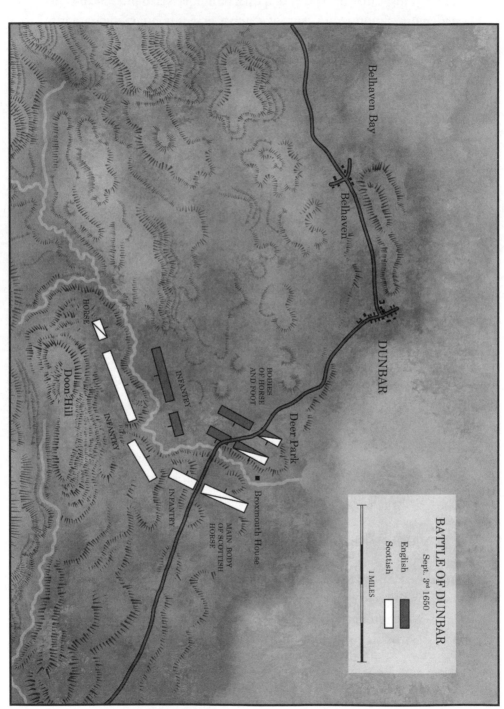

Map 1: Battle of Dunbar. (*Courtesy of Chloe Rodham*)

BATTLE OF DUNBAR

Sept. 3rd 1650

English
Scottish

1 MILES

Belhaven Bay

Belhaven

DUNBAR

Deer Park

Broxmouth House

Doon-Hill

HORSE

INFANTRY

INFANTRY

INFANTRY

INFANTRY

BODIES OF HORSE AND FOOT

MAIN BODY OF SCOTTISH HORSE

expressing constancy and resolution to this side, the Lieutenant-General caused him to be mounted, and with two troopers to ride about to view their gallant Army; using that as an argument to persuade him to their side; and, when this was done, dismissed him to us in a bravery. And indeed the day before we fought, they did express so much insolency and contempt of us, to some soldiers they took, as was beyond apprehension.[3]

Humanity only stretches so far. The campaign, in Cromwell's view, had been forced on him and had soaked up resources Parliament could ill afford. In the aftermath, a cash windfall could not be overlooked and, after all, as God had granted the victory he must approve the windfall. He needed to make sure these men could not launch a further attack.

There is general agreement as to where the battle occurred. This, among battlefield historians, is comparatively rare but topography more or less fixes the action. Despite this, Thomson's *Atlas of Scotland* from 1832 shows the battle being fought on the south side of Doon Hill. Young and Adair show Cromwell deploying further north eastwards than either Reese or Reid. Further, they suggest four crossings of the burn by the English forces, on either side of the main road. William Seymour creates a far broader frontage by indicating Parliamentary thrusts all along the line of the stream. This seems rather unlikely – and contradicts the contemporary account.[4]

As you head north along the present A1 past Cockburnspath, the slab-sided mass of Torness Nuclear Power Station rears like a granite cliff from Dunbar Point. It is a brutalist monument incongruous in the pleasant coastal landscape. A few miles further on and the cement works (astride a portion of the battlefield) look even worse. If you can accept these dual assaults on the aesthetic, it gets better. Turn right off the main road onto the old one (now the A1087) and you come to the simple memorial bearing an inscription from Carlyle: '3rd September 1650 here took place the brunt or essential agony of the Battle of Dunbar'.[5] Some new signage, at the time of writing, has just been erected (thanks to the efforts of the Scottish Battlefields Trust).

'Essential agony' – that sums it up. Carlyle displays his customary genius for just the right phrase and it is in the right place. But the agony was not over, far from it; for many of those Scots, it was only just beginning. The shocking awfulness of battle, a symphony of suffering, was about to get its long requiem. The Dunbar prisoners have no voice but those who endured similar horrors since do speak to us:

> The hours dragged by, as we knew they must. The drop-outs began. It seemed a great many of the prisoners reached the end of their endurance at about the same time. They went down by twos and threes. Usually they made an effort to rise. I never can forget their groans and strangled breathing as they tried to get up. Some succeeded. Others lay lifelessly where they had fallen. I observed that the guards paid no attention to these. I wondered why. The explanation wasn't long in coming. There was a sharp crackle of pistol and rifle fire behind us.
>
> Skulking along, a hundred yards behind our little contingent, came a 'clean-up' squad of murdering buzzards. Their helpless victims sprawled darkly against the white of the road, were easy targets. As members of the murder squad stooped over each huddled form, there would be an orange flash in the darkness and a sharp report. The bodies were left where they lay, that other prisoners coming behind might see them.
>
> Our guards enjoyed the spectacle in silence for a time. Eventually, one of them who spoke English felt he should add a little spice to the entertainment. 'Sleepy?' he asked, 'you want sleep. Just lie down in the road, you get good long sleep!' On through the night we were followed by orange flashes and thudding sounds.[6]

This testimony is from a far more modern death march – Bataan in spring 1942 – but it gives a flavour of the hopelessness and terror of such a grinding calvary. Those Scottish soldiers who stumbled south in the wake of their defeat would have been shocked and demoralised, many with minor injuries which, left untreated, could swiftly become serious. We can safely assume that some, if not all, of those who died at Berwick-upon-Tweed had succumbed to injuries sustained in the fight. We know too that men were shot en route so the sound of gunfire would have been as familiar and terrible to them as to the Americans later caught up in the sadistic hell of Bataan.

What About Cromwell?

So what did Cromwell now intend should happen to his Scottish prisoners? Psalm 117 (one of the shortest) was chosen by Cromwell as his rallying and regrouping anthem on the battlefield at Dunbar. As the words rang out from the dry throats of men still intoxicated by the red mist of battle, the Psalm steadied and reassured them; victory was theirs and who could doubt that this was surely God's work? 'There is no reason to doubt the sincerity of Cromwell's faith displayed on the battlefield of Dunbar – Cromwell chose the phrase "The Lord of Hosts" as the parliamentarian rallying cry and call sign on the battlefield. His religious beliefs underpinned his actions at Dunbar, as they underpinned his whole military career.'[7]

Those too badly injured and the camp followers he released. These people were not a threat, nor did they have any economic value, no need for them to be a drain on the Treasury. The able-bodied were different. He could not afford simply to parole them as this would leave the Scots with the nucleus of a future army – even at this stage, the war was far from being won. Secondly, they constituted an economic windfall; these able-bodied, primarily young men were worth money. There was a variety of uses to which they could be put: recycled for garrisons in Ireland, hired out as mercenaries, used as forced labour in England or in the burgeoning American colonies where workers were urgently needed.

Cromwell clearly saw the Scots' renewed allegiance to the House of Stewart as contrary to God's will and yet was careful not to overstate this when dealing with their parliament. He would assert he did not want war with Scotland, based on past allegiance and yet it could be suggested that Cromwell himself was continuing in the tradition of James VI and Charles; the attempt to create a united Britain, a common republic:

Cromwell's surviving letters and speeches generally do not emphasise this religious element, do not seek to portray the Scottish campaign as a form of religious crusade with anything approaching the same strength and bitterness as Cromwell's colouring of his Irish campaign of 1649–50 ... religion cut both ways and at times made Cromwell uneasy, troubled or unsure. In summer 1650, as part of a delegation dispatched to persuade an uncertain Sir Thomas Fairfax to lead and command the proposed campaign to Scotland, Cromwell chose instead to emphasise the secular and practical rather than the spiritual motivation for and goals of the venture – the Scots, he argued, were evidently planning to invade England to restore the Stuart monarchy, and so it would be better to march north to ensure that the fighting, violence and bloodshed should take place on Scottish rather than English soil.[8]

Dunbar reinforced Cromwell's belief that his actions were guided by divine providence. As Peter Gaunt points out, this spurred him on to take bigger risks. In 1651, he allowed Charles II, leading a Scots army, to march into England. This could easily have backfired – he was lucky it did not. Worcester is often considered Cromwell's masterpiece. '*Gott mit uns*' is a powerful tool, and always has been. Faith is a powerful rallying cry. Cromwell was no cynic, he was a genuine man of faith and his confidence in divine intervention was completely sincere. Two great victories, the second on the anniversary of the first, to the naturally pious mindset of the mid-seventeenth century could not be just coincidence.

Still, his quarrel with the Scots was essentially dynastic and constitutional rather than religious. Scottish Presbyterians were not Irish Catholics and he never showed any animus towards the rank and file:

Scotland was very different, in the eyes of Cromwell and of many of his parliamentarian compatriots. As always, it is impossible completely to separate religious and military strands and Cromwell's attitude towards the Scots sprang not only from a shared or at least overlapping faith, a belief in essentially the same Protestant God, but also from recent military and political developments. After all, Scotland not England had led the way in resisting Stuart tyranny in the late 1630s and, by bravely and courageously rising against Charles I and by inflicting a crushing military defeat upon him, they checked his power in England, helped to restore government with parliaments south of the border and opened the way for both reform of, and effective resistance to, royal policies in England.[9]

Cromwell was always uneasy about the imposition of Presbyterianism in England and Wales and the Scots were still good and steadfast Protestants. After beating the Engagers at Preston, Cromwell was welcomed by the resurgent Presbyterians. What he seems to have wanted was a compliant neighbour more or less on the same wavelength. There can be no suggestion he actively wished, at any point, to invade Scotland. He needed their friendship not subjugation: 'The Scots were "brothers" who, having been shown the errors of their way by God's reproof at Preston, were now to be treated in a civil way, with love, to remove any remaining prejudice and to re-establish harmonious relations under a shared God'.[10] If he did indeed seek some form of English-dominated pan-British republic, then he clearly preferred to achieve this by peaceful means.

He was naïve in thinking the Scots would not resent the killing of the King – a lengthy history of opposition to Charles' intermeddling in Scottish affairs should not have necessarily implied the Scots were ready for regime change. He misread their mood completely:

> Hence we see Cromwell expressing regret about the Scottish campaign, attempting to convince the Scots that the war was unnecessary, giving voice to a belief (almost certainly unfounded) that the majority of the Scots had no quarrel with the new English republic but had been led astray by the false arguments, deceptions and concealments of their political and religious leaders. Repeatedly during the campaign of 1650–51 Cromwell stressed that the dispute between England and Scotland rested upon political not religious divisions. During the winter of 1650–51 Cromwell very visibly attended Presbyterian services in Edinburgh and Glasgow.[11]

We have no reason to doubt the sincerity of his expressed regrets at having to fight the Scots. These are a constant feature not just of his public utterances but also appear in private correspondence. The Scottish prisoners from Dunbar were not popish imps of Satan but misguided former allies who had been led badly astray. We have no evidence to suggest Cromwell intended to mistreat his captives. That they were shockingly abused is clearly a matter of undisputed fact and Cromwell, as commander, must bear ultimate responsibility. But we cannot say he was intending sadistic and deliberate excess. For purely economic reasons if no other, he wanted these men in good health, sick, dying and dead they were no use to him whatsoever.

The Total Loss to the Town

Dunbar today is a pretty town, the thirteenth-century belfry at Friar's Croft, the courtyard of 71–5 High Street and the seventeenth-century Town House (Tollbooth), also on the high street (now the town museum), were there at the time of the battle. As was the church, though the present building (shrouded in scaffolding at the time of writing) is a much later example of good no-nonsense nineteenth-century Presbyterian stolidity. The place was walled though quite what state these ramparts were in during 1650 is not clear. Defoe, writing over half a century later, describes them as being in poor condition. There appear now to be no visible traces.[12] The aptly named Cromwell House, dating from the eighteenth century and facing the harbour, was demolished in 1987.[13]

Shattered stumps of the castle's walls still crown the anchorage. The place was important, seat of the Dunbar Scottish Earls of March, significant figures in high medieval polity. Here, the lively Black Agnes successfully defied an English siege, even though her husband was on their side. In the early 1560s it was re-fortified and garrisoned by the French but after Queen Mary's disastrous liaison with the mercurial and unstable Bothwell, the Scots Parliament, in 1567, decreed the place should be thoroughly slighted. The more recent fort on the headland was built in the late eighteenth century to see off energetic privateers such as John Paul Jones.[14]

That the town suffered is clear from the evidence offered by subsequent compensation claims. Of course, there are many willing to grab an opportunity offered by recompense and we might view the payments in this light but there's no doubt Cromwell's men did damage. Some of this was inevitable. You cram so many men, horses, guns, equipment and materiel into a small town and there'll be breakages. Besides this was effectively enemy country and soldiers, however well behaved, tend, at best, to be careless. Cromwell used the church and churchyard as an artillery park. Even lighter guns weighed in at over an old imperial ton and they were both heavy and hard to manoeuvre; tired, hungry, fearful gunners may not be that careful either.

Men need billets and horses need stabling, armies are locusts, they strip a place bare. And Cromwell had another agenda. The sight of burning buildings, of chattels carried off, of outraged citizenry might have been just what was needed to draw the Scots down from Doon Hill in defence of the locals. We also know from compensation claims elsewhere just what damage was done by Cromwell's men. East Lothian Council Archives holds the accounts and details of those who put in claims for the losses they had sustained during the occupation of Dunbar before and after the battle of September 1650. There are 182 names on the list – a mix of men and women (the latter made up about 15 per cent of the total). They were heads of households, a snapshot of Dunbar's population and, via the details of the claims, form a picture of the economy of the burgh.

East Lothian, and Dunbar in particular, suffered greatly before and after the battle even if, as it seems, the levies and regiment due to be raised by the county did not participate in the concluding engagement. Some East Lothian troops may have been involved in skirmishes running up to the battle and others were involved in a guerrilla campaign in the aftermath. But in Dunbar itself they were more pragmatic.

An appeal must have been made to the authorities, the result being that a body of notaries public took evidence from householders and property owners of Dunbar to account for the losses that they sustained during Cromwell's occupation. And a large part of this evidence has survived. Almost all the claimants (the townspeople) were small-scale farmers as well as householders with a trade: grain, malt and livestock feature strongly as do spoilage of 'yards' and 'kaill'.

The town council minutes for 1651 contain a full list of all of the individual claims submitted by citizens of the burgh in respect of losses incurred due to damage/requisition by Parliament's forces during the course of the 1650 campaign and after. The total sum claimed is in the amount of 134,638.00 pounds Scots or 22,460.00 pounds sterling.[15]

These meticulously recorded individual claims range from a few pounds Scots in value to several hundred. For example, one George Maxwell claimed £1,212 (pounds Scots – the Scots pound was worth about one-twelfth of a pound sterling). Some of the expenditure relates to the subsistence of garrison forces left behind after the victory; for example, Thomlinson's Foot Regiment was stationed in Dunbar from 31 January–16 April 1651 and the council claimed a sum of 5,000 pounds Scots (800 pounds sterling) for its subsistence.

Local author R.J.M. Pugh, in his *History of Dunbar*, records that as late as 1663 the town of Haddington was paying an annuity to the local doctor's widow for her late husband's care of the hurt 'sojers [soldiers] at Dunbar fecht [fight]'. Pugh also comments on the erection of the battle monument (latterly moved due to encroachment by the cement works). It was put up initially by the Cromwellian Association in 1951 (as reported in the *Haddingtonshire Courier*, 5 January of that year). Carlyle, who was a native of Dumfriesshire, had married the local doctor's daughter in Dunbar and attended a commemoration on the field on the anniversary in 1843.[16]

Pugh also tells us there was a campaign medal issued by Parliament and one survives in Dunbar Golf Club. The obverse carries a bust of Cromwell and is inscribed 'The Lord of Hosts Word at Dunbar Septem y (e) 3 1650'. The reverse shows the House of Commons in session. In 1651 when claims were being assessed Maus Ferguson demanded £31 for the loss of her hens, Thomas Purves wanted rather more, £12,020. The whole bill amounted to a whopping £134,638 2s. 6d. (Scots).

We get a real flavour of the behaviour of Cromwell's army from some of the other claims lodged after the event. Here is the Scottish Parliament's record of a claim made by Margaret Fraser, Lady Gleneagles and her son, John Haldane. Her husband and another son had both died at Dunbar:

At Perth, 18 December 1650; Our sovereign lord and estates of parliament, having heard a supplication given in to them by Dame Margaret Fraser, lady Gleneagles and John Haldane, now of Gleneagles, her son, showing that whereas it pleased the king's majesty and committee of estates to grant them an exemption from all quarterings, both local and transient, upon the consideration of their supplication, wherein they did represent that their said lamentable condition through their suffering for adherence to the cause and covenant, to the loss and spoiling of their goods and means by the former rebellions, and now lately at the last said conflict near Dunbar, her husband and son had lost their lives in the defence of religion, king and kingdom, therefore craving that, in respect of their singular condition, their lands may be liberated from all quarterings and public dues, as the said supplication at more length bears. Which, with the report of the committee of bills relating thereto, being taken into consideration by our said sovereign lord and estates of parliament, they do except the whole lands belonging to the laird of Gleneagles from all quarterings, both local and transient, in respect of their singular condition, and ordain the said lands to be deleted out of the roll of quarterings, and discharge the general quartermaster and all officers, quartermasters and soldiers to give order for quartering others or quarter themselves upon any part of the said lands belonging to the said laird of Gleneagles as they will be answerable.[17]

At the outset, in 1639, there appears to have been a marked enthusiasm for the cause, the sort of response Kitchener would get in 1914. This kind of gung-ho spirit tends to wane after contact with reality. It was far less prevalent in 1643 and even more so seven years later. The archaeological evidence from Durham would suggest that the prisoners from Dunbar were (mainly) young men who had not seen previous military service.[18]

The old if impecunious nobility still had influence. The Covenanting movement was orchestrated by four social strata; magnates, barons, burgesses and ministers, meeting as a general 'Table' where any number of peers could sit but only restricted numbers of the rest.[19] The lords still wielded considerable power in their own fiefdoms and would always be the focus for recruiting regiments, often with their affinities providing the officer cadre. The demands of maintaining status in failing markets led to ever increasing indebtedness and it was often successful bourgeoisie who acted as bankers. A powerful lord like Argyll was easily able to raise a brigade 5,000-strong in 1638; Campbell of Glenorchy had recruited as many as 172 men from only 5 parishes into his clan regiment.[20]

The old ties of feudal obligation were breaking down as the laird system replaced the old relationships, particularly after the re-ordering of the Estates had given the Shire Commissioners (mostly lairds) a new and powerful voice in the government of the country.

Traditionally, beneath the great lords in the pecking order were the lairds, those minor gentry. Their influence had steadily increased since the Scottish Reformation and the ensuing Civil War of 1568–73. Increasingly, these were those who had status based on property ownership rather than feudal superiority. And their connections were based on shire communities rather than kin affinities. This was inevitable for that was where they had found their power base. Michael Lynch sums it up aptly:

> What was different about the Wars of the Covenant was that they involved the whole of society, noble and non-noble, rural and urban. Regiments were raised by burghs and lairds of modest means as well as by nobles, shires or clans; even the lawyers of the College of Justice raised two regiments, of horse and foot, in 1643–4, as did the ministers, who were each liable for a fully-armed soldier…. Such a war demanded organisation of the machinery of the state as never before. It was the lairds who were the main civil servants of the Revolution.[21]

Subsequently, the Wars of the Covenant embraced all levels of society. Scotland and her citizens had to make a supreme effort after 1638 – a truly national struggle, one which required all levels to participate, not necessarily that willingly. As we've seen, recruitment by 1650 proved increasingly difficult. The war had drained both resources and motivation and, of course, the men called to the colours in that year were being expected to fight for the successor of a king they'd expended so much blood and treasure fighting against, to support a royal prerogative the Covenant had challenged, and we can doubt that even the most naïve recruit had much faith in Charles II's acceptance.

A Different Elite – the Officers

Scotland had always exported military muscle. Scots had fought for France in the Hundred Years War, they'd journeyed from the Western

Isles to form a kind of Samurai in Ireland – the Galloglass, and they'd fought throughout the Thirty Years War. More than a few, such as Leven, had reached high rank, a hardcore of hardbitten professionals, often rich in bloodlines but less so in credit lines. The officer corps in Scotland differed from its equivalent in England. As we'll see, the Durham prisoners were almost exclusively other ranks – at some point officer POWs were segregated. The list of those who died at Berwick appears to include several officers so the split took place either there or later.

Under the conventions in England, an officer, ideally a 'gentleman', was given a commission to a certain rank and was then expected, certainly if senior, to raise local forces, forming a regiment which normally bore his name – Newcastle's White-coats, for example. Yet many officers in the English service were lacking in experience, pedigree and standing being more important. Well might Cromwell famously quip: 'I had rather have a plain, russet-coated Captain, that knows what he fights for, and loves what he knows, than that which you call a Gentle-man and is nothing else'.[22]

Scotland was luckier in that it had this significant pool of professional mercenaries to draw from. This didn't mean that seasoned professionals commanded every unit. Higher command at regimental level was still awarded to men of influence: it was their social and economic sway which gave them the power to recruit from tenantry and affinities. Field officers were drawn from the professionals, even down to company level, where a gentleman captain would be advised by NCOs who'd seen overseas service. This was a fairly good system and meant there was a core layer of experienced soldiers embedded in each tier of command.

More subtly, it created necessary balances between those who might, while amateurs, be fired with high ideals and those who fought just for wages and loot. Most who'd served in the religious wars in Germany or the Low Countries had run out of crusading zeal a long time before. To most of these the Kirk was just a fact of life, not a cause to die for. Politically they also had no particular animus towards the King or, as in 1650, no especial loyalty to his successor. The marriage between Charles II and the Estates was cynical in the extreme for both sides and the simplistic appeal of the Covenant in 1638 was diluted by a dozen years of conflict and growing war-weariness. A Presbyterian

Minister, Patrick Adair, as early as 1642 was none too impressed with the Covenanting zeal of the forces sent to Ireland: '[the soldiers] had no inclination towards religion except insofar as the times and State who employed them seemed to favour it'.[23]

The system was far from foolproof, mercenaries expect to be paid so cash, usually in short supply, had to be found for their wages. The definition of foreign service could be quite elastic, as in 1640 when General Monro had been deployed to Aberdeenshire to quell local Royalist sympathisers. The mission proved quite lucrative and the Colonel felt he needed the mobility of an attached unit of cavalry to maximise opportunities for pillaging. The local shire committee found an officer, Arthur Forbes, to command this new yeomanry troop:

> who, though he were none of the wisest nor best commanders yet his father, Mr John Forbes, sometimes minister at Alford his suffering banishment in King James the Sixth's time for opposing episcopacy, and his son Arthur being seized upon at sea anno 1639, was cast for sometime into prison at Newgate, in London, by the King's warrant, was sufficient recommendations to prefer him.

It wasn't successful. Forbes' bandits behaved badly in their only fight, and ran away but not before robbing their own side. Forbes forfeited his brief tenure and was ingloriously cashiered.[24]

Dour Covenanters tended to take a dim view of near apostate soldiery. Early in 1647, the army had been given a makeover, 'new-modelled', a bit like the English Parliamentary forces a couple of years earlier. This process involved a series of amalgamations with a plethora of under-strength units being merged. This probably didn't unduly bother the rank and file but it led to redundancies among officers, many of whom became supernumeraries. This did offer Argyll an opportunity to retain only those who were ideologically sound (or at least appeared to be). However, barely a year later when Hamilton and the Engagers gained ascendancy most transferred their loyalties without demur; paymasters before prophets.

After the Preston debacle an Act of Classes was passed which sacked all those who'd collaborated with the Engagers and a new commission for purging the army was established in June 1650, though it's questionable what real effect this actually had, with some units ignoring it completely.[25] Walker's classic dismissal of the politically correct replacements may only be half true and it seems more likely that Leslie's army at Dunbar was competently officered. The fact so many appear to have been absent from their posts at the crucial point was clearly a factor in his defeat.

Rank and File – Soldiers of the Covenant

Scotland, until 1650, had not suffered the chaos of civil war to the same extent. There had been the scrapping at the outset, Montrose's campaigns, Hamilton's folly and the debacle at Preston. Yet, as we've seen, Scotland possessed, at the outset, an experienced corps of professional fighting men who'd won their spurs in the indescribably bloody and savage conflicts raging in Europe. The Scots army (a more correct term than 'Covenanting Army' as this was a truly national call out) was raised by conscription. That is not to say that there weren't any men who volunteered but the system itself was geared to compulsory national service which, for all its limitations, could be and was very effective.

In each separate sheriffdom a 'committee of war' was set up and the members, collectively, had responsibility for raising and equipping forces. Their first task was to assess, by muster, how many able-bodied men were available and then to summon these for service according to a centrally imposed quota. Mainly this was a government directive but sometimes senior local commanders might have sufficient executive power. The committee had to ensure their men possessed proper weapons and gear with forty days' rations. If their period of service extended beyond this initial call-up, then the government was responsible for their subsistence. Frequently this system didn't work well and, with sustained operations such as the lengthy siege of Newcastle upon Tyne in late summer/ autumn 1644, the soldiers were badly under-supplied.

We have no record of whether or not the rank and file had been willing recruits but we do know that the Scots army had had problems recruiting sufficient numbers for the campaign. Twelve years of war had taken their toll – it was no longer possible to call out all men between the ages of 16 and

60. This new system of organising recruitment by shire committee was, in part, recognition of the increasingly important role of shire representatives as much as it was an acceptance that the production of food and the economy had to be protected. It was not exactly the start of what would later be termed 'reserved occupations' but the basic idea was there.

It is interesting to note that the presence of a Stuart monarch at the head of a Covenanting army was not enough to bring out some of the more traditionally Royalist areas such as Aberdeenshire and Kincardinshire:

> The Scots infantry regiments raised from the summer of 1650 were generally smaller than those of the English. Only small numbers were raised from Edinburgh, Berwickshire and Roxburghshire to join the Teviotdale men, and very few came from Haddingtonshire. Support for the king was weak in Dumfriesshire, the South-West as a whole, and parts of Ayrshire, so that few men were recruited from these areas. Larger numbers came from Fife and Kinross, Linlithgow, Stirling and Clackmannan; Perthshire, Forfarshire (about 600 men). Regulars from the respective clans led by Lovat and Argyle from the Highlands took part. Only about 110 men were raised from Aberdeenshire and the Mearns.[26]

The people were weary of war generally.

In England during the latter stages of the First Civil War local ad hoc militias or 'clubmen' had been formed to see off whoever's army happened to pass by, King or Parliament. Scotland, if less ravaged, had seen atrocities, Montrose's female camp followers foraging prior to the Battle of Kilsyth in 1645 had been cut up by Covenanter cavalry, and worse, several hundred had been callously murdered by drowning in the wake of his *Gotterdammerung* at Philiphaugh. War is cruel. When Bolton in Lancashire was stormed two years before, the inhabitants suffered dreadfully:

> the soldiers spoiling all they could meet with, nothing regarding the doleful cries of women or children, but some they slashed as they were calling for quarter, others when they had given quarter, many hailed out of their houses to have their brains dashed out in

the street, those that were not dead in the streets already, pistoled, slashed, brained or trodden under their horses feet ...[27]

The fact the original Conscription Act had to be bolstered by further statutes on 24 June and 3 July 1650 indicates how sluggish recruitment was. Trying to rapidly increase a modest standing force of 3,000 infantry and 2,500 cavalry to an ambitious complement of 19,000 was asking a lot from a poor country which had been at war, on and off, for a dozen years.[28] Incentives were lacking, a young man taken from the plough, the bench or counting house was swapping a difficult life for a far harder and uncertain one to fight for a king he had never seen.

Military service had little to recommend it and this was about homeland protection – which you could argue was a reason for going for many – but it also meant the general lure of loot was lacking. The conscript could look forward to long, hard marches in bad weather over worse roads, burdened with weapons, pack and accoutrement. His plain, hodden grey uniform was probably of variable quality like his footwear, both would suffer during the campaign and replacements would be scarce, as were regular rations and decent tentage and medical facilities. The awful summer weather would ensure their uniforms got wet and stayed that way, chafing and cumbersome, shoes would leak, chilblains, colds and fevers dogging them.

To the experience of Dunbar must also be added the psychology of defeat, the despair and humiliation of surrender, beaten by an enemy they had probably considered already defeated. A survivor of Essex's defeated army at Lostwithiel six years earlier recalls the harsh treatment prisoners received:

Then came our misery. For when we had laid down our arms, and came to march through the enemy's army, we were inhumanely dealt with: abused, reviled, scorned, torn, kicked, pillaged, and many stripped of all they had, quite contrary to the articles ... they took away our cloaks, coats and hats, calumniating us by reproachful words and threats ... and after a day or two march, they stripped many of our officers to their shirts, taking away their boots shoes, hose etc.[29]

They must have been fully aware of the awfulness of their situation. As conscripts they had been fighting on home turf for their country. Now they were effectively stateless, a commodity to be sold on and traded. They would be abused, reviled, pillaged and stripped by the Parliamentarians, kicked, beaten, spat upon and worse; all of their personal items, cloaks, passable headgear, timepieces, even the pathetic personal keepsakes that a man clings to as a reminder he has a home, taken. Added to the normal disdain shown by victors who have got through by the skin of their teeth, there was an added racial element, 'as for those Scots – I rate 'em as sots'.[30] To Cromwell, these men and the few women who we know had remained with them were an ongoing risk, to be neutralised and, if possible, used to fund the costs of the exercise.

Highlanders and Mosstroopers

And there are about five hundred sick in the castle, and about six hundred yet in health in the cathedral, and most of which are, in probability highlanders, they being hardier than the rest.[31]

Highlanders were problematic, with a recent track record of fighting against the Covenant rather than for it. The Civil War had changed the effectiveness of highlanders as soldiers. Montrose's deputy Alistair MacColla had re-invented their tactics so the 'highland charge' became an effective and disciplined manoeuvre. The 'Year of Miracles' had witnessed the defeat of numerous Covenanting forces. Culturally, there was a widening gap across the Great Glen as the lowlanders came increasingly to look down on their culturally backward contemporaries, part fearful, part contemptuous. They made good soldiers though, and while we cannot be sure of how many highlanders served in the Covenanting Army of 1650, there was clearly more than a few.

The 'mosstrooper', that descendant of the border reiver, used the arms which had proved so effective during the long intermittent conflict that had only ended with James I's ferocious intervention in the first decade of the seventeenth century. Their chosen weapon was the lance; mounted on an ash shaft some 13ft (4m) in length, used couched for thrusting or hurled over arm like a javelin. Cumbersome matchlocks received little favour as they were essentially unsuited to the cavalry arm. Wheel locks, when introduced, proved more practical, though expensive. The well-off might carry a brace of pistols secured in holsters worn each side of the saddle, in addition to sporting a carbine or caliver which, as the sixteenth century wore on, had replaced the crossbow or latch as a missile weapon. How many mosstroopers carried firearms during the Dunbar campaign is not clear, but for Cromwell's men this was a new type of opponent, skilled, ferocious and elusive.

It is difficult to identify mosstroopers among the captured at Dunbar. Looking at the names of those who died and were buried in Berwick only one name, Featherstone, belongs to one of the border families.[32] If any were captured, they would have been prime candidates as escapers during the forced march south to the border; independent-minded and on their own home turf, fleeing from the law was an instinctive reflex. The march south might be dictated by commerce and policy but it would feel like retribution.

Chapter 5

The Trail of Tears

It is high time for me to put an end to you ...
Oliver Cromwell, speech dissolving the
Rump Parliament, 1653

There are all too many war crimes still within living memory: the long trail from Dunbar to Durham is a much older one and its victims have no voices. It is only with the aid of archaeology that we can begin to piece together details of the lives of those who made it as far as Durham: the men who left their bones there, tumbled into mass graves and were literally swept under history's carpet for nearly as many years as there are days in the year.

As for those Scots ...

There was no Geneva Convention in the seventeenth century. The fate of the defeated generally lay in the hands of or even at the whim of the victor. Contemporaries were shocked at Henry V's callous cull of knightly prisoners at Agincourt. Killing nobility was ungentlemanly and besides, it was uneconomic, the dead cannot be ransomed. At Philiphaugh on 13 September 1645, at the dismal end of Montrose's 'Year of Miracles', Irish troops and camp followers attempted to surrender to David Leslie.[1]

Though the battle was over, the killing was not. Leslie gave way to the exhortations of the group of ministers who were anxious that the Lord's work be seen to be done. By the Lord's work they meant the systematic massacre of captives who were marched to nearby Newark Castle and summarily shot in batches, lined up against the barmkin wall (where the bullet marks are still discernible). In order to conserve valuable ammunition, the women and children were flung into the river and held under with lances till all were drowned. Only the three senior officers – Stewart, Laghtnan and O'Cahan – were spared.[2]

Officers generally fared better; they could be ransomed or exchanged, sometimes persuaded to change sides. At Dungan's Hill (in Ireland) in August 1647, two years after Philiphaugh, a Parliamentarian force caught the Irish Confederates' Leinster army on their line of march; the subsequent battle (details of which are unclear) resulted in a crushing defeat and the deaths of over 3,000 Confederates.[3] Parliament's losses were trifling in comparison but it seems that many Irish were killed after they had tried to surrender. The actual act of capitulation had to be accepted by the other side before the losers could claim POW status. It was all fairly unpredictable.

That was Ireland of course – the Scots were different, former allies and co-religionists, at the very least. Yet, there was still lingering anti-Scots sentiment in England. Not helped by 300 years of border warfare, it had been given fresh impetus by more recent memories of Scots armies coming through Northumberland in 1640 and again in 1644. These were not pillaging expeditions but they had expected, like all armies of the period, to live off the countryside. Leven's two successful campaigns had seen Northumberland, Newcastle, Wearside and Durham all occupied. Both times they had had to pay the expenses of the Scots army and further sums had been required to get them to leave. The occupied do not like occupiers especially if the former are Northern English and the latter Scots.

A comment made in a letter from Robert Watson, one of the Earl of Northumberland's officers, to the Earls Steward in London has a heartfelt ring to it: 'I hope now theire is no feare of Scottes invasion'.[4] It should also be borne in mind that many of Cromwell's soldiers had fought in Ireland and the habit of casual brutality, once acquired, is not easily shed. The Irish were regarded as sub-human *untermenschen* and while the Scots were not viewed in quite this way, a hint of the same inhumanity lingers.

It is a mindset that can have horrendous consequences. Consider, for example, what happened to the French town of Oradour-Sur-Glane in the summer of 1944, as the Allies were building their Normandy bridgehead. The 2nd SS Panzer Das Reich was ordered north towards the battle.

Slowed by resistance activity, the SS decided on reprisals. They massacred over 600 citizens of this small town as a blanket retaliation. The victims had not taken part in the killing of German soldiers; they were effectively selected at random and made an example of. The Germans had committed other atrocities in France, but this was on a different scale. Like Cromwell's troops in Ireland, these men had seen service in a brutalising environment: the division had fought extensively on the Eastern Front. It was that experience of war they imposed – 'Russian' rules were far harsher and atrocity was the norm.[5]

Christopher Browning, in his arresting study of the Holocaust, *Ordinary Men: Reserve Police Battalion 101 and the Final Solution in Poland*, shows how easily the process of brutalisation works; how horror becomes commonplace.[6] 'Ordinary' men do terrible things. Cromwell's soldiers were ordinary men as were their Scottish victims. How many of those who were pulling the triggers on the way to Berwick had served in Ireland and now just casually adopted a similar reflex?

Marching

And here they are, in that cold September, the wreckage of their nation's defeat. Men, for the most part, young and untried in war, that, only a day before, had been part of an army confident of victory and who never saw that thundering, shattering defeat loom near. Stripped of weapons, already hungry, they struggle in their long, unkempt column down the rutted slime that passes for a road. No banners, no drums, no colours and no hope, unkempt, unwashed, unfed. The stink of defeat clings like a shroud.

Nobody favours the loser:

As an Army nurse returning from Vietnam in 1968, our entire planeload of veterans were held on the plane for two hours until it was safe for us to go into Travis Air Force Base. We were told to take our uniforms off after leaving the airport. I was also in uniform in Washington, D.C., and had eggs thrown at me by protesters. No matter that I did not agree with the war, I still deserved respect for my service.[7]

Success they say has a thousand fathers, failure is an orphan. The defeated become pariahs in their own land. Now they stumble south, their journey punctuated by pistol shots as those who fall out are killed without compunction.

> After the Battel at Dunbar in Scotland, my Lord General writ to me, That there was about Nine thousand Prisoners, and that of them he had set at liberty all those that were wounded, and, as he thought, disabled for future Service, and their Number was, as Mr Downing writ, Five thousand one hundred; the rest the general sent towards Newcastle, conducted to Berwick by Major Hobson, and from Berwick to Newcastle by some Foot out of that Garison, and the Troop of Horse ...[8]

It is always difficult to calculate numbers involved in these situations;; exact figures for the Dunbar prisoners will never be known. But if we take Hesilrige's figure of 9,000 (which is not far off Cromwell's own estimate of a thousand more, although, of course, 10,000 is a suspiciously round figure), then somewhere between 3,500 and 4,500 were released immediately with 5,500 being marched off south.[9] Those let go comprised the severely wounded and camp followers. This must have been a diverse group, soldiers' wives and some children, sutleresses, all manner of tradesmen; smiths, farriers, armourers, gunsmiths, joiners and carpenters, coopers, drovers, medics and musicians – all sorts followed an army of the time. How many of these there were and how many wounded we just don't know. What we do know is the likely rate of casualties to dead for the time and that allows us to come up with an estimate. If the total Scottish dead were just under a thousand, then at least twice that number would have been wounded, probably half of them seriously.

In the Great War an average foot battalion of a thousand men on the march required roughly a mile (1.6km) of road. This was on the hard granite pave of Northern France and Belgium; more room would be needed on the rutted, mud-garnished track our Scots took. If there were 5,000 men and women trudging, then that's a minimum of 5 miles (approximately 8km) for the entire column. They don't look much like soldiers, ragged as scarecrows, already stinking, their hodden grey soaked and tattered, and boots if they had any, already giving out. 'Men marched asleep. Many had lost their boots/But limped on, blood shod. All went lame, all blind/Drunk with fatigue.'[10]

Some of the injured would, in the following days, weeks or even months succumb to their injuries or to complications arising from them. Those able to do so, would walk, or be carried back, to their homes. And a pitiful sight they were. One eyewitness, Anne Murray, writing a few days after the fight, was making her way to Fyvie Castle in Aberdeenshire (scene of one of Montrose's battles six years earlier), when she met up with some walking wounded. She was so moved by their dreadful plight she set up what might later have been called an advanced dressing station at Kinross, where she treated sixty or so of them.[11] One had suffered a severe head wound, so bad that sections of the brain were exposed. Another youth had been transfixed by a sword thrust. Entry was from behind, beneath the right shoulder and the point had exited on the left side of his chest. The wound was lifting with maggots. Another had a gunshot wound to the arm which was turning gangrenous. They stank; the charnel-house reek of death enveloping them like a shroud. Clearly some, perhaps most, would not survive.[12]

Berwick

In the long course of the border wars Berwick-upon-Tweed changed hands no less than fourteen times. A prosperous and important Scottish seaport for the North Sea trade, Longshanks more or less destroyed the town as well as slaughtering a large number of its luckless inhabitants in 1296.[13] Things did not get any better from then on.

Berwick became a forward operating base for both nations with the modest fortifications being added to, extended and upgraded till the town was one of the most reinforced in Britain. Edward I himself, Bruce and then Henry VIII all added their own signatures. In Elizabeth's day the whole place was given a state-of-the-art makeover, shrunk in size but studded with high-tech artillery bastions and massive battered (sloping) walls in the latest style. The medieval castle now lay some distance north of the walls and was very run down.[14]

It may be the prisoners were housed in the castle itself or marched inside the ramparts. Their first sight of the walls then, as they marched down Castlegate, would have been the mighty Brass Bastion guarding the eastern corner next to the sea, the jutting flat arrowhead of Cumberland Bastion in the centre and Meg's Mount rising over the western sweep down towards the Tweed. Scotgate pierces the wall below Meg's Mount and the long winding column would have tramped beneath its arch just as we do today. Ravensdowne Barracks weren't yet built and the POWs may have been herded up by Palace Green, next to the present Commonwealth church.[15]

How many were there at this point? Hesilrige indicates losses along the way:

> I believe they were not told at Berwick and most of those that were lost, it was in Scotland, for I heard, That the Officers that marched with them to Berwick, were necessitated to kill about Thirty, fearing the loss of them all, for they fell down in great Numbers, and said, They were not able to march; and they brought them far in the night, so that doubtless many ran away.[16]

If any of the Scots was minded to make a run for it then clearly north of Berwick was the time. Once south of the border they were effectively in 'enemy' territory. Sir Arthur refers to thirty having been shot out of hand, more might have been as easily 'put to the sword'; bullets after all cost money. The guard was pretty weak even with four troops of dragoons and so chances for escape were plentiful.

From Dunbar to Berwick is nearly 40 miles (64km). That is a very long way for men who are already hungry, wet and exhausted to march in a day, over very bad roads at the end of a wet and dismal summer. There is no record of an overnight halt on the first leg of their journey and Hesilrige does tell us they reached Berwick late at night. So it's quite possible they had been force marched from Dunbar without a halt. That would have been a harsh experience.

From Dunbar the road bellies south just in from the coast then rises up to the narrower defile at Cockburnspath where Leslie had established his earlier blocking force. That would be the best place to make a run for it. More towards the coast the ground slopes down towards the rocky shore and the fishing village at Cove. Inland it rises towards the old French camp and the defile of the Dunglas Burn could offer a tempting escape route, difficult for cavalry or dragoons to follow with plenty of good hiding places.[17] Escapers must have known there could not be any sustained pursuit, troopers having neither the time nor resources to chase them.

Still that leaves the question of why so many of them did continue to march rather than seeking their freedom. The answer probably lies in a number of causes: their physical condition, the demoralising effect of defeat, knowing they had little chance of shelter or welcome further south. There is too a peculiar psychological factor which affects the prisoner of war en masse: we see similar quiescence in large groups of captives throughout history. It takes a degree of confidence and self belief to flee as well as the courage to try your captors' mood. There's no doubt of the courage these men had displayed but the very act of surrender depletes your store of self esteem.

Although Berwick was only a temporary halt, some still died there and the burial record offers some tantalising insights:

July – 15th Thomas Rosse soldier: August – 18th Robert Layne trooper; 26th Robert Thompson quartermaster: September – 9th Thomas Huxtable trooper; 10th Henry Wallace trooper; 17th William More soldier; 17th John Greenway soldier; 17th Richard Lyndinge soldier; 18th Samuel Corden captain; [see prisoner list Samuel Gordon Lieutenant/Ensign of Foot]; 19th Edward Layone corronitte [cornet] 19th Thomas Dee trooper; 19th William Fidler trooper; 20th George Frank soldier; 20th George Wilson soldier; 22nd Robert Walker trooper; 23rd Henry Crawforth trooper; 24th Roger Fokeser dragoon; 24th Robert Blackwell trooper; 25th Peter Chiseman soldier; 26th William Wiard trooper; 27th Henry Sargnale trooper; 28th Roger Featherston trooper; 29th Frank Gizzpe trooper: October – 1st Joseph Room soldier; 1st John Falkiner soldier; 1st Robert Archibald woeuds [probably indicates he died of wounds]; Alyson Trotter Scot woman; 3rd John Lucas trooper; 4th Richard Bankes trooper; 4th George Bullie trooper;

5th Thomas Taylor trooper; 6th Samuel Gaskin soldier; 6th Robert Anerston doctor [***]; 6th Franke Gizzipe trooper [double entry with 29 September]; 7th Richard Fowler soldier; 7th Hugh Morton soldier; 7th John Stemie belonging to the Artillery; 7th Thomas Floyd trooper; 7th Henry Blancher trooper. 9th John Collie trooper; 10th Jacob Prigg trooper; 10th John Dudine trooper; 12th Henry Aisker soldier; 13th Bart Copp trooper; 14th George Hill trooper; 17th Edward Houston trooper; 22nd Mattthew Faking trooper [?Young]; 23rd William Dude soldier; 23rd Henry Hendry trooper; 24th Gilman Taylor Capt; 28th John Stobs a capt man: November – 2nd Edward Kinniston soldier; 2nd Woyson Tration [?] a scot woman; 30th Henry Neat/Neald trooper.[18]

Looking at these names, there are fifty-odd recorded deaths. The first three all died before 3 September so we can safely assume these are probably members of the garrison or they might just be Scottish prisoners from earlier in the campaign. Again, we do not know how many of these there were. Berwick was the obvious holding ground for all POWs: there must have been men swept up in the course of the campaign. Not all who marched had necessarily been taken just at Dunbar – there will have been others caught up in the slog south. Assuming those who are listed after the date of the battle are all Scots (and we do not know they are – a Featherstone is very unlikely to have been on the Scots side, for instance) then the register includes several officers and two women.

This suggests to us that, by this point, there had been no segregation of the officers. It is clear that women also accompanied the prisoners. How many we don't know, Sir Arthur makes no mention of any at all. This begs the question of whether Cromwell deliberately included women in his haul; they had a cash value too as indentured servants, or were these wives/camp followers allowed to accompany the male prisoners? This makes a degree of sense; they could have acted as nurses and/or cooks (if there had been anything to cook that is).

We also have to consider what happened to Cromwell's own wounded. He only admits to a very modest loss but they must have numbered several hundred who would either have to be evacuated by sea or transported back to Berwick (their nearest forward operating base) in carts (and a truly awful, grinding journey that would be in un-sprung wagons).[19] On this basis we cannot say for sure that all of the recorded deaths are Scots. We can certainly say Captain Gordon is a Scot as he is on the list of captured officers (see Appendix 2). Many are listed as troopers and therefore clearly cavalry, not necessarily Scots, though, as most of the Scottish prisoners are more likely infantry, cavalry survivors having got clear away. The implication has to be that these are English troopers who subsequently died of wounds or sepsis.

Next, what did they all die of? Wounds and subsequent complications have to be the most likely causes. Hunger, exhaustion and illness, possibly even deliberate brutality, might also have taken their toll. The Scots were already famished before the battle and the physical toll of the forced march from Dunbar would have been considerable. What killed the two women? We have no idea, most probably sickness and/or fatigue. There are no surviving burials or any later note of them; the Scots just disappear from record. No local tradition or memory, as far as we're aware, survives anywhere except Durham itself.

Berwick was a major garrison but only a staging post for the Scottish POWs. All who were fit were on the move again after that one night, still un-watered and un-fed. Their escort changed, unspecified troops were drawn from the garrison strength and attached to guard the column. Off they went into the vestiges of that dismal summer and onto the long road south.

Alnwick

Allied prisoners from the Durham Light Infantry, captured at the time of Dunkirk, would likely know how they felt:

> The speed of the Russian advance after the successful summer offensive of 1944 led to hurried evacuation of the more easterly camps westwards. This would be a forced march, any distance from 300 to 800 miles through the teeth of a continental winter. Some were to be moved by train but this, of itself, posed dangers as the RAF now controlled the skies; 'the senior British officer said we would not move under any circumstances unless the top of the cattle

trucks were painted in white "POW", in order to avoid being shot up …'.[20]

It was an undiluted nightmare:

Rodney Gee was less fortunate: he had to march. He was considerably older than his fellow captives, being in his mid-forties: 'To carry my goods, I made a rucksack from a pair of trousers. Columns of marching men attracted the Allied aircraft overhead that could not recognise the columns as marching POWs. We refused to march by day due to the danger from the air and we marched by night. After two nights we refused to go on as we were too weak; the Germans feared an uprising of Poles, internees and forced labour people'.[21]

Although these are accounts from the Second World War, the unpleasant realities of forced POW marches do not necessarily change. At least the Dunbar men did not have to worry about aerial surveillance.

We have virtually no information about the march till they arrived at Morpeth but it seems to have been conducted in relatively easy stages; Berwick to Belford (16 miles/26km), then to Alnwick (16 miles/26km), on to Morpeth (20 miles/31km), next Newcastle (14½ miles/23km), Chester-le-Street (11 miles/18km) and finally into Durham (8 miles/12km). Easy stages if you are fit, particularly for men used to walking everywhere. If you are dehydrated, starved, exhausted, possibly wounded, maybe sick, then it would be a living hell. There is no mention of executions by the roadside and probably few attempts at escape. We do not know of any encounters with locals but people would probably have come out to see them go by. It's probably reasonable to suggest the Scots would get no sympathy; ancient memories were still alive and more recent ones still fresh; all bad.

We do not even know how they interacted among themselves. Hesilrige reports that the men displayed very little corporate spirit, more dog eat dog: 'some were killed by themselves, for they were exceeding cruel one towards another. If a man was perceived to have any Money, it was two to one but he was killed before morning, and Robbed; and if any had good clothes, he that wanted, if he was able, would strangle him, and put on his clothes'.[22] This was at Durham, of course, where desperation would have mounted. Whether such murderous internecine squabbling happened earlier we cannot say. This kind of ordeal is not the best form of team-building. And after the battle, there could be no certainty that men who had come from the same area, who had joined up together would remain together.

However, they must have been some connections which will have helped the marchers to pull together rather than be at each other's throats. We know from the transportee records that there were relatives among them, including a few sets of brothers and a number of men with the same surname (who might also have had a connection).

Berwick to Belford is a reasonably flat route; the road hugs the coastal plain passing by Haggerston. The current ruins are from the late nineteenth century when it was remodelled by Norman Shaw.[23] What was there in 1650 would have been a great deal more modest and vernacular. Lindisfarne would have risen on their left, the mound of Beblowe crag, crowned by a Henrician fort, also given a later makeover by Lutyens.

This was not a gentle landscape. Northumberland, less than half a century after King James' pacification of the border, was not a place you would want to visit.[24] Life there was poor and it was hard, full of small huddled farms and fishing hamlets – folk had little to spare even if they wanted to. The men still had their officers we surmise, it's likely they were not separated out until Newcastle. We can only hazard a guess at the order of march – possibly they remained in their companies and regiments. Nor can we say if any women stayed with them, very possibly yes but clearly, as there is no reference to them, not many. The sum of what we really don't know is considerable.

Then the road would have climbed up into Belford and down out again. Most of the pleasant high street is no older than the eighteenth century but the overall ribbon spread was probably similar a hundred years before; though the buildings would have been meaner and more crowded. The hall too is much later and grander, built by James Paine (*c*. 1754–6).[25] It was probably in the grounds of whatever was there before that the prisoners were corralled in. No tents or bedding were provided; they just dropped into exhausted oblivion. No food or water either, except for whatever they could find.

The harbour, Dunbar. (*Authors*)

Dunbar from Doon Hill. (*Authors*)

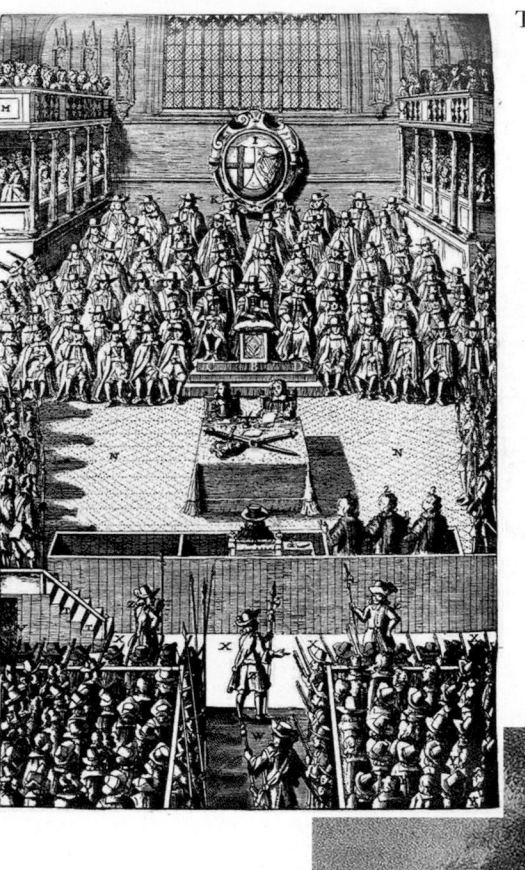

The Trial of Charles I. (*Public domain*)

David Leslie, by unknown.
(*Public domain*)

Oliver Cromwell, by Circle of Adriaen Hanneman. (*Public domain*)

Sir Arthur Hesilrige, by unknown. (*www.npg.org.uk*)

Looking up Doon Hill. (*Authors*)

A typical Dunbar cottage. (*Authors*)

Dunbar churchyard. (*Authors*)

THIS MEMORIAL IS ERECTED
IN MEMORY OF THOSE MEM-
BERS OF THE 19TH COMPANY &
OF THE LOTHIANS & BERWICK
-SHIRE IMPERIAL YEOMANRY
WHO FELL IN SOUTH AFRICA
DURING THE WAR 1900-1
THEY BRAVELY & WILLINGLY
GAVE THEIR LIVES AT THE
CALL OF DUTY FOR THEIR
QUEEN & COUNTRY & THEIR
SORROWING COMRADES AND
FRIENDS DESIRE THROUGHOUT
ALL TIME TO COMMEMORATE
THEIR SPLENDID DEVOTION

DULCE ET DECORUM
EST PRO PATRIA MORI

The other Dunbar war memorial, (*Authors*)

Dunbar remembers. (*Authors*)

The entrance to Dunbar harbour from the landward side. (*Authors*)

Dunbar harbour today. (*Authors*)

Looking out to sea from Dunbar harbour (*Authors*)

The old harbour at Dunbar. (*Authors*)

The ruins of Dunbar Castle. (*Authors*)

The monument to the men of Dunbar. (*Authors*)

Inside the walls of Berwick. (*Authors*)

The churchyard at Berwick.
(*Authors*)

The road from Berwick. (*Authors*)

The walled garden at Morpeth Castle today. (*Authors*)

The interior of St Nicholas' Cathedral, Newcastle upon Tyne. (*Authors*)

The nave at Durham Cathedral. (*Authors*)

Durham Cathedral. (*Public domain*)

In memory of the Scottish soldiers captured at the Battle of Dunbar and imprisoned in Durham, who died and were buried here in the autumn of 1650.

The memorial in the cafe at Palace Green Library. (*Authors*)

A sign to the battlefield. (*Authors*)

Re-enactors portraying the Scots Army, 2012. (*Courtesy of Adam Barr*)

Charles II and Catherine of Braganza, by Frederik Hendrik Van den Hove (*c.* 1630–71?). (*Public domain*)

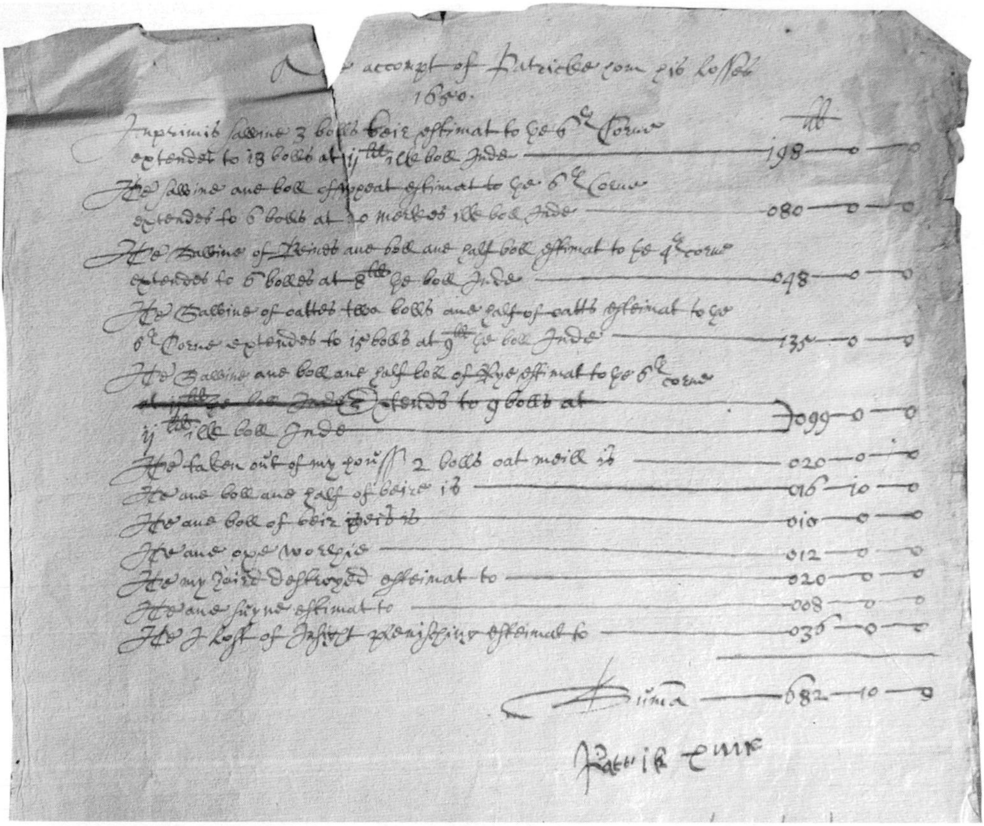

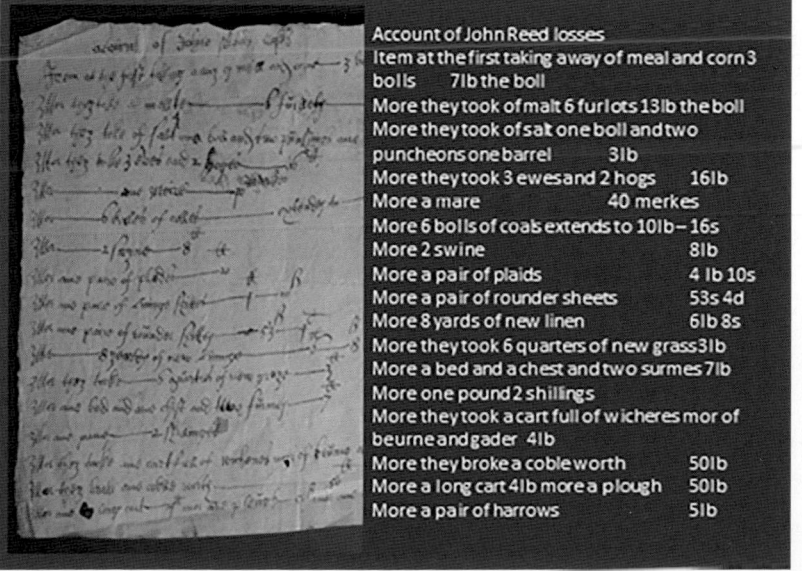

One of the Dunbar claims. (*Courtesy of East Lothian Council Archives*)

Account of John Reed losses
Item at the first taking away of meal and corn 3 bolls   7lb the boll
More they took of malt 6 furlots 13lb the boll
More they took of salt one boll and two puncheons one barrel   3lb
More they took 3 ewes and 2 hogs   16lb
More a mare   40 merkes
More 6 bolls of coals extends to 10lb – 16s
More 2 swine   8lb
More a pair of plaids   4 lb 10s
More a pair of rounder sheets   53s 4d
More 8 yards of new linen   6lb 8s
More they took 6 quarters of new grass 3lb
More a bed and a chest and two surmes 7lb
More one pound 2 shillings
More they took a cart full of wicheres mor of beurne and gader 4lb
More they broke a coble worth   50lb
More a long cart 4lb more a plough   50lb
More a pair of harrows   5lb

A transcription of a Dunbar claim. (*Courtesy of John Malden*)

Seal of the Massachusetts Bay Colony, by unknown, Michael G. Hall, *The Last American Puritan: The Life of Increase Mather, 1639–1723*, p. 133. (*Public domain*)

The Ranney House, Middletown, from Charles Collard Adams, *Middletown Upper Houses: A History Of The North Society Of Middletown, Connecticut, From 1650 To 1800, With Genealogical And Biographical Chapters On Early Families And A Full Genealogy Of The Ranney Family* (The Grafton Press, 1908). (*www.archive.org*)

Some of George Darlings' descendants. (*Courtesy of Misty Scheidt*)

Next morning, shaken awake, mustered into line, probably with the help of musket butts and boots, they went down the hill out of Belford and south towards Alnwick. The ancient seat of the mighty, frequently over mighty, Percies which they had held since the early fourteenth century (give or take the odd attainder) rises on the flank of the Aln Valley, the northward approach bulked out by the impressive mass of the great castle. As they trudged down towards the Lion Bridge with the walls rising beyond they would have passed the memorial to another Scottish visitor – Shakespeare's Malcolm Canmore, who came once too often in 1093.[26] Eighty years later a successor, William the Lion, also came to grief here, routed and captured by the Umfravilles. Probably none of the reeking, tattered column had ever heard of either or was likely to care.

They were probably housed inside the walls, within the old outer wards. The Earl (the Percies weren't elevated to their present dukedom until the 1770s) would not want Cromwell's detritus too close to his apartments. Still no food or water was offered. It's possible to surmise the rough handling would escalate as the men became more exhausted and even more taciturn, scrapping among themselves for any real or imagined morsel someone might have hoarded. The Dunkirk spirit is best reserved for movies; it's less obvious in desperate reality. Maybe some of the guards were decent men who shared their own pretty meagre rations but there would never be enough to go round. We don't know if any died on the way from Berwick to Belford or from there to Alnwick, Sir Arthur does not tell us.[27]

Morpeth

More from that dreadful winter of 1944–5:

> Joseph Weddle was another who endured the harsh journey west in the unrelenting cold of January 1945: 'Some of the lads coming into the camp, especially the Indian soldiers, were in a bad way. The lads had a whip-round to give them some of what we had. The German officers got us lined up. We had a flat float, the kind of cart with tyre wheels pulled by a small pony. This carried the Germans' equipment. We didn't know where we were going, just moving away

from Danzig because the Russians were pushing through. We were told to keep together and see what happens. When you got tired, you just rested. Even the refugees, Germans and Poles were on the roads with their horses, carts, barrows, marching, marching, marching!'[28]

For the DLI 'Pals' survival meant sticking together:

Weddle and his pals stuck together, a close knit team: '... it was bitterly cold, and the wind! Jokers, grousers and habitual aggressors stumbled on together ... Most of us had British overcoats, which were a godsend.' Even the most brutal of the guards began to relax the iron bonds of discipline. It was becoming obvious to all the war was coming to an end: 'Sometimes we went into large barns, no lights. You had to be there to believe it. When you're cold you always want to go to the toilet and you're in the middle of a crowded barn. You couldn't see. Somebody would try and light a match! The barn was full of straw. You couldn't find your pals on the way back. Some shouted, "Stop down there and go to sleep." Then you got somebody's boot in your face. Some didn't bother, just pissed in the straw where they were. That was the worst part in the larger barns.'[29]

Morpeth has had two castles, the original motte on Ha' Hill then the present fort built later, possibly after King John had destroyed the first one. This is about 200m south or the original and probably dates from the thirteenth century.[30] The castle, of which now only the gatehouse and sections of curtain walling survive, had changed hands a few times and had been besieged by Montrose in spring 1644, before the Earl of Callendar re-took it for Parliament. It's possible some of the POWs had been there then.

when they came to Morpeth, the Prisoners being put into a large walled Garden, they eat up raw Cabages, Leaves and Roots, so many, as the very seed and the labor, at Four pence a day, was valued by sufficient men at Nine pounds; which Cabage, as I conceive, they having fasted, as they themselves said, near eight days, poisoned their Bodies, for as they were coming from thence to Newcastle, some dyed by the way side ...[31]

There is an assumption that this walled garden was adjacent to the castle possibly on the level ground outside and on the east (no trace remains), though it may have been Hepscott Park. What is clear is that the starving soldiers tucked into the raw cabbages growing there, roots and all. While this might have temporarily sated their desperate pangs it would be the death of so many of them. They may well have picked up infections here – it was still common to use night soil as a fertiliser in this period and certainly there is no evidence they were able to wash their booty before wolfing it down. It seems likely that the immediate effect was that their shrunken stomachs couldn't cope. Hesilrige tells us that they began dying almost straightaway, though there is no record of any deaths in Morpeth.[32]

By now their dreadful calvary must have seemed never-ending, filthy, stinking, lice-ridden, starving and exhausted, brutalised and beaten by their guards, reviled by the country folk. These men have no voices, we have no memoir from any of them – not even officers (we can assume the higher ranks were still with them at this point). As Sir Arthur notes, most had not eaten in over a week. During that time they had fought a major battle and marched for days without sustenance or respite. Now it was down the long road to Newcastle, scene of the long, bitter siege in the autumn of 1644. Some of them might have been there, some of them might have got the irony.

Newcastle

If the Scots had left us any record, it might have read something like this:

Frederick Bedlington was another who endured the long, freezing march west as the German scurried to avoid the Soviets' inexorable advance: 'The roads were lined with the dead of concentration camp prisoners, many of whom had been shot as they got too weak to walk. We made sledges in the camp prior to the march on which to carry our goods. The march took us into the Czech mountain region. The

people were very friendly. When the food ran out we had to live off
the land and what we could steal from the farms and houses. I was
beaten up for attempting to steal a pigeon at one farm. I entered
one Czech household and was fed by the family. We marched into
Bavaria. We broke into a potato cellar in one farm then made a fire
and roasted the potatoes.[33]

Newcastle, like most major towns, still possessed functioning medieval
ramparts. The place was walled to defend the town primarily against the
Scots. Those long and bitter centuries of the border wars from 1296 to
c. 1568 witnessed endemic conflict which flared incessantly at skirmish
level and quite frequently burst into full-scale conflagration with a litany
of major battles; Halidon Hill, 1333, Neville's Cross, 1346, Otterburn,
1388, Homildon, 1402, Flodden, 1513, Solway Moss, 1542 and Pinkie,
1547. By the time of the Civil Wars most of these fortifications, while still
standing, had been neglected. Only Berwick with its powerful thrusting
bastions represented the Renaissance ideal of an artillery fort. Medieval
walls were not built to withstand shot – as Newcastle had discovered
in 1644. Mighty Norham, which had resisted the Scots for two years
in the early fourteenth century, fell after a five-day bombardment from
James IV's formidable train in 1513.

Six years earlier Newcastle's ancient ring of defences had taken a
fearful pounding from Leven's guns and mines. We don't know to what
extent, if any, repairs had been carried out. The rickety suburbs beyond
had been torched by the mayor to clear fields of fire and the town had
suffered terribly in the hungry aftermath of the siege and storm. It had
then been occupied till 1647. It seems safe to assume the Scots would not
be popular visitors.

John Mabbitt points out that the extent and quality of Civil War
defences, surrounding and augmenting earlier walls, was patchy and the
archaeological work which has been undertaken to reveal more has not
been comprehensive.[34] Most Civil War works were thrown up in a hurry
and on a budget. Some, nonetheless, were extensive and complex:

By the middle of the seventeenth century many of these medieval
walls were in varying states of ruination. Despite some notable

refortifications during the sixteenth century, the walls of many towns had begun to decay or had been encroached on by new development. In military terms the medieval walls were obsolete by comparison to the bastioned defences of the Low Countries and Italy which had been built in the sixteenth century.[35]

Langton, in looking at patterns of urban settlement, comments that the walls of Newcastle still constituted a form of social demarcation, with those of the poorer sort residing in the suburbs outside. Writing in the sixteenth century, Leland had noted that: 'The strength and magnificence of the walling of this town [Newcastle] far passes all the walls of the cities of England and of most of the towns of Europe.'[36] As Mabbitt also observes, it had been customary for townsfolk to fund the maintenance of their defences, and mural towers studding Newcastle's ramparts bore the names of individual guilds.

This is at least in part confirmed by Gray in his *Chorographia*.[37] Labour, willing or conscripted, was supplied by local residents and artisans and was needed to raise such outworks as the sconce known as the Shieldfield Fort which had featured in the Siege:

Thomas Wouldhave appointed overseer of the works. Any who refused to come to pay 8d per day, everyone to come at six in the morning. A drum to call them and go with them to work, to bring shovels etc to work with. Moved that the town undertake the work of the Shieldfield fort as a testimony of their love and respect for Parliament for funds vouchsafed to the corporation, ordered that all the earth and sod work to be done by the burgesses at their cost … To be drawn up and entered at the next Common Council.[38]

With the emergence of a new mercantile *hautebourgeois* elite in the sixteenth century the walls, intended purely for defence, became a symbol of civic identity and pride: 'The key to the continuing importance of the medieval walls was their importance in maintaining civic identity through the embodiment of a legitimacy granted to the town as a corporate body'.[39] This was not just hubris, the walls were, in every sense, a concrete statement of the city's ancient rights, tangible resistance to notions of centralism, be these uttered by King or Parliament. The damage inflicted by the Scots was an insult to civic dignity, not just a military humiliation.

That walls still had a military role was underlined by the debacle of 1640. Conway's ill-judged decision to stand at Newburn left the city completely exposed. Had he perhaps chosen to remain behind the walls, Leven would have faced a far more difficult choice, the dragging drain of a siege or risk of infantry assault. Further repairs were carried out after the Restoration when various properties and other 'obstructions' abutting the walls were removed.[40] This was just as well, they continued to be of use: they were last put in a defensible state during the final Jacobite alarum in 1745.

In 1644 the walls still stood some 12ft in height, with a thickness of 8ft, by a ditch or fosse some 22yd (20m) wide and 8ft (2.4m) in depth. Gates were 'embattled' and the circuit studded with strong towers 'between each of which, there were for the most part two watch towers made square with effigies of men cut in stone upon the top of them as though they were watching, and they are called garret, which had square holes over the walls to through [throw] stones down'.[41] In terms of the overall circumference, Hutton's plan gives a distance of 2,740yd (2,505m) from Closegate to Sandgate; a later measurement carried out in 1745 which includes the Quayside totals 3,759yd (3,273m) and 1ft.[42] Once the circuit was complete, responsibility for ongoing maintenance was assigned to the twenty-four wards, each responsible for its adjacent gates and intervening towers.

Memories of the long siege and bitterly contested storm were still fresh. It had taken a long time to get rid of the Scots; the loss, deprivation and humiliation were still fresh. This must have been a bitter moment for any of the prisoners who had taken part in the occupation: perhaps some had cause to hope they would not be recognised. They could hope for no sympathy from the Geordies, quite the reverse. They would be a symbol of turned tables, at best.

Marched in their straggling 5-mile column, the Scots were crammed into St Nicholas' Church, mainly in the nave. There, diarrhoea and sickness spewed out of them and fouled the space. Those not already infected would be lucky to escape, a reeking vile sewer of poisoned waste streaming through the church. Some died here:

Burials – September 1650: 13th Thomas Wilson a soldier died 12th; 16th John Strong a soldier died 15th; 17th James Matthews a soldier died 16th; 26th 'This month 7 soldiers moor buried whose names was not knowne: October – 1st 2 soldiers whose name is unknown; 2nd Robert Walton a soldier died 2nd, Henry Wayte a soldier died 2nd, 14th 2 soldiers buried whose names not known to us; 23rd a soldier died 23rd; 27th a soldier died 27th: December – 2nd a soldier; 18th William Leader a soldier: 1651 – January: 20th a soldier.[43]

Hesilrige had already confirmed that some were sick by the time they marched from Morpeth:

for as they were coming from thence to Newcastle, some dyed by the way-side, and when they came to Newcastle, I put them into the greatest Church in the Town, and the next morning when I sent them to Durham, about Sevenscore were sick, and not able to march, and three dyed that night, and some fell down in their march from Newcastle to Durham, and dyed.[44]

The clean-up costs can be reckoned from Newcastle's Chamberlain's Account Books (1642–50) – note the use of Roman numbers:

Paid for ringing at 3 churches the 5th September for the defeat given to the Scotch army jxs ijd;[45] 10th September appointed day of thanksgiving … the marvellous deliverance … Dunbar … where their army was totally routed though in number 3 tymes as many as ours ix£ vs xd Paid constable for West Spitle Tower for candles & coles for the guards that watches the Scotch prisoners js jxd Cole and candles for the guard at Nicholas Church for 2 tow candles to burn roughly viijs.[46] Paid for clensing of Nicholas Church where the Scotch prisoners was kept on whole night V£ js xjd.[47] Paid for carrying 9 of the Scotts prisoners wch was died out of the Mazindew [nave in dew?] iijs.[48]

By now these men were sick as well as starved. Newcastle was anxious to see them on their way – the fear of disease running high. The town had experienced an outbreak of plague that year, conveniently blamed on witches. Thirty alleged suspects had been tried and half of those hanged on the Town Moor during the middle and latter part of August.[49] Nobody wanted a fresh outbreak so these gaunt, ailing scarecrows would be hustled out as quickly as possible.

Men would now be dropping regularly on the march south through pleasant undulating ground towards Chester-le-Street. It's possible any who fell out were again pistolled on the spot. Maybe the bodies were collected in carts for mass interment or just shoved into shallow graves by the roadside. Either way these men (assuming it was all men by this point) have no memorial, no carefully tended graves with name, number and unit. Their lives are a blank page, their deaths a perfunctory footnote. Yet, all left family behind, people who would wait anxiously for weeks, months, years, praying for some deliverance till hopes finally faded and they were denied a graveside to mourn by. In the words of the twentieth-century phrase, they were 'known unto God'.

The anonymity is hard for modern minds to comprehend. In our time we've seen the flag-shrouded coffins of casualties from Afghanistan driven slowly and with proper solemnity through Royal Wootton Bassett amid the poignant respect of the silent crowd. Awful as such losses are, there is some comfort in this collective mourning. The families of these lost soldiers never had that, never would. The gaping holes in their lives were never filled with any kind of closure, however painful.

Their march to Chester-le-Street and then on to Durham was in short stages, perhaps a testimony to how weakened they had become. These unlucky and undesired visitors passed through the smaller town and then on, leaving no trace or local memory.

As you head south the towers of Durham Cathedral rise up like a vision of the Kingdom of Heaven, God's peace upon the land, as they have done for a thousand years. Did the Scots view these solid Norman spires, more authoritative than dreaming, as some sign, if not of salvation, then at least of a respite? If they did, they would have been very wrong. This was journey's end, in the most final sense for all too many of them. Their experience had been terrible but now it was about to get much worse.

Chapter 6

Land of the Prince Bishops

You have no more religion than my horse. Gold is your God. Which of you have not bartered your conscience for bribes?
Oliver Cromwell, speech dissolving the Rump Parliament, 1653

Quicquid rex habet extra, episcopus habet intra – The King's prerogatives outside are the bishop's inside

The sweeping authority of the Prince Bishop was of no concern to the starved and exhausted soldiery who stumbled beneath his walls. Indeed, there was no bishop, Parliament had secularised his fiefdom and torn down the ornaments of his church, the ancient cathedral was just a big, handy building and the Scots would discover few signs of God's Grace or Christian charity. The welcome they got, if any turned out, would have been very far from friendly. Though some spark of pity remained: we know Hesilrige was able to recruit local women to nurse the sick when some of them were moved to better conditions in the castle.

Palace Green

In 1069 William the Conqueror appointed Bishop Walcher of Lorraine both bishop and earl, the first in a string of Prince Bishops that would for centuries control both city and surrounding county. In 1072 he ordered the building of a castle on the volcanic plug where its successor still sits. This was probably a timber motte but soon rebuilt in stone. The King had gone north to subdue Malcolm Canmore.[1] The Scottish king was forced to bow his knee in fealty (the re-stirring of a very long quarrel). Inhabitants of Durham would see much of their restless northern neighbours over the next several centuries.[2] Walcher was heavy-handed

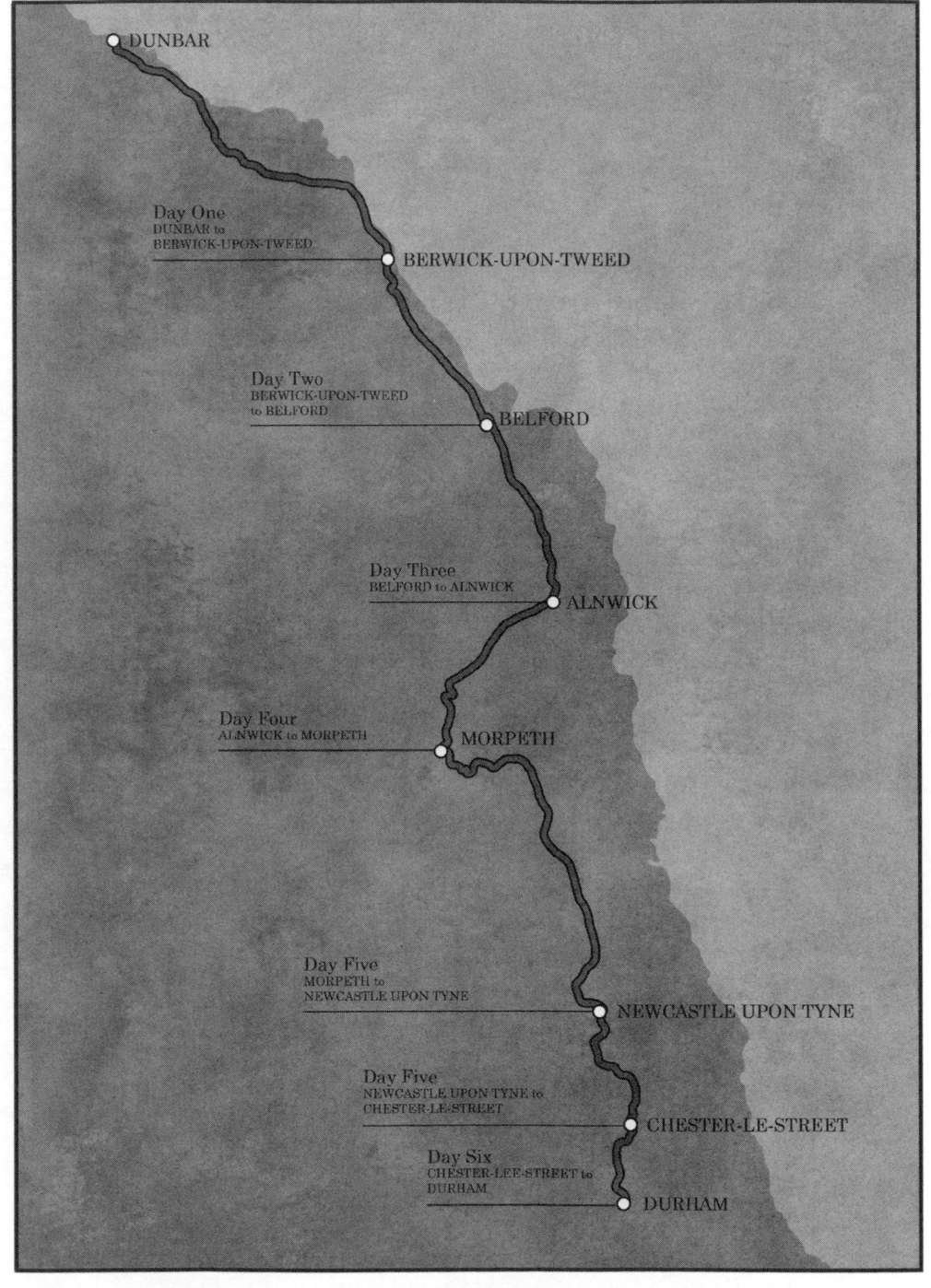

Map 2: The Prisoners' Progress. (*Courtesy of Chloe Rodham*)

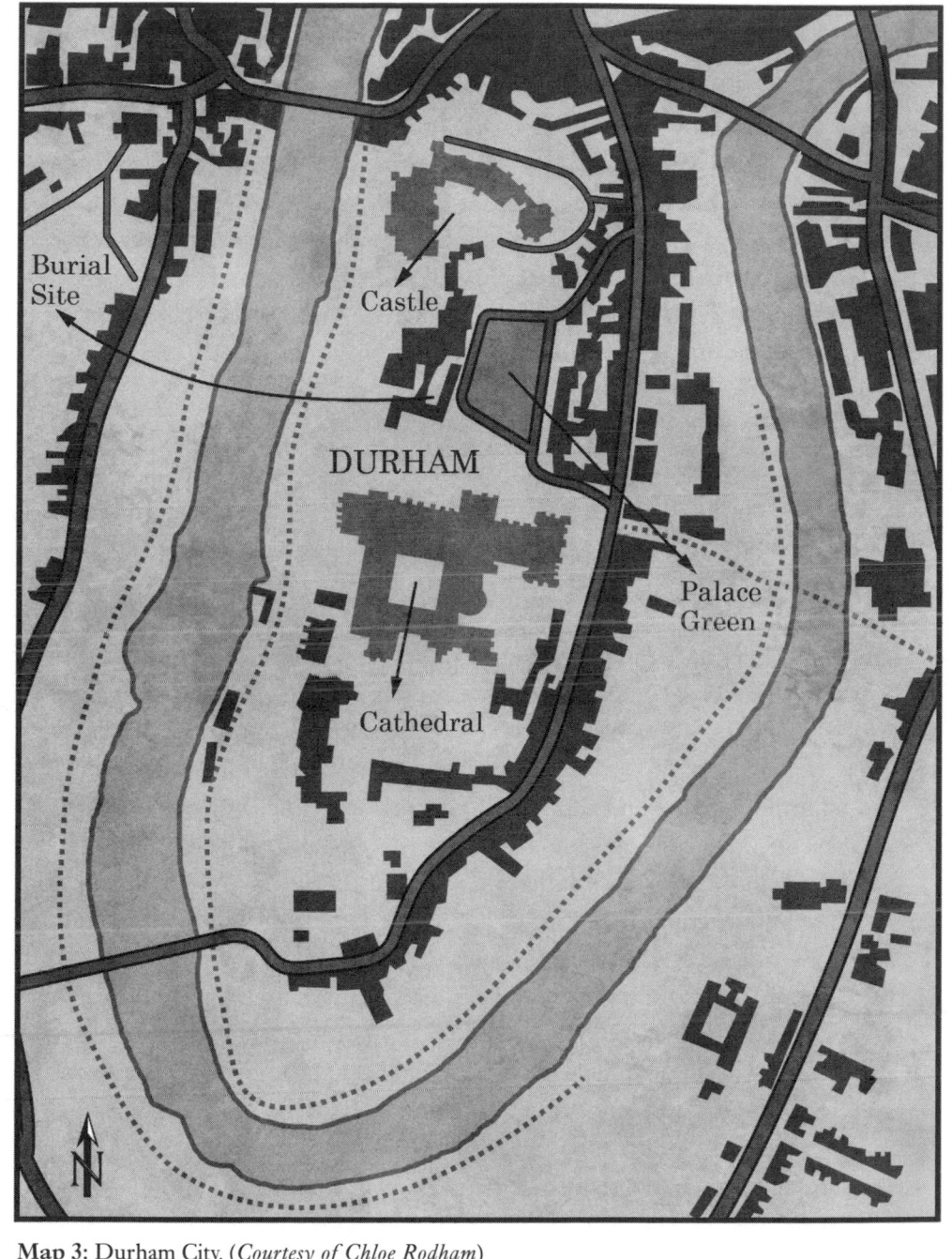

Burial Site

Castle

DURHAM

Palace Green

Cathedral

Map 3: Durham City. (*Courtesy of Chloe Rodham*)

and his northern subjects showed their resentment in fairly certain terms when they wiped out bishop and entourage at Gateshead eight years later. William's limited store of patience was exhausted and the harrying of the north saw a broad strip of the area wasted.[3]

This place was very much a fortress, the whole peninsula already protected on three sides by rearing bluffs above the broad stretch of the River Wear. Today it is the home of the chopping but tranquil blades of rowers but then it was a moat. The defended site extends to around 28 acres (11.3 ha). On the west flank of Palace Green, tatty bothies of humble peasantry were replaced by a suite of facilities supporting the office of Prince Bishop.[4]

All of the ecclesiastical buildings including the great mass of the cathedral, its many offices and all the buildings enclosed by both of the outer baileys, north and south, were encompassed by the enceinte or defended zone.

We see Durham as pretty serene, an island of blissful, unchanging tranquillity, holiness and beauty. In 1650 it was rather different, ragged, uncared for, part-abandoned, with a rather post-apocalyptic feel to it. The Civil Wars had been a cataclysm. This was a terrible, sapping conflict which affected the north of England for a decade and had, in its wake, swept away the very foundations of pre-war society. The King was dead; the Church belittled and despoiled, people were tired, hungry, fearful and resentful. These Scots had been here twice before, in 1640 and four years later, both times as conquerors.

The conflict had pushed taxes up 1,000 per cent; 150 towns and scores of villages were attacked; thousands of properties were damaged or destroyed. Depending on where you lived, anywhere between 10 and 20 per cent of the male population (and many women) had been involved in fighting, 85,000 had died in battle or skirmish, at least 100,000 more suffered sickness and starvation and 6 per cent of the population had died. Overall, the Wars of the Three Kingdoms wasted the population of the UK more intensely than the Great War of 1914–18 would.[5]

During the preceding decade beginning with the humiliation of Newburn, prebends such as John Cosin, the future bishop, had, a harbinger of worse to come, been stripped of their livings. In 1645 the Book of Common Prayer had been done away with, the clergy were effectively purged. On 23 April of that year (St George's Day) Parliament had appointed preachers to Durham, their wages to be paid from the sequestered assets of the Dean and Chapter.[6] Almost four years later and the great cathedral was abandoned, the final resting place of the greatest northern saint, a mere shell; a second stripping of the altars.

Death Comes Now to Durham

Cromwell was in dire need of resources. The Scottish campaign had, after all, been very expensive at a time when Parliament was essentially broke. He wrote to Hesilrige on 5 September, two days after the battle:

> After much deliberacion, we can find no way hoe to dispose of these prisoners that will be consisting with these two ends. (to witt, the not loosing, & the not starving them neither of which would we willingly incur) but be sending them into England, where the Council of State may exercise their wisdom & better judgment in so dispersing & disposing of them, as that they may not suddenly return to your prejudice. We have dispatched neer 5000 poore wretches of them, verie of which it's probable will dye of their wounds or be so rendered unserviceable for time to come by reason thereof. I have written to the Council of State desiring them to direct how they shall be disposed of, and I make no question but you will hastne the prisoners up southward, and second my desires with your owne to the Councill.[7]

Sir Arthur Hesilrige (1601–61) was one of the famous five members, elected to the Short and then Long Parliament in 1640. He had been active in hounding both Strafford and Laud (though ultimately he was no regicide). Of impeccable Puritan credentials, he had been a stubborn opponent of the King, summoned on various counts for refusing to pay fines and taxes and even, for a brief sojourn, incarcerated. His career as a soldier in the wars had been at times unfortunate. He fought well at Edgehill and served with Waller against Hopton in the South West. His heavily armoured cavalry, 'lobsters' as they were derided, had, despite the weight of their kit managed to flee convincingly at Roundway ('Runaway')

Down. The King quipped after Sir Arthur had resisted flurries of blows and got clean away that if he had been as well supplied as he was fortified, he could have withstood a siege.

With significant injuries sustained in the melee, despite his spread of plate, he had not got off unscathed. Yet, he had held Waller's left at Cheriton and done well enough at 2nd Newbury.[8] While in the South West he had shown a taste for iconoclasm and despoiled the great cathedrals at Winchester and Chichester. He supported Cromwell in 1644 over army reform and he had given up his commission after the passing of the Self-Denying Ordinance (which he supported). In December 1647 he was appointed Governor at Newcastle and did creditable service in the Second Civil War. He held the town and clawed back Tynemouth Castle from turncoat Henry Lilburne.[9]

His Puritan principles did not preclude wholesale speculation and, like others, he shamelessly gobbled up confiscated estates. In partnership with his son, he manipulated his position to add to his rapidly swelling portfolio, spending some 22,500 pounds sterling and acquiring manors in Bishop Auckland, Middleham, Easingwoodburgh and Wolsingham.[10] His rapacity brought him into conflict with Freeborn John Lilburne, equally cantankerous, and they ended up in bitter litigation (which Hesilrige won).[11]

John raged against his opponent, alleging he was a worse tyrant than Strafford. Like Freeborn John, Hesilrige had a real knack for alienating his contemporaries. He backed Cromwell to the hilt in 1650, though they later fell out over the dissolution of the Rump. Clarendon, admittedly partisan, branded him absurd, bold, rash, hare-brained and devoid of tact.[12]

Cromwell is cannily diplomatic when he writes to Hesilrige, who had been unhappy at Pride's Purge and pointedly declined to sit in judgement on King Charles. He had been returned to Parliament in February 1649 and sat as a member of the Council, a man of some consequence, and by now an ostentatiously wealthy one. 'I know you are a man of business', Oliver began. 'This not being every dayes work, will willingly be performed by you, especially considering you have the commands of your supervisers.'[13]

Maybe Cromwell suspected this whole matter of the prisoners' disposal was a poisoned chalice; in any event he was keen to pass the responsibility on:

Sir I judge it exceeding necessary you send us up what horse and foot you can with all possible expedicion, especially considering that our men fall verie sicke & if the lord shall please to enable us effectually to prosecute this business to the which he hath opened so gratious a way, no man knows but that it may produce a peace to England, & much securitie & comfort to God's people, wherefore I pray you continue to give what furtherance you can to this worke, by speeding such supplies to us you can possible spare, not having more at present, I rest ...[14]

It is Sir Arthur's long, self-justifying letter to the Council that provides us with a series of insights into the prisoners' sufferings, couched in suitable humanitarian terms, though it is really intended to be exculpatory:

and when they came to Durham, I having sent my Lieutenant Colonel and my Major, with a strong Guard both of Horse and Foot, and they being there told into the great Cathedral Church, they could not count them to more then [than] Three thousand; although Colonel Fenwick writ to me, That there were about Three thousand five hundred, but I believe they were not told at Berwick and most of those that were lost, it was in Scotland.[15]

Already, he is trying to ensure he cannot be blamed for the number of deaths. And, in fairness, it is clear the wretched men brought their own death sentences with them. We know the flux was already present in both armies before the battle commenced. The conditions of the march and of their confinement were bound to make it worse.

Hesilrige was aware that large numbers of the group died miserably on his watch and was at great pains to shove the blame elsewhere:

When I sent them first to Durham, I writ to the Major, and desired him to take care, that they wanted not anything that was fit for

Prisoners, and what he should disburse for them, I would repay it. I also sent them a daily supply of bread from Newcastle, and an allowance equal to what had been given to former Prisoners: But their Bodies being infected, the Flux encreased amongst them. I sent many Officers to look to them, & appointed that those that were sick should be removed out the cathedral Church into the Bishops Castle, which belongs to Mistris Blakiston, and provided Cooks, and they had Pottage made with Oatmeal, and Beef and Cabages, a full Quart at a Meal for every Prisoner.[16]

It's not insignificant that Susan Blakiston is listed as the owner of Durham Castle. Formerly widow of Richard Chambers, an affluent north-eastern trader, she had married John Blakiston (1603–49) in 1626. Blakiston was one of the leading local politicians of his day and, with Hesilrige, a man of influence. Born in Sedgefield, County Durham, he was the third son of Marmaduke Blakiston, Prebendary (honorary canon) at York Minster. His father had been a noted Arminian (follower of the High Curch Dutch theologian Jacob Arminius) but during the decade before the outbreak of civil war, John drifted into the Puritan camp, becoming markedly anti-Episcopalian.

Blakiston was elected as MP for Newcastle in 1640, though he did not take his seat until early 1641 (due to a contested vote). He became Mayor of Newcastle in 1645 and Coal Master of Newcastle with a handsome stipend of £200 per annum. He differed from Sir Arthur in holding strongly radical views. Appointed to the High Court, he sat as one of the King's judges and was twelfth out of forty-nine signatories to his death warrant. He then featured on various committees dealing with confiscated estates and, like Hesilrige, wasn't shy about helping himself. John died in June 1649 but clearly his widow was still in possession later in the following year. There is some uncertainty how he came to be in possession of Durham Castle. It has been suggested that Thomas Andrewes, Lord Mayor of London, bought Durham Castle for just over £1,200 in May 1649 and then sold it on to Blakiston or perhaps Blakiston bought it outright. Possibly the latter as he died in June so scarcely had time to complete the purchase.[17]

During the tenure of Bishop Neile (1617–27), the place had been in a pretty sorry state. He gave the north end of the west range and those rooms at the northern end of the great hall a much-needed makeover to the extent that, in the time of his successor Bishop Morton (1632–46), the castle was fit enough for entertaining the King in 1633 and again six years after.[18] It is hard to say how it was faring eleven years later, but it was presumably good enough for the 500 sick Hesilrige refers to. Of course, it is possible there was simply nowhere else to put them and of course it was adjacent to the cathedral.

Sir Arthur makes it plain that men were dying wholesale despite his best humanitarian efforts and this is almost certainly true:

> They had also coals daily brought to them; as many as made about a hundred Fires both day and night, and Straw to lie upon; and I appointed the Marshal to see all these things orderly done, and he was allowed Eight men to help him to divide the coals, and their Meat, Bread and Pottage equally; They were so unruly, sluttish and nasty, that it is not to be believed; they acted rather like Beasts than Men, so that the Marshal was allowed Forty men to cleanse and sweep them every day.[19]

This sounds fair and would have struck the right note with its intended audience. But there appears to be evidence that the prisoners in the cathedral were not supplied with coal – perhaps this tender care was merely window dressing:

> But those men were of the lustiest Prisoners, that had some small thing given them extraordinary: And these provisions were for those that were in health; and for those that were sick, and in the Castle, they had very good Mutton Broth, and sometimes Veal Broth, and Beef and Mutton boild together, and old Women appointed to look to them in the several Rooms: There was also a Physitian which let them Blood, and dressed such as were wounded, and gave the sick Physick and I dare confidently say, There was never the like care taken for any such Number of prisoners that ever were in England.[20]

What was killing these men – dysentery or typhus? Symptoms of dysentery (an infectious disease of the intestines, especially the colon) appear between a few hours and five days after ingestion of contaminated bacteria. Rarely is infection passed from person to person. A common cause is human faeces in water or, most likely in this case, used to fertilize that fatal crop of cabbages in Morpeth. An untreated sufferer may produce 10–20 litres of diarrhoea a day with mortality rates of 50 to 60 per cent.

A closer understanding of what happened can be gained by looking at the impact of another disease – typhus. This is a terrible affliction, feared by all armies. As late as 1945 concerns about a typhus epidemic persuaded British 21st Army Group to agree to a German proposal they should accept responsibility for and take over the camp at Bergen-Belsen. Nothing could have prepared them for the vision of Hell they stumbled into:

> Some of the huts had bunks, but not many, and they were filled absolutely to overflowing with prisoners in every state of emaciation and disease. There was not room for them to lie down at full length in each hut. In the most crowded there were anything from 600 to 1,000 people in accommodation which should only have taken 100 … The compounds were absolutely one mass of human excreta. In the huts themselves the floors were covered and the people in the top bunks who could not get out just poured it on the bunks below.

Newcastle and Durham cathedrals would have looked very similar, and no wonder the burgesses on Tyneside had needed to spend so much on the clean-up.

For those 300 years later in North Germany, nothing in nearly 6 years of terrible war could compare:

> We took a look around – there were faeces all over the floor – the majority of people having diarrhoea. I was standing aghast in the midst of all this filth trying to get used to the smell, which was a mixture of post-mortem room, a sewer, sweat, and foul pus, when I heard scrabbling on the floor. I looked down in the half light and saw a woman crouching at my feet. She had black matted hair, well

populated and her ribs stood out as though there were nothing between them, her arms were so thin that they were horrible. She was defecating, but was so weak that she could not lift her buttocks from the floor and, as she had diarrhoea, the liquid yellow stools bubbled over her thighs.[21]

It has been suggested that some, possibly a significant number of those who died, were victims of 're-feeding syndrome'. This was another feature of the relief of Bergen-Belsen. Soldiers entering the camp and trying to help handed out chocolate and bully-beef to starving inmates. These were meant to be acts of kindness and compassion but often proved fatal.

Deprive someone of food or drink for more than five days (the Scots soldiers had been suffering this for nearly two weeks) and the human body starts to conserve energy by reducing organ function and cellular activity. Sudden feeding or re-hydration triggers insulin production and affects the function of electrolytes (which control the flow of water into and out of cells and spark nerve function: the impulses which control breathing and heart function among other things). It is particularly important that electrolytes are replaced at a steady rate when you start replenishing fluids and nutrients, which is why babies with diarrhoea are now given liquid with salts and sugar in judicious amounts. It is why the famine diet given to Bergen-Belsen patients ended up including the same ingredients as well as vinegar to appeal to Eastern European tastes. Get it wrong and you run the risk of flooding the body with fluids causing cardiac arrest.[22]

The fact is that you can't force food into someone who is suffering from starvation. Did that apply to the Scottish prisoners? Most had not eaten for a few days prior to the battle, then endured the long march. What was needed was a proper famine diet administered slowly enough to let their systems recover. Hesilrige might have been killing some of his charges through kindness; in the circumstances the very blackest of ironies.

Iconoclasm

Hesilrige continues his woeful saga blaming the Scots themselves for their disorderly conduct:

Notwithstanding all this, many of them dyed, and few of any other Disease but the Flux; some were killed by themselves, for they were exceeding cruel one towards another. And the Disease of the Flux still encreasing amongst them, I was then forced, for their preservation, if possible it might be, to send to all the next Towns to Durham, within four or five miles, to command them to bring in their Milk, for that was conceived to be the best Remedy for stopping of their Flux, and I promised them what Rates they usually sold it for at the Markets, which was accordingly performed by about Threescore Towns and places, and Twenty of the next Towns to Durham continue still to send daily in their Milk, which is boiled, some with Water, and some with Bean flower, the Physitians holding it exceeding good for recovery of their health.[23]

During their earlier triumphal occupation, the Scots were castigated for damage to the cathedral's interior, and as losers they got blamed again. It is possible that some of those incarcerated in 1650 had been there before as occupiers. Now they were accused of vandalising the old Neville family tombs in the south aisle, supposedly as revenge for the 1346 Battle of Neville's Cross. It's unlikely many or indeed any of them had even heard of this long-ago defeat or cared. There's a very good chance much of this alleged iconoclasm was the zealous work of reformers in the previous century. How would unarmed men with no access to tools effectively carry out such destruction? Would they, hungry, sick and despondent, have had the will or the energy to do it and, even if they had, why antagonise their captors further?[24]

It seems more likely that they simply used whatever wood they could find for fires, driven by necessity. This is far more understandable. A survey from 1653 talks of the 'building of a new font somewhat suitable to that which the Scots destroyed' and from the same time the *Rites of Durham* claims the Scots 'defaced the Chime Bells and cloke [clock] and all taken away'.[25] Such bold larceny sounds far more like the work of occupiers than captives. The library-keeper, one Isaac Gilpin, accused the prisoners of 1650 of filching and burning manuscripts. If it happened, this was likely to use as fuel rather than plain wantonness, and one does have to wonder how they got access to any manuscripts in the first place.

Only five years after the last occupation, the Dunbar prisoners were dumped in the cathedral. With an interior space of 4,000m² it was about the only structure big enough to house so many. By the standards of the time the number of prisoners equalled the population of a medium-sized town. The authors of the *Rites of Durham*, writing mid-decade, attempted to define precisely what had been vandalised and when: 'But in the yere 1650: this Abbey churc[h] was made a prison for the Scots and quite defaced w[i]thin ... But in the year 1655 the Clocke and Chyme was repayred againe w[hi]ch was taken downe and preserved from the s[ai]'d ruyne'.[26] So the clock was seemingly taken down to prevent damage and put back up again later. This account also mentions a brass lectern, clearly a piece of some value, which went missing but (see below) this appears to have been taken by one of the supervisors appointed to manage the prisoners. After all, how would they possibly get such a hefty piece away? '[T]hey burned upp all the wood worke in regard they had no coals allowed them'. This was driven by pure desperation. In 1640 the Scots had lifted '4 paire of faire Organs belonging to the quior'.[27] This was proper looting, systematic and probably planned. The plain fact was that by 1650 there was not much left to steal or destroy and that which was destroyed was done so purely out of need.

We know the Scots had none of their officers with them. But despite Hesilrige's claims of indiscipline there would have been some senior NCOs and old soldiers present who would have been capable of taking charge. These men, all of them, however unprepared and unwilling, were at least soldiers and likely to have given a good account of themselves in the battle. Discipline would not have been wholly lacking. It does seem that they used the west end of the nave for living and the east (and colder) end as a toilet. Analysis suggests that a film adhering to the floor slabs may represent urine deposits.[28] To put it bluntly, they slept in one end and pissed in the other. Scorch marks possibly from braziers might substantiate this idea.

Damage to the Neville tombs might have resulted just from general crowding and that end of the cathedral allowed access to lofts which communicated to the library, so putting the manuscripts, such priceless treasures, in reach as a handy additional source of fuel. Though, of course, one has to ask how sick and starving men were able to make the necessary climb.

If the Scots, as Hesilrige smugly points out, were unruly and inclined to vandalism, their guards were not much better. One of these was named Robert Brewin who had been appointed the year before: 'Robert Brewen shall be Bridewell Keeper for the Town for one year paid 20 nobles provided he behaves himself honourably ... January 1649/50 "Robert Brewen Master of the Bridewell to have 10/-" he putting in good security ... to set poor people on work'.[29] Brewen seems to have been easily as light fingered as any larcenous Scottish POW and his office allowed him to get away with it and provided handy scapegoats:

Ther was lowe downe in the Quere another lettorn of brasse [undoubtedly the same one as referred to previously] ... standing in the midst against the stalls ... Which same stood theire until the yeare 1650, when the Scotts were sent prisoners from Dunbarr fight, and put prisoners into the church, where they burned upp all the wood worke, in regard they had no coals allowed them. And there was a fellowe, one Brewen, appointed to looke to the Scotts, by Sir Arthur Haslerige baronet, then Governor of Newcastle, and the fower northeran counties, which conveyed this said brasse lectterne, and eagle away, and many other thinges appertayninge to the church, and sould them for his owne gaine, a man of badd conscience, and a cruell fellowe to the poore prisoners ... In the yeare 1650, this Abbey church was made a prison for the Scotts and quite defaced within, for ther was to the number 4500 [?] which most of them perished and dyed ther in a very short space, and were thrown into holes by great numbers together, in a most lamentable manner.[30]

This character was clearly something of a survivor, hence an astonishing entry from the *Newcastle Courant*:

we have the following surprising account from Boyle in Ireland, that there is living there one Brewen, aged 109, who carried arms in the Parliament forces, 1641. He retains his old set of Teeth, ... of which he has a new set. About … years ago he cast one of his old teeth, and has a new one in its place; he lost his sight suddenly about 16 years ago; but has lately recovered partly the sight of one eye.[31]

Home Front

Dunbar, for the Scots nation, was a major disaster, and the following year they came back and did it again at Worcester. For families of the POWs there was nothing but the anguish of waiting, with many living out their lives and going to their graves not knowing what had happened to their fathers, sons, brothers or husbands. There was no Red Cross, no solemn but serene Commonwealth War Grave Cemeteries with row upon row of neat Portland headstones. They were just gone; loss and penury their only legacy.

In the wake of Dunbar the Commissioners of the General Assembly of the Church of Scotland ordered a day of national fasting in atonement for God's displeasure. More helpfully, individual parishes began collecting donations which rapidly extended across the board.

- On 31 October the Assembly wrote to the presbyteries of St Andrews and Cupar in Fife, detailing the sufferings of the POWs in Durham and reporting 500 pounds (Scots) of death monies had been raised and were to be remitted to the Dean of the Guild of Stirling.[32] Parishes had already been trying to help the wounded and traumatised survivors who'd come back, firstly from Dunbar and then Worcester.
- Kirk Session minutes record calls for relief for POWs held at Berwick, Newcastle, Durham, Tynemouth and (oddly) in the Tower. Ministers used their pulpits to stimulate charity from their congregations, though most probably had little enough to give.
- On 3 November, at Kircaldy, notices were read out from the pulpit and a team of eight collectors formed to bring in donations.[33]
- On the same day in Burntisland, the sum of 100 pounds Scots (the value of the Scottish pound had fluctuated against sterling but James VI and I had fixed the exchange rate as 12:1) was raised for prisoners at Berwick and Newcastle.[34]

- Two weeks later, again at Kirkcaldy, the minister announced that a collection would be made on the following Sabbath. In fact, the sum of 26 pounds 6s. 8d. (Scots) was raised. On 1 December the minister was able to inform the Assembly he'd remitted 50 merks (a merk/mark was equivalent to 13s. 4d.) to the Dean of Guild of Stirling.[35]
- During March and April 1651 the presbyteries circulated to their constituent parishes copies of a petition received from the captured officers at Tynemouth begging relief. St Mungo's Alloa and Tullibody raised 8 pounds Scots and ensured the money got through; they naturally obtained a receipt.[36]

What about those left behind? Men left wives and families who were every bit as much casualties of war. There were no established funding mechanisms for war widows or those left destitute. Women had to throw themselves on the mercy of the Church. Helen Smith, widow of John Young killed at Dunbar, appealed to her Kirk in Culross who awarded her 12s. per month, and this was probably the best that could be offered.[37] Some would want to re-marry but wouldn't know if their husbands were dead or alive as POWs. As late at 1655, the Synod of Fife was debating the position and deciding that a war widow had to either obtain clear evidence of her husband's death or seek a declaration from the courts to that effect.

Last Rites

The moment of truth for Sir Arthur was when he had to tell the council how many he had lost, almost 50 per cent or more depending on whose figures you accept:

> Gentlemen, You cannot but think strange this long preamble, and to wonder what the matter will be; in short it's this, Of the Three thousand prisoners that my Officers told into the Cathedral Church at Durham, Three hundred from thence, and Fifty from Newcastle of the Sevenscore left behinde, were delivered to Major Clerk by order from the Councel, and there are about Five hundred sick in the Castle, and about Six hundred yet in health in the Cathedral,

the most of which are in probability Highlanders, they being hardier then the rest, and other means to distinguish them we have not, and about Sixteen hundred are dead and buried, and Officers about Sixty, that are at the Marshals in Newcastle.[38]

Mass burials were mostly associated with plague – Daniel Defoe gives a good account of this.[39] But these were not civilian. These were men a very long way from their own parishes, not likely to be welcomed anywhere in Durham. Their worth was as a live commodity. To Hesilrige they were an embarrassment, he was not supposed to lose so many. In addition, large numbers of corpses are a health hazard.

Not for them the heroic, Homeric, torch-lit send-off. Mass graves, shallow and scraped in a hurry, men fearful of contagion, probably soldiers, dumping reeking corpses into the pits. They had been dying at the rate of hundreds per week – a significant daily total. The graveyard squads would be busy, cloths wrapped over their faces against the smell, smoke possibly to ward off contagion, fetch 'em, strip 'em, dump 'em, cover 'em up; get it done. Stripped of everything except their anonymity, bodies trundled on carts from castle to pit. This job was best done quickly and as near to hand as might be managed. No weeping widows, no cortèges, no dignity. This was disposal not interment. And there they lie, pale and stiffening, wasted frames with bare bones protruding, skeletal faces, pinched, aged, unshaven and universally blank, their once-youthful bodies hideously marred by the intensity of their suffering.

A last word from Sir Arthur:

I cannot give you on this sudden a more exact Accompt of the prisoners, neither can any Accompt hold true long, because they still dye daily, and doubtless so they will, so long as any remain in Prison. And for those that are well, if Major Clerk could have believed that they had been able to have marched on foot, he would have marched them by Land; for we perceive that divers that are seemingly healthy, and have not all been sick, suddenly dye, and we cannot give any reason of it, onely we apprehend they are all infected, and that the strength of some holds it out till it seize upon their very hearts. Now you fully understand the condition and the number of the Prisoners,

what you please to direct, I shall observe, and intend not to proceed
further upon this Letter, until I have your Answer upon what I have
now written.[40]

Having reckoned up the losses and assuring he couldn't be blamed,
Sir Arthur then had to think about what to do with the survivors:

My Lord General having released the rest of the Officers, and the
Councel having given me power to take out what I thought fit, I
have granted to several well-affected persons that have Salt-works
at Sheels, and want Servants, Forty, and they have engaged to keep
them to work at their salt-pans; and I have taken out more about
Twelve Weavers, to begin a Trade of Linnen cloth like unto the
Scotch-cloth, and about Forty Laborers.[41]

Chapter 7

A Brave New World

Ye sordid prostitutes, have you not defiled his sacred place, and turned the Lord's temple into a den of thieves by your immoral principles and wicked practices?

Oliver Cromwell, speech dissolving the Rump Parliament, 1653

The origins of transportation lie in the Vagabonds Act of 1597. Peace with Spain had left large numbers of demobbed soldiers and sailors to wander the country. Panicked by a rising crime wave, Parliament agreed that persistent rogues could be shipped to parts 'beyond the seas' at the behest of members of the Privy Council.

It was no accident that the author of the Act, Sir John Popham, Lord Chief Justice, came up with this option of personalising the transactions. Popham had been among those who responded to the offer to take up Irish land confiscated from the rebellious Desmond family and 'plant' it with English Protestant tenants. Sadly for Popham, another magnate had got there first and his eighty tenant families had to head off again. Still the idea of building a fortune by supplying the poor as labour in developing territories had been born. Nor was he to be alone in spotting the potential of the overseas colonies.

Two joint stock companies were created in the early years of the seventeenth century: the London Company (whose patron was Robert Cecil, renowned Chief Secretary of State) and the Plymouth Company (so-called because its investors were drawn from the South West of England). The London Company became responsible for the Southern American development below what would become New York. The increasing importance of its interests in Virginia would see it renamed the Virginia Company over time. Popham was heavily involved in the Plymouth Company which had holdings in New England.

This was the era before modern banking and business financing measures were established. An emerging merchant class (people of the middling sort as they were known) were growing increasingly frustrated at the difficulties in making a return on their profits. Your money might be safe stored in a locked chest but it was not generating any interest. The opportunity the Colonies offered for investment was highly attractive, if risky. Cargos lost to the whims of the waves were the price to be paid if you were to make your fortune grow.

The investors in these companies, of course, included men of rank and substance. But they also proved a draw for the Merchant Venturers of emerging towns such as Bristol and Newcastle as well as for those minor gentry who were looking to trade to provide an income. Men like Oliver Cromwell who swapped his role as landowner for that of businessman.

Crown control of the economy made it difficult and frustrating to build a fortune at home. Charles I, that embodiment of the Divine Right of Kings, thought it perfectly proper to allocate a share in the price of saucepans, for example, to one of his cronies. Over time, the attempt to introduce economic change would be one of the factors leading to the Wars of the Three Kingdoms.

Early efforts to settle the New World were disastrous. It rapidly became clear that the hoped for mineral largesse of Spanish and Portuguese South America was not going to be replicated on the northern continent. And the combination of convict labour and gentlemen adventurers had not prevented the destruction of early settlements such as Jamestown.

'While the Spanish in America slaughtered for gold, the English in America had to plant for their wealth'.[1] There was no gold or silver on the East Coast so it was natural to turn to farming which required labour, skilled labour if possible. They needed migrants.

Sir Thomas Smythe, Treasurer of the London Company (effectively the CEO), was canny enough to appeal to both patriotism as well as self interest. 'To plant an English Nation there [in Virginia], and to settle a trade in those parts, which may be peculiar to our nation, to the end we may thereby be secured from being eaten out of all profits of trade by our more industrious neighbours [the Dutch]'.[2] Alongside the fervour, skilled craftsmen and tradesmen were offered housing, food, clothes, cash and a land grant to settle in the New World.

Farming, especially of crops such as tobacco or sugar, was labour intensive and the indigenous peoples failed to provide a sufficient workforce – thanks to the impact of new diseases brought from Europe by the settlers and the cultural resistance of the existing communities.

Ideally, labour needed to be cheap (free would be even more desirable) and willing to work hard for long hours. Better still, would be labour that had no choice about working hard for long hours.

In Britain there was a perceived problem of surplus population – the rootless, the unemployed, the criminal, the unattached. And, of course, the dissident – those who not only disagreed with the way society was organised but sought to change it.

Removing them solved two problems, restoring domestic harmony and providing for the development of wealth and Empire. Increasingly in the Americas the ideology of the Colonies, of the relationship between Britain and her overseas holdings, would develop over the course of the next century. Far more so than in the West Indies, where, initially at least, the focus was on economic drivers.

Transportation also offered a means to increase the population in the colonies in general. It was anticipated that many travelling out as indentured servants would remain, whether they had gone voluntarily or not. The period of indenture varied from three years to life, reflecting the differing paths that brought the labourers to their destination. Most had a time limit placed on the indenture – they were meant to gain their freedom eventually. That would come to be the key difference between the indentured servants and the black slaves who so often worked alongside them in the early days.

Not such an unlikely strategy in reality. Regardless of circumstance, there is a natural human tendency to have regard for a place you have helped to build, particularly if you have formed relationships with others there: perhaps even acquired a new family.

Many went willingly, entering into the contract to pay their passage to a new life in a new world. They were going to a world that had its own dangers, aside from those inherent in the nature of the contract. In the early decades of the seventeeth century half of those who went as bonded servants would be dead before their contract was up. Treatment could be brutal and there are recorded cases of men and women worked to death. Jordan and Walsh open their excellent book by recording the discovery of a seventeenth-century skeleton in Maryland in 2003. The remains were those of a boy who had died in about 1660, possibly of TB. His spine suggested years of toil. But what was most striking about him was the location of his burial: in a hole under a pile of household waste in what had been a cellar. Was this the concealment of a murder? Or an indication of how little value was placed on this particular life?[3]

Vagrants and criminals provided a rich source for forced migration – some 70,000 of them were sent to the Americas and Barbados before the American Revolution made this option unavailable (America refused to receive them from 1783). From 1788 Australia became the government's destination of choice for their surplus population.

Our Dunbar men were soon to be followed by thousands of Irish as Cromwell's campaigns took their toll. It has been argued that Cromwell was pursuing an ethnic cleansing programme there. Numbers are difficult to assess – some have put the figure as high as 50,000. Nor did the 1650s see the end of the process, transportation of troublesome insurgents would go on for another 100 years.

The ready market for indentured servants fuelled private enterprise. We know of at least one well-organised London gang which was paid £2 for every healthy male they kidnapped and deposited on board ship. Perhaps this is where Robert Louis Stephenson got his idea for 'Kidnapped'. It is difficult to be precise about numbers: Blumenthal cites a contemporary source who claimed 10,000 a year were taken.[4]

This was a brutal time and, as far as the companies developing the Colonies were concerned, the bottom line was the only concern: individuals were effectively regarded as chattels. 'Secretary Kemp wrote in 1638 to the Secretary of State, Windebanke, "of the hundreds of people who are now transplanted, scarce any are brought but as merchandise, and sold to the planters as servants." And to be a servant then was to be the virtual slave of a soulless system.'[5] This harshness was also reflected in the Colonies by the tough treatment of anyone who stepped out of line. The Quakers of New England were a prime example. The General Court of Boston ordered that Quakers who could not pay exorbitant fines should be sold as bondsmen or bondswomen in Barbados or other of the English possessions, including Virginia. Three men and one woman who defied such banishment were hanged on Boston Common (1659–61).[6]

Convicts, with longer terms of bondage, were potentially more profitable purchases than other indentured servants. The Virginia planters needed labourers, and took what they could get – whether kidnapped, self-sold, or convict. As an 1896 article in the *American Historical Review* noted: 'All were bought for tobacco and set at work raising more. As Virginia's staple was tobacco, it naturally became a centre of white as well as black servitude, whether its victims were indented or not, and criminal or not. All fared alike.'[7]

An account of the 'Number of Souls in the Province of Maryland in 1755', appearing in the *Gentleman's Magazine* for 1764, gives figures for convicts: 507 male convicts, 386 women convicts, 67 boy and 21 girl convicts, a total of 981, still serving their term, of which about 39 per cent were female.

Presumably the proportions held true for those who had already served their time and remained in the state. 'Eliminating 30 percent on the total percent of the total population listed as Negro slaves, and about half of the remainder as under 16 years of age, the adult convicts comprised about 6.3 per cent of the adult whites.'[8]

It was not unusual for large groups to be transported instead of facing prison or the gallows – the Dunbar men were just some of many. Hundreds in the late seventeenth century were consigned to Jamaica, but most were shipped to Maryland and Virginia. At least 4,500 were 'pardoned' for the Colonies between 1661 and 1700.[9] Women and children also had a value: not least as a means to persuade male colonists to stay and marry. It was a two for one offer – a man taking on a maid would pay 120lb of tobacco but would get an apprentice (usually a child) for only 20lb.

It is estimated that between 1620 and 1775 some 300,000 'free willers' (self-indentured servants) to the Americas accounted for 2 out of 3 migrants from the British Isles.

The transportation of Scots prisoners was to be repeated after the Battle of Worcester in 1651 when 8,000 more were taken captive. The Council of State instructed the Committee for Prisoners to grant a licence to send these men to the West Indies. Here, the crop was sugar rather than tobacco, equally valuable and requiring equally back-breaking labour.

The Sugar Trade

The Portuguese introduced sugar plantations in the 1550s off the coast of their Brazilian colony, located on the island Sao Vicente. Production rapidly spread as the Caribbean conditions for growing the cane were equally good. It was not long before the rest of Europe started to appreciate the tremendous wealth to be accrued from the cultivation of this cash crop using the plantation system and began colonising the remaining American territories, hoping to capitalise on the lucrative cultivation and trade of natural resources.

Sugar was the most important crop throughout the Caribbean, although other crops such as coffee, indigo and rice were also grown. It created a unique political ecology; the relationship between labour, profits and the physical environment in the Caribbean had European powers vying with each other for political and economic control. Also, of course, over time it would lead to vast numbers of black Africans being transported as slaves. Environmental consequences of the trade exacerbated international conflict. Huge amounts of timber were needed for sugar refinement. As forests were reduced it became necessary to try to take over territory which was still ligneous. By the middle of the seventeenth century competition was escalating as the sugar trade threatened to stagnate.

Ironically (and horribly) it was the wide-scale destruction of the native populations which had cleared the way for the plantations. Local populations died at unprecedented rates due to the influx of old world diseases brought by colonists. Estimates of these population losses vary from 8.4 million to 112.5 million.[10]

Sugar changed the nature of society in the Caribbean as well as the structure of the local economy. Large plantations offered economies of scale, a lesson that would be learnt in the Americas as well. Like tobacco and, later, cotton, sugar was most efficiently grown on large plantations with many workers. Slaves from Africa were imported and put to work. For example, prior to 1650 more than three-quarters of the islands' population was white. In 1680, the median size of a plantation in Barbados had increased to about sixty slaves. Over the decades, the sugar plantations began expanding as the transatlantic trade continued to prosper. By 1832, the median–size plantation in Jamaica had about 150 slaves, and nearly 1 of every 4 bondsmen lived on units that had at least 250 slaves.[11]

For about 100 years, Barbados remained the richest of all the European colonies. The colony's prosperity remained regionally unmatched until sugar cane production expanded in larger countries, such as Saint Domingue and Jamaica. As part of the mass sugar industry, sugar cane processing gave rise to related commodities such as rum, molasses and falernum (a sweet syrup used in Caribbean and tropical drinks that tastes of almond, ginger, lime and sometimes vanilla, cloves and allspice).

The English government was also concerned that Barbados' continued trade with Dutch sailors for foodstuffs could result in them relying on the Dutch for survival; so the English government increased the tax on Barbadian tobacco to higher levels than that from Virginia. Combined with the poorer quality, this was the death knell for Barbadian tobacco farming with imports to London plummeting.

Ironically, it was a Dutchman that came to the rescue of Barbados' economy. Pieter Blower was the first man to bring sugar cane to the island in 1637. Initially, it was only grown on a small scale and used as feed or to create rum.

However, with the weakening tobacco cash crop, in 1642 the Barbadian planters started to grow cane for use as sugar. The Dutch were keen to expand their trade routes. Seizing their opportunity, they provided planters with cheap loans, insurance and inexpensive equipment. They also took them to Brazil to see how sugar cane should be grown for cultivation as sugar crop.

The Dutch also realised that the planters were short on labourers. They had recently taken over the West African slave routes from the Portuguese and were looking to find new sales points. This changed the makeup of Barbadian society. As did the influx of transportees from Ireland, in particular but also from groups offered transportation as an alternative to other punishments in the Cromwellian period. There is some evidence that besides the officers from Dunbar held at Tynemouth and eventually sent to the island, many of the prisoners from Worcester were destined for the Caribbean.

Here, indentured servants and African slaves lived and worked beside each other, sharing many things (work tools and diet, for example) while also maintaining cultural and religious differences from each other and from their English masters. Over time those relationships would move from a recognition of differences based on religion, culture and free/unfree status towards a simpler model of difference based on race. At that point the areas of connection and collaboration would break down between the two groups.[12] But, for a while at least, the potential for alliance and resistance seemed very real.

Jenny Shaw opens her book on the Irish and black African workers of Barbados with a description of an Irish Catholic labourer in the 1650s sentenced to twenty-one lashes for 'slandering' English colonists by threatening to drink their blood. Cornelius Bryan was clearly a trouble maker, and was ordered to leave the island within a month. As far as we know, he never obliged and seems to have prospered in situ. His will of 1687 states that he left behind a wife, Margaret, and six children. By then he owned 22 acres of land and thirteen enslaved black Africans.

Shaw argues that Cornelius and the thousands of other Catholic Irish transported by Cromwell occupied a space somewhere between 'civilised and uncivilised, white and not white'. Subject to the same harsh treatment as the black slaves they worked alongside, they were distinguished from them by the prospect of freedom at some stage. And with it, the possibility of improving their lives, of becoming themselves, the owners of the very type of plantation they had once worked.

The irony is that indentured labour returned with the end of slavery in the nineteenth century. As Britain and America looked to new territories for sugar cultivation, they carried the trade to islands in the Indian and Pacific oceans, to Australia and Africa. Wherever it took hold, the planters encountered trouble sourcing enough local labour. The answer was imported indentured labour. 'From one sugar region to another – from Brazil to Hawaii – the sugar plantation became the home of alien people – people who had been uprooted and shipped vast distances to undertake the intensive gruelling labour on sugar plantations.'[13]

Indenture

Indenture was meant to be time limited but the Dunbar men were dependent on the goodwill and honesty of their 'employers'. They had little recourse if they were not freed as promised. Jordan and Walsh cite a group of Scots sent to the West Indies after the Battle of Worcester complaining in 1656 that their indentures were being illegally extended to seven years. The London Committee of Enquiry which investigated the matter upheld their sentences.

It was a dangerous business just getting there. The shipboard mortality rate for forced transportees has been estimated at between 15 and 30 per cent. Nor did it improve when they landed.

Within a five-year period after landing, from 35 per cent (women) to 50 per cent (men) of the 1620–80 indentured newcomers died. Among prison-vented men and women the death-rate was higher, then and thereafter. Arrival records (cited by Smith) show that when the Honour arrived at Annapolis in 1720, twenty of her sixty-one convicts had died. Thirty out of eighty-seven died during the voyage of the Gilbert in 1722, and thirty-eight out of ninety-five on the Rapahannock Merchant in 1725. Whether British or Irish, this grievous mortality prevailed to the mid-18th century.[14]

Despite deplorable conditions on ships transporting convicts, it was a loss to contractors when the death rate on the voyage was high. Walter Hart Blumenthal cited the work of Sir Walter Besant from 1902. Besant had looked at 3 original documents concerning 3 ships transporting convicts in 1740/1. The voyages took 2 months or more. Of 153 convicts on board one of these ships, 61 died and 8 were landed sick. The remaining 84 were soon sold. On the second ship, with 108 on board, 37 died. On the third craft 50 were put on board and 15 died. The proportion of the sexes is not stated. Most of the convicts were '7-year' passengers; a few had been remitted from the gallows but sentenced to 14 years' servitude.[15] Of course, we have to bear in mind that the nature of the vessels and their destinations had changed in the intervening ninety years.

Why did the Dunbar prisoners not fight back? Jordan and Walsh record a number of attempts to take over the transport ships, particularly when the practice became a major business with up to 200 at a time being shipped overseas. Indeed, this was a real fear in 1618 when 100 'dissolute' youths were packed off to the Americas on the personal orders of James I. No record of any trial exists. So anxious was the Treasurer of the London Company, Sir Thomas Smythe, about the prospect of mutiny that he had to be summoned to a table banging by James' Secretary of State, Sir George Calvert: 'The Kings desire admitted no delay'. Smythe, still wary, decided to keep numbers manageable – the cargo was sent out in small groups on four ships. Perhaps once onboard ship, it was felt to be a foregone conclusion and at least offered hope rather than death. Physically weakened after months of imprisonment, many of the Dunbar men might well have fell ill onboard ship. Seasickness was no incentive for action.

> Not all fared badly. Many years later, one of the Scots who settled in New Jersey from around 1680 onwards wrote home that he had had a drink with one of the 'old buckskin planters', a Scot who 'was sent away by Cromwell to New England as a slave from Dumbar [*sic*]. Living now in Woodbridge like a Scottish Laird, wishes his countrymen and his Native Soyle very well tho' he never intends to see it'.[16]

There was a familiar element awaiting the men of Dunbar as they found themselves in the New World, though not necessarily a comfortable one. The Congregationalists of New England did not just vary from the Scots Presbyterianism in organisation. Their world view, their sense of the proper order of society was at variance with the relatively relaxed practice of the Scots. That's rather entertaining given our perception of Calvinism these days but there is plenty of evidence that Puritan New England viewed its Scots addition as morally slack. The Innes trial recounted in the final chapter of this book is a prime example of this.

Avihu Zakai has suggested that the Puritan settlers of the Massachusetts Bay area viewed their settlement as a sacred task. Their 'Errand into the Wilderness' was identified with the 'Errand of the

Church of the Wilderness' in the Book of Revelation. All aspects of human life were to be based on the word of God, creating a culture that must have felt in many ways familiar to the men of the Covenant coming from Scotland in the 1650s. By then, of course, the practicalities of taming and managing the new settlement had pushed this initial ecclesiastical fervour into the background but it seems likely to have persisted as a founding ideal.

Nowhere was this more comprehensively illustrated than in their relationships with the native peoples they encountered in the Americas.

The founders of the Massachusetts Bay, New Haven, Connecticut and Rhode Island colonies in the 1630s were families with young children and their university trained ministers. Their aim, according to John Winthrop, the first governor of Massachusetts Bay, was to create a model of reformed Protestantism, a 'city upon a hill', a new English Israel.

That idea made clear the religious orientation of the New England settlement, and the charter of the Massachusetts Bay Colony stated as a goal that the colony's people 'may be soe religiously, peaceablie, and civilly governed, as their good Life and orderlie Conversacon, maie wynn and incite the Natives of Country, to the Knowledg and Obedience of the onlie true God and Saulor of Mankinde, and the Christian Fayth'.[17]

To illustrate this, the seal of the Massachusetts Bay Company shows a half-naked Native American, dressed in a leaf loincloth and holding a bow, depicted as entreating more of the English to come over and help them. The attitudes summed up by the seal go a long way to explain the increasingly strained relationships between incomers and the First Peoples. The Indian wars, exacerbated by escalating tensions over land ownership and use, were to have a direct impact on the lives of the Dunbar men in America.

The witch trials, so much a part of our image of Puritan New England, will have come as no surprise to the Scots prisoners – over 3,000 Scots had been brought to trial for the same offence in the seventeenth century.[18] Like many other Europeans, the Puritans believed in the supernatural. Every event appeared to be a sign of God's mercy or judgement, and people believed that witches allied themselves with the Devil to carry out evil deeds and deliberate harm such as the sickness or death of children, the loss of cattle and other catastrophes.

Hundreds were accused of witchcraft in Puritan New England, including townspeople whose habits or appearance bothered their neighbours or who appeared threatening for any reason. Women, seen as more susceptible to the Devil because of their supposedly weaker constitutions, made up the vast majority of suspects and those who were executed.

The most notorious witchcraft cases occurred in Salem Village in 1692. Many of the accusers who prosecuted the suspected witches had been traumatised by the Indian wars on the frontier and by unprecedented political and cultural changes in New England. Relying on their belief in witchcraft to help make sense of their changing world, Puritan authorities executed nineteen people and caused the deaths of several others. It is interesting to note that the son of one of the Dunbar transportees, James, son of George Darling, testified at the Salem trial in 1692.

Chapter 8

Bringing Up the Dead

They throw in drummer Hodge, to rest
Un-coffined – just as found; his land mark is a kopje crest
That breaks the veldt around,
And foreign constellations west
Each night above his mound

Thomas Hardy (1840–1928)

One of the most arresting images from the Lost Lives Exhibition (produced by the Durham Team in 2018) was the facial depiction of one of the buried soldiers. It is unnerving and uncanny as such reconstructions always are. Nobody can say it's totally accurate, we can never know, but he looks right somehow. And there he is, pretty much like any ordinary young chap; if you had to guess his nationality, you would probably say Scottish. You can see plenty like him now on the streets of most towns and villages north of the border. He looks as if he would be at home in the crowd at a football match. He was likely born in about 1629 and probably spent his early childhood in the Highlands or possibly the south west.

He might have been anaemic and moved to a different area sometime in the early years of the next decade. He had consistently poor dental hygiene and a herniated vertebral disc suggests a hard life of heavy humping. Latterly, he had experienced a lack of vitamin C and spells of malnutrition. Of all the dead found, he was the only one to show evidence of possible battle injury, a slash or cut above the left eye. This had not killed him; it had healed long before death. We do not know for sure what the cause of death was – the odds are high it was dysentery that did for him. He was perhaps 21 years old.[1]

Looking at him, you have no sense that you are staring at the dead. He looks very much alive, as he might when he was captured rather than after the rigours and trauma of forced marching, starvation, brutality and finally disease. We feel we ought to know him or at least his name. For over three-and-a-half centuries he had been forgotten, tumbled into a mass grave and swept under history's carpet. We know nothing about his family, not even his name. We can guess that there would have been someone back in Scotland to mourn his loss. He left us no words, no hint as to his identity and his story was never told. All we have of him we owe to science.

The fact that we can look on his face after so many centuries is a tribute to the exacting and detailed work carried out by the scientists and archaeologists of the Durham Team. You will find a detailed analysis in their book, *Lost Lives, New Voices*. It is a compelling read, providing a guide to the forensic techniques they used as well as drawing a vivid picture of the life led by the Dunbar soldiers based on the evidence of their bones. Their achievement is all the more impressive when you realise the scale of their task. There appeared to be between seventeen and twenty-nine skeletons in the two graves; they were so incomplete it was impossible to say exactly how many. There were also over 1,000 pieces of bone which could not be tied to a particular body.[2]

For all those years pleasant Palace Green had kept its secret, the dark underlay beneath the veneer of studied, studious, genteel calm. A bit like the mad woman in the attic, you knew she was up there but really didn't want to find out. However, in November 2013 work began on digging out for a new cafe space at the southern end of the west flank of Palace Green Library. There have been buildings on this site for a very long time; some we see today are traces of fifteenth-century survivals. A scrubby no-man's-land of enclosed yard lay between library buildings east and north and the 1960s' Pace Building standing west. An ancient alley, 'Windy Gap', scoots away to the south. A builder's nightmare; the working area is enclosed and as archaeological traces were inevitable, diggers were on standby.

Work began on 5 November, with a deeper excavation going ahead three days later. It was on the 21st that three skulls were uncovered. When bones are found, there are protocols to be followed – this may, of course, be a recent crime scene. A licence to exhume is required from the Ministry of Justice which triggers a meticulous dig; it becomes the kingdom of the trowel. As the layers of soil and silt were pared back to reveal evidence of skeletons, it became obvious that these were very likely part of mass burials and of considerable age: no modern police detective would be needed. The remains had been hastily interred in a tumbled east–west alignment, haphazard and entwined. However objective you may be as an archaeologist, there's something special about bones. Those of us who have uncovered these human traces would surely all admit to a particular thrill, a frisson that other finds just don't engender.

Two separate grave-pits were subsequently identified, the first in the north-east corner which held eighteen bodies and the second eleven. All appeared to have been interred together and none was complete, nor were they laid out in the accepted funerary practice of the day; an orderly pose, and strict alignment. These were random and disordered, chucked into the pit in a hurry and with scant respect. There were no traces of any personal effects, clothing or shoes. Were these people nobody had cared about or were they under such pressure to get them interred that they had no time for the usual rituals?

The site itself, while close to the cathedral, was not hallowed ground. In the seventeenth century, the cathedral boundary had stopped just short of the yard. This was castle ground: a service area. There had been other remains found in the past, particularly around the music school. There is no way of confirming or disproving if they were linked to the Dunbar prisoners, and it's quite possible they date from other periods: Durham has been inhabited for a very long time and as a consequence all sorts of local myths have evolved. Local legend held that a conical mound in the cathedral cemetery was some kind of tumulus. It's not, it was thrown up around 1830 as a viewing terrace and extended for the 2nd Boer War memorial later on.[3]

Much has changed on Palace Green since 1650 and a lot of what we see today dates from Bishop Cosin's post-restoration makeover and subsequent development. The location of the mass graves is marked along its western flank by the line of Bishop Flambard's castle wall and, to the east, by Palace Green itself with Windy Gap in the south. This area was historically covered by a range of domestic and ancillary buildings serving the Prince Bishop's extensive household.

As far as could be ascertained, all the remains were male. Subsequent DNA analysis suggests these all came from a specific grouping rather than representing a cross section of the population, with a number of them having isotopes consistent with being Scots. It's very much a question of balancing the statistics. Andrew Millard, in a lecture on the forensic science given in 2017, used a distribution grid to illustrate his conclusions: only five of the bodies could be definitively identified as Scots – the others were most likely so. Having said that, three of them came from outside Britain. That's interesting: were these the sons of Scots who had served abroad in the various wars of the seventeenth century and who had started families there?[4]

The age range and gender bias further implies a military connection, consistent with evidence yielded by other mass graves at sites such as Towton (uncovered in 1996). Having said that, these aren't battlefield graves as such, none of the dead appeared to have died violently, unlike those at sites such as Towton or Visby in Sweden.

By and large they had not led easy lives; there were signs of childhood deprivation, nutritional deficiencies and illnesses. They had not had sedentary occupations either, many showed clear signs of hard physical labour. One-third had potentially suffered from rickets – a deficiency of vitamin D, calcium or phosphate which results in weak and/or stunted bones and possibly stunted growth.[5] This condition is more likely to be found the further north you go: shorter days and cloudier conditions make access to the sunshine needed to produce vitamin D less likely. It is far less common in the Britain of the twenty-first century because vitamin D is added to food, particulary to flour – almost eradicating what had been a widespread affliction.

There was evidence of scurvy too, caused by a lack of vitamin C. These young men had the added misfortune of being born into that dire seventeenth-century 'heyday of famine' when outbreaks of measles, scurvy, TB, typhus and whooping cough stalked the land like a posse of grim reapers.

Could they have been Scottish soldiers from 1644/45, from the earlier army of occupation? It's possible but if they'd been buried by their own side, we might have expected more attention and some records of their loss. It seemed unlikely that they were plague victims (which might have accounted for the hasty burial). There were outbreaks of plague in Scotland in the 1640s (Alan Junkin, an American descendant of one of the Dunbar transportees, found mention of it in the parish records of his ancestor).[6]

Plague was present in England as well, and struck Durham in 1644. Yet, parish records suggest relatively few were dying, certainly not in such large numbers as would necessitate mass interment. During a particularly long outbreak (1587–9) most people had continued to be laid to rest in parish cemeteries – any overspill was taken out of the city to be buried on the moor.[7]

The dead may not be able to talk, but science can give them a voice and help us to understand more about their lives. The team at Durham used bio-archaeological observation, biochemical and microscopic analysis of bone and residues found in the skeletons' dental calculus, together with isotropic analysis to piece together a medical/physical 'biography' for a number of them.

SK6 (names are the one thing science cannot provide) was older than most of the others, past 46, a real veteran. He was born before 1604 probably from the western sector of the central lowlands and spent his childhood there or in Caithness, perhaps even Orkney. His diet, a balanced mix of plant and animal protein, was fairly good overall yet he was only 5ft 4in (166cm) tall. He had had a hard life, with lots of tough manual work and may well have used his teeth as tools – a fisherman perhaps? He had the beginnings of osteoarthritis, a long-term vitamin C deficiency and showed signs of the onset of a form of arthritis, diffuse idiopathic skeletal hyperostosis (DISH). DISH is often associated with obesity and it is very common for sufferers to also develop cardiovascular conditions.[8]

That's it, an unfinished symphony, unwritten biography. He was nobody well known, just your average squaddie, older certainly but without much evidence of previous military experience; possibly one of the newer recruits. What evidence we have, both from the excavation and from the American records, suggests a higher percentage of younger men among the prisoners of war. Maybe the older generation had managed to slip away after the battle; wiliness comes with experience. Of course, it is also likely that Cromwell was aware that younger men would fetch a better price. That men of his age are being conscripted at all suggests the Estates were indeed scraping the barrel.

SK21 was a good deal younger (in the 18–25 category), so born between 1625 and 1632, somewhere between Falkirk and Aberdeen. He'd suffered dietary stress in childhood alongside vitamin D deficiency, consequently afflicted by rickets; his historic consumption of oats suggested a potential highland homeland. He certainly smoked a pipe and, along with living in smoky conditions, this gave him sinusitis. He had also led a demanding physical life.[9]

It was a tough century, life was hard for most. By 1650 a dozen years of war had impoverished and wearied most. It shows in the physical remains of the Durham burials. These were conscripts, young men, some very young, dragged from their ploughs, nets or benches to soldier. They were not hardened professionals and in the end they were reduced to mere commodities, dumped anonymously when they were beyond being of any use. We get a glimpse of just how tough life was from the gloriously titled 1614 survey of the 'wairris and commodaties that ar shippit and transpported further of this kingdom yeirli'.[10] This is a statement of Scotland's trade but also provides data on the economy as a whole. Exports were far smaller than their English equivalent – only 736,986 pounds (Scots) to 30 million (Scots) for their southern neighbour. What is truly interesting is that it shows an economy in a state of transition. Raw wool, once the mainstay of the Scots economy had shrunk to only 7 per cent of total exports. The market for hides and skins would follow it in the 1670s. The growth sectors were fish, coal, salt and grain. All of these were industries that paid badly, and were brutally demanding. Most people still worked the land. And it was a subsistence economy – only in a few areas such as Fife was food produced which was surplus to local needs.

Diet was basic. The compensation claims for Dunbar list the food supplies taken by Cromwell's men. The vast majority of it is grain – suggesting that cereals were an important part of the daily supply. Like northern England, wheat production was secondary to oats and barley (which grow better in cold, damp climates).

Price rises from the mid-sixteenth century onwards had hit the poorest hardest. Michael Lynch has calculated that general prices rose fourfold between the years 1550 and 1625. But agricultural prices rose even faster – nine-fold in the case of Fife where barley rose from 16*s.* to 140*s.* a boll during this period, driven by the deliberate depreciation of the coinage by the Crown. In Edinburgh the official price of bread (which was controlled by the Council) rose eightfold. Wages did not keep pace with inflation, nor did the income of those who farmed but did not own land.

There is a reason why the bodies of the Dunbar men found at Durham show signs of childhood privation. This was the period when the Scots diet moved from one based on meat to one high in cereals supplemented by whatever protein was available together with whatever vegetables would grow in such a climate. Kale (cabbage) was sturdy enough to thrive and was clearly ubiquitous.

The monition of cursing issued by Bishop Gavin Dunbar of Glasgow against the border reivers in 1525 gives us a good indication of what the diet was at the start of the sixeenth century (and of how restricted it became). It specifically refers to 'cail yards' (cabbage patches):

> I wary [curse] thair cornys, thair catales, thair woll, thair scheip, thair horse, thair swyne, thair geise [geese], thair hennys, and all thair quyk gude [livestock]. I wary thair hallis, thair chalmeris [rooms], thair kechingis, thair stanillis [stables], thair barnys, thair biris [byres], thair bernyardis, thair cailyardis [vegetable patches], thair plewis [ploughs], thair harrowis, and the gudis and housis that is necessair for their sustentatioun and weilfair.

In some areas, the word 'kale' would also be the word for broth – an indication of its importance in the diet. There were regional differences – lowlanders had less access both to dairy products and fresh meat, for example. The danger period was childhood. If you survived that a typical Scot had a fair chance of living to the age of 50–70.

Alongside this economic change was an alteration in the nature of land holding. The old feudal system was giving way to a new economic order: the rise of the middle classes (or middling sort as they were called at the time). The departure of so many of the old nobility to the London court of James I in 1603 had left a gap: an opportunity grasped by new money. Merchants, burghs and those minor gentry who were now consolidating their holdings as lairds and flexing the political muscles they had acquired over the years from 1575 were effectively driving the political process.

Famine, Fear and the Rise of a Middling Sort

Famine is ugly. In our time we view this as an affliction of developing countries but seventeenth-century Scots were very well acquainted with the phenomenon and the archaeological evidence from the Palace Green burials confirms this. Poor harvests occurred in 1621 and the following year, and famine prices endured from 1620–5. The Highland region suffered notably in 1604, 1623 and in 1650, while the north was afflicted in 1634–6. Want was punctuated with outbreaks of plague to which hungry folk succumbed more quickly

These years cover the time period within which many of the Dunbar prisoners were born. The closing years of the seventeenth century were even leaner – the 'ill years' of the 1690s when economic recession and a succession of failed harvests produced great hardship and rocketing mortality rates. It is estimated perhaps between 5 and 15 per cent of the Scots population died as a result – in areas such as Aberdeenshire, this climbed as high as 25 per cent.

> These were grim times indeed: The crops were blighted by easterly 'haars' or mists, by sunless, drenching summers, by storms and by early bitter frosts and late snow in autumn. For seven years this calamitous weather continued – the corn rarely ripening; the green, withered grain being shorn in December amidst pouring rain or pelting snow-storms. Sheep and oxen died in their thousands, and a large proportion of the population in rural districts was destroyed by disease and want.[11]

Poor Law relief had been introduced by statute first in 1574, then 1579 and 1592, a governmental response to the ills of an itinerant, mendicant poor. The Kirk was a prominent player and the scheme was run by local magistrates. Deacons and other worthies drew up lists of eligible poor in their parishes and oversaw draconian treatment of those who were deemed undeserving. Famine put the whole system under immense strain and the 'ill years' were so bad it broke down altogether in many areas.

For those not of the middling sort, as so many of our soldiers were, life was getting harder. The old feudal system may have been harsh but those working the land had a place in it. The new order had less time for affinities of kinship or obligation. In the absence of an independent income or landholding, most had no choice but to seek work labouring for another. It was the start of a process that would see thousands leave the land looking for work in urban areas, a route that would end in the clearances as old loyalties finally dissolved.

In the absence of a written record left by our soldiers, we have to find other ways of understanding their mindset; trying to find out how they may have viewed themselves and their place in the world; the way of thinking that led them to respond to the call to fight, rather than getting out of there as quickly as possible. One of the striking events organised as part of the Lost Lives Exhibition in the summer of 2018 was a storytelling session. A Scots storyteller from the Dunbar area recounted tales which have been passed down through the oral tradition; stories that our men would have heard round the fire. Myth shapes our understanding from an early age. Far more than an entertainment, they embody the values and expectations we want to pass on. In many ways you can judge a society by the tales it tells.

Heather Yuill is a master of her art. She held the room riveted for 2 hours, spinning stories, playing the harp (much as the travelling harpists of the seventeenth century would have done) and elucidating the provenance and history of the material she used.

Surprisingly, many of the stories feature saints: men like Kentigern (St Mungo), the sixth-century apostle of Strathclyde, whose tale is a political one as well as a spiritual one – his father died fighting the Bernicians of northern England in AD 597. Another tale recounts how the Scots acquired the Saltire as their flag. The Scottish Flag Trust tells the story:

Tradition has it that the flag, the white saltire on a blue background, the oldest flag in Europe and the Commonwealth, originated in a battle fought in East Lothian in the Dark Ages.

It is believed that the battle took place in the year 832AD. An army of Picts under Angus mac Fergus, High King of Alba, and aided by a contingent of Scots led by Eochaidh (Kenneth mac Alpin's grandfather) had been on a punitive raid into Lothian (then and for long afterwards Northumbrian territory), and were being pursued by a larger force of Angles and Saxons under one Athelstan.

The Albannach/Scots were caught and stood to face their pursuers in the area of Markle, near East Linton. This is to the north of the modern village of Athelstaneford (which was resited on higher ground in the 18th century), where the Peffer, which flows into the Firth of Forth at Aberlady, forms a wide vale. Being then wholly undrained, the Peffer presented a major obstacle to crossing, and the two armies came together at the ford near the present day farm of Prora (one of the field names there is still the Bloody Lands).

Fearing the outcome of the encounter, King Angus led prayers for deliverance, and was rewarded by seeing a cloud formation of a white saltire (the diagonal cross on which St Andrew had been martyred) against a blue sky. The king vowed that if, with the saint's help, he gained the victory, then Andrew would thereafter be the patron saint of Scotland. The Scots did win, and the Saltire became the flag of Scotland.

When Kenneth mac Alpin, who may have been present with his grandfather at the battle, later united Picts and Scots and named the entity Scotland, Andrew did indeed become the patron saint of the united realm. Kenneth mac Alpin, King of Scots and Picts, Ardrigh Albainn, was laid to rest on Iona in 860AD.[12]

The men who gathered at Dunbar, regardless of their politics, regardless of their background, had been reared on tales of pride in their homeland, to believe that God was on their side in defending her and that they were united in a communal effort with profound historical roots. It's the best sort of patriotism: one that takes pride in one's heritage.

Chapter 9

Where is Home?

Not what they want but what is good for them ...
Remark by Oliver Cromwell

Those of us who come from migrant families know the peculiarities of a dual heritage: particularly marked when the country that became home also made the move necessary, as in the movement to England of Irish families in the nineteenth century or the forced transportees from Dunbar and Worcester sent to an America that was still a British colony. That sense of connection does not necessarily diminish with the generations: family legend and the twenty-first-century passion for knowing where we came from can actually enhance it.

That is what is so interesting about talking to the many descendants of the Scots prisoners. They have developed a remarkable body of information about these men and present it with a passion and understanding that brings it to life. *Lost Lives, New Voices* is a great source of information about what happened to our Dunbar men when they reached their destination: we are not going to repeat it here. Instead we want to focus on the history put together by their descendants and the local historians of the areas they settled in.

In doing so we hope to demonstrate the impact they had both in their own time and subsequently. Because they still do have a direct influence on how people see themselves and the pride they have in their ancestry. Here is an example, a quote from a piece posted by Teresa Rust. She is the descendant of two men identified as probably coming over with the Dunbar men and is married to somebody with the same antecedents. She is Executive Director of the Scottish Prisoners of War Society, an American body dedicated to investigating and recording the details of the men transported in the 1650s after the battles of Dunbar and Worcester. It is an invaluable source of information as well as a fascinating read. It must also take an incredible amount of work to maintain: the number of descendants has been estimated, by Chris Gerrard, at close to 500,000.[1] The John Hamilton of Concord Descendant Tree on Ancestry.com was showing over 12,000 descendants and spouses in 2015.[2] Teresa Rust maintained and researched that tree for many years.

> Now that I am starting to read a lot about the Scottish prisoners as a whole group, it is becoming apparent that they were for the most part thrifty and hardworking and within a generation many had already established themselves well. What is it about the Scots that they have this sort of drive and ambition?
>
> Of course, our prisoners were strong men to have survived what they did and still be fit to labour as indentured servants.
>
> Take for example Daniel Blacke/Black. The following is from American Ancestors Online: 'In 1654, the Middlesex County Court in Charlestown ordered that: "Daniel Blacke Scotchman servant to Mr. Wilton Simes [William Symmes?], being lawfully convicted for assaulting & beating his master, is by this Court committed to prison, until further order of Court."
>
> Simes was probably the son of Charlestown's minister, Zechariah Symmes, one of the town's most prominent citizens. The Symmes family farm, covering much of present-day Winchester ... Blacke undoubtedly labored there cutting hay in the meadows. No further records about Blacke's imprisonment have been located, but he must have overcome this episode of violence and moved on after his indenture, for his name turns up again later in Topsfield. A New York governor, Frank S. Black, traced his ancestry to this Scots war prisoner.'
>
> I would love to get the back story to this event! He is convicted of this assault and sent to prison but one can't help but wonder what the details really were to this 'assault.' I can only imagine his frustration as a proud Highlander being bossed about by a Puritan Englishman.[3]

That is fairly typical of the material you get from the descendants, detailed research combined with an understanding of these people as individuals. And, so often, you can also get a sense of how their own lives have been impacted by their ancestors and of the connection they share. In addition, strikingly, again and again, we find that the Scots prisoners had a profound influence on their new country shaping its politics and its history.

They have given us a detailed picture of the journey undertaken by our men. Take transportation lists, for example.

There is no ships' passenger list for the *Unity*. The Scottish Prisoners of War Society website has a list, compiled for the *Lost Lives, New Voices* book, with over 180 suggested names of men found in New England who appear to fit the criteria of a Scottish prisoner of war. They have been placed into four categories: Definite, Probable, Possible and Doubtful.

A 1902 researcher has given us a great deal of detail about the process of sending the first shipment of prisoners out on the *Unity*, which sailed for the colonies in November 1650. We know that she had shipped out of Boston on 6 February (there is a bill of health for that day). The captain, Augustine Walker, came from Charlestown. We don't have a lot of information about him: we know he was admitted to the church in 1640, and that he and his wife Hannah had four children. He died before 8 August 1654.[4] Clearly a lot of trade was being carried out from Charlestown – it was the home of the master of a later ship, the *John and Sara*. The transportees it carried were handed over to Thomas Kemble, a Charlestown merchant who acted as broker. There were to be other links between the two vessels – John Beex (Beech), transporter of the Scottish prisoners aboard the *Unity*, was also a consignee for the second ship.

The Committee of Both Kingdoms suggested using the men as labour in the coal mines or transporting them to America, France or Ireland. In preparation for this the prisoners were moved to London. On 11 November Heselrige was told to deliver 150 prisoners to Augustine Walker, who would take them to New England. The *Unity* sailed in the winter instead of waiting for spring, so the trip was rough and the prisoners had scurvy, but all arrived safely in Boston near the end of December.

Captain Augustine Walker and the brokers/consignees, Beech and Foote, consigned most of the Scottish prisoners to two businesses in Maine and Massachusetts in which Beech had an interest. Sixty-two of the Scots are known to have been sent to the Saugus Ironworks at Lynn, Massachusetts (one of the first iron manufactories in North America). The rest were sold as indentured servants to local residents. Fifteen men were sent to Berwick, Maine, while a few others, exact number not given, went to nearby York, Maine. They got £20–£30 per man.[5] The typical cost for passage across the sea was £5, so the voyage made quite a profit – about £1,500 (approximately £105,000 in today's terms). Unity Parish in Berwick, Maine was founded by the Scottish prisoners and the names of areas within it commemorate both one of the battles with the English and the name of the ship that carried them to America.[6]

On 24 March 1651, the Council wrote to Hesilrige with orders to move on the Scots still held at Durham Castle. As a consequence, 300 were to be delivered to Colonel Rokeby and 200 to Lieutenant Colonel Killigrew, who had been licensed to transport them, on the condition that they should not be used for anything that might prejudice of the Commonwealth.[7]

Assistance was to be given in shipping them away from Newcastle to London. The lot under Rokeby were destined for France. Arriving in London, they were confined in the Tiltyard at Greenwich and the East India House and yard at Blackwall. Among the troops detailed to guard them was a troop of horse under the command Major Stephen Winthrop, the fourth son of Governor John Winthrop of Massachusetts. You have to wonder if that played a part in deciding on their destination.

The men had been housed on board vessels lying in the Thames where their treatment still seems to have been open to criticism:

> At this time complaints were heard in regard to the treatment of Scotch prisoners aboard vessels lying in the Thames, and the justices about Blackwall were ordered to receive some sick Scotch prisoners into their pest houses, to be cured at the expense of some persons who had fetched them from the North for transportation to the foreign plantations.[8]

A commission was formed in September of that year to deal with actually sending the non-commissioned men to the plantations. The captives from Worcester, held at Liverpool, Chester and Stafford, were ordered to Bristol for transport.

It took a while. On 2 December 1651, disease had broken out among men still left in London. Angry enquires ensued: why were they still there and how was potential infection to be contained. It's at this point that a subsistence allowance is ordered; 4*d*. a day for privates and 5*s*. per week for officers.[9]

Approximately 900 of the surviving Scottish prisoners went to Virginia, Massachusetts and the Barbados colony in the Caribbean and another 500 were indentured the following spring to Marshall Turenne for service against the French army.[10]

We have more details including a passenger list for the *John and Sara*.

London This 11th of November, 1651; Captain John Greene;
Wee whose names are under written freighters of your shipe the John & Sara doe order yow forthwith as winde & weather shall permitt to sett saile for Boston in New England & there deliver our Orders and Servants to Tho. Kemble of Charles Towne to be disposed of by him according to orders wee have sent him in that behalfe & wee desire yow to Advise with the said Kemble about all that may concerne that whole Intended voyage using your endeavours with the said Kemble for the speediest lading your shipp from New Eng; to the Barbados with provisions & such other things as are in N.E. fit for the West Indies where you are to deliver them to Mr. Charles Rich to be disposed of by him for the Joinet accont of the freighte's & so to be Retou'ned home in a stocke undevided thus desiring your Care & industrie in Despatch and speed of the voyage wishing you a happy & safe Retourne wee remaine your loving friends
Signatum et Recognitum
John Beex
Rob't Rich
Will Greene
in pneia Jo Nottock: notar Publ;
13 May 1652
Entred & Recorded Edward Rawson Recorder[11]

The consignors were Robert Rich of London, John Beex and William Green. In this ship was a quantity of provisions, ironwork and household items, free of duty by ordinance of Parliament, shipped by Robert Rich, who had, a year previously, shipped on the *Speedwell* a cargo comprising mostly linens and cloths valued at over £2,000.

Stackpole, Thompson and Meserve's 1913 history of the town of Durham, New Hampshire gives us more detail about the distribution of the 272 Scots dispatched on the *John and Sara* to Thomas Kemble of Charlestown.[12]

Kemble was part owner with Valentine Hill of mills at Durham Falls and Lamprey River. He also owned lands in Maine and had an extensive lumber business, ideal work for fit young Scots once they had recovered from the horrors of the journey. Richard Leader had charge of some more Scots at the Saugus Ironworks at Lynn and later, in 1652, took some of them with him to work in the mills at South Berwick, then called Great Works.

Richard Leader (1609–61) was an English businessman engaged in trade between America, England and Scotland. We don't know how he acquired his knowledge in metallurgy, but it is likely that he had some contact with the Irish ironmaking industry. He fell out with the undertakers of the Saugus Ironworks (Company of Undertakers for the Iron Works in New England) and moved to South Berwick saw mills, which he managed on behalf of John Becx and Co. Clearly he was convinced by then of the capacity of the Scots prisoners. Leader brought twenty-five of his bonded workers with him at a cost of £20 to £30 each and put them to work on a gang of up to twenty saws. The increased output inspired the name Great Works for the site and the river.

Five years later Leader sold out his interests and freed his servants, many of whom were granted land in Kittery. One of those indentured servants was James Warren, who had come over on the *Unity*. James was granted land on 15 August 1656. He received 50 acres with 48 poles. One pole, or rod, equals 16.5ft (one-quarter chain). However, the land proved to be of poor quality but he later acquired better holdings.

By 1656, Leader was in Barbados, where he engaged in sugar refining and salt manufacturing. In a letter from 1660, he complained about the island's climate and stated that if it were not for the slave labour available in Barbados, he would prefer to reside in New England. He also wrote that he intended to leave 'this western world' for Ireland, as he saw 'no place either for profit or pleasure so good as Ireland', which was remarkable considering conditions there following the Cromwellian war. Perhaps he had some sentimental attachment to the country. He made it back to New England all the same, dying in Kittery in December 1661.

James Warren prospered, holding a number of public offices and leaving a substantial amount in his will. His son Gilbert received 40 acres of land, while another son, James, got all the other land and buildings including the homestead, He gave to his daughters, Margaret and Grisel, and granddaughter, Jane Grant, 5s. each and to his grandson, James Stackpole, some cattle. To his wife, Margaret, he gave the rest of the estate.[13]

His granddaughter Catherine married the son of another Scots prisoner whose descendants have documented his life – Robert Junkins. Catherine had been born a Stackpole suggesting that the writer of the Durham history was himself a descendant. Two of his descendants have been most helpful in the writing of this book. Jean Seeley pointed out that he was probably born in Berwick, which was also the name given to the upper part of Kittery in Maine where he died in about 1702. The other descendant, Michele Fuller, is equally dedicated to researching the history of the Scots prisoners.

So far I have found 3 grandfathers that came over on the Unity. Duncan Stewart, Peter Grant and James Warren. Their children and grandchildren moved to Maine and almost 400 years later still live there. I have been researching my line for over 30 years and just recently came across James Warren in my line. His daughter, Jane, married Peter Grant's son.[14]

Stackpole et al. note that many of the indentured men were granted land in the towns where they had worked once their period of servitude was up.

The records of Dover, under date of 5 October 1652, have the following: 'Given & granted unto Mr. Valentine Hill, his heires Executors administrators or assigns foure acres of land adjoining to Goodman Hudsons Lott for his Scots.' Later, about 1663, we find another record as follows, 'Layd out and Bounded to Henrey Brown and James Ore fower ackers [acres] which were given and granted unto Mr. Valentine Hills seven Scotes in the yeir 1652. Said land lyeth on the northern side of the land that was granted to Hudson and now in the hands of Edward Patterson.' It bordered on the 'freshet,' that is, the mill-pond above the dam at Durham Falls, and was on the south side of the river, and on the Newmarket road. It is probable that they worked by shifts in the mills, having three days in the week to work in their gardens. They were not allowed to marry till they got their liberty. Some of them never married. Some married daughters of their employers. Some married Irish maids who had been kidnaped and brought over as house servants and to swell the population of the colonies.[15]

David MackHome, John MackHolme, Glester MackTomas and Alexander Tompson are listed among the 272 Scottish prisoners transported to Boston, Massachusetts aboard the *John and Sara*. Spelling at the time was rather inexact but even by seventeenth-century standards these variations on Scots names are striking; clearly somebody has spelled these phonetically. You can imagine an English speaking recorder trying to make sense of what he was hearing, particularly if he was listening to a Gaelic-speaking highlander.

The chroniclers of the McThomas clan looked at the four names above and came up with a very different version:

Additionally, Chief Andrew MacThomas of Finegand suggests that the individual listed as 'Glester MackTomas' should perhaps be understood to be 'Alistair' as 'Glester' does not mean anything and is not a recognizable Scottish Christian name. Therefore, due to the phonetic spelling referenced above, perhaps these four men are better understood to be David McComie, John McColm, Alistair MacThomas, and Alexander Thomson.[16]

These men were not the only ones who had their surnames misheard. You can view a copy of the passenger list in 'Suffolk Deeds'.[17] This is an 1880 compendium of archive material produced by the City of Boston and is an early reflection of the work of the descendants of the Scots prisoners. Members of the Suffolk County Bar presented a petition to the Alderman of Boston:

> To the Honorable the Board of Aldermen of the City of Boston : —
>
> The undersigned, members of the Suffolk Bar and others, respectfully call the attention of your Honorable Board to the worn, mutilated, and illegible condition of the early records of deeds of the County of Suffolk.
>
> Your petitioners represent that, in addition to the ordinary causes of decay, said records have been so seriously affected by the introduction of steam heat and gas into the hall in which they are now kept, that their destruction is only a question of time.
>
> Your petitioners further represent that such destruction – undermining as it will the very foundation of all the titles to real estate in said county – may result in incalculable loss to said City of Boston, and the real-estate owners therein : that measures should be immediately taken for the preservation of said records ; and that this can best be done by printing the same.[18]

It is clear from their introduction to the volume that the documents were in a vulnerable condition:

> It is greatly to be regretted that our early records were not written in the first instance on parchment, instead of being intrusted to such perishable material as paper. This volume of Suffolk Deeds has been printed none too soon. Beside the ancient chirography, which is sufficiently forbidding even to experienced antiquarians, and which renders it illegible to most people, the book has suffered extremely from the destructive effects of time. The paper has been in many places completely eaten through by some corrosive substance in the ink. In others it has become blackened and discolored by age, and has grown so brittle that it has cracked and fallen into small

pieces. Frequent handling and inspection during the two centuries and a half of its existence have worn away the edges and corners, and fairly rubbed off portions of the writing near the too narrow margin. In years past unskilful attempts have been made to patch up some of the crumbling pages by pasting along the edges strips of thick paper. These have partially, and in some cases wholly, covered up the writing beneath

The poor condition of the paper under them made it unadvisable to attempt to remove these strips, and the book has been printed as it now is, without alteration, emendation, or addition, except as herein stated. The words and parts of words so lost are denoted by brackets. Boston, Nov. 13, 1880.[19]

Among the names that appear on the passenger list are John, Allester (*sic*) and Dan Mackhellin. There are also five Robinsons and one John Macklude. The request to preserve and publish the early deeds of Boston includes the following names: McClellan, Robinson, Mcloud. It is easy to conceive that the latter were possible descendants of the former with names spelt correctly rather than phonetically.

Survivors from Dunbar were sold into forced labour in mines, forges, mills and plantations in New England and elsewhere in the Americas. Of the 350 men destined for transport to New England, only about 150 arrived in Boston, where they were sold for between £20 and £30 each. Some were sent to cut lumber at that remote sawmill on the Salmon Falls River in what is now South Berwick, Maine, and others were sold as indentured servants, for terms of six or seven years. Those who built lives here 400 years ago are remembered by local landmarks such as the McIntire Garrison and Scotland Bridge in York, as well as the town names like Berwick and Durham we have already encountered.

Another of the misspelt names was that of William Forbes, variously given as Furbish or Furbus, who along with his brother Daniel was sold to Samson Angier of Kittery, Maine, both for £30. William remained with Samson while Daniel was either sold or given to his brother, Edmund Angier of Cambridge, Massachusetts.[20]

William Furbush seems to have been indentured for about eight years and then settled, as did a number of the transportees, in Dover, New

Hampshire. He seems to have been a strong-minded man of independent views and this was to get him into trouble a number of times. He was not the only one. B. Craig Stinson in a fascinating article on the Scottish Prisoners of War Society website gives us a glimpse of how they were perceived by their neighbours:

> Often we see the Scots earning their first taxable land in existing English towns but soon selling and relocating to unoccupied land where they could cluster together in new communities. These places soon took names that identified their residents, including the Parish of Unity and Scotland Parish. Scottish settlements tolerated a more boisterous lifestyle that determined to be free from Puritan authority and mores. When the English authorities did intervene in these places it was often to attempt to enforce church attendance or to fine the Scots for drinking or using coarse language. According to several written accounts of these unwelcome encounters, the constables were often met with curses from the Scottish men and more than once with fists from the Scottish women.[21]

Quakers began proselytising with some success, in Dover in 1662. The Congregational minister, John Rayner, made the mistake of entering into a public debate with them, which he lost. He was clearly determined not to make the same mistake when they returned later in the year. This time an order for the arrest of three Quaker women had been sought and issued by one of the deputies of the Court – one Richard Waldern.

The women were summarily convicted of entering the town (Quakers had been banned) and a savage sentence imposed: their hands would be tied to a tailboard, then having been stripped to the waist, they would be flogged ten times with a three-corded whip. They were then to be dragged through the snow and ice to the next town, where the beatings would be repeated, a journey through eleven towns covering 80 miles in total.[22]

> At Dover while the flogging was being administered, the Rev. Mr Raynor 'stood and looked and laughed at it'. Whereupon, Eliakim Wardwell ... reproved the reverend gentleman for his brutality.... For this offensive behaviour he was put in the stocks along with

William Fourbish, who had also manifested irreverence by rebuking the pious Rayner.[23]

Sinton, as a descendant of Furbush, was clearly both moved by the story and, quite rightly, proud of his ancestor. 'Perhaps, in addition to the cruelty of the local clergy and the bravery he witnessed from the Quaker women, William Furbish also recalled his own 80-mile forced march from Dunbar, Scotland, to Durham, England, just twelve years earlier'.[24]

William was in trouble again in 1679, by which time he had moved 4 miles from Dover. The constable had attempted to seize his household goods:

> 1 July 1679, (4:2:133), Wee present William Furbush for abuseing of the Constable & sleighting of his pouer & sayd hee could not answere what hee did in his office & he sayd Furbush tooke up a dreadful weapon & sayd that hee would dy before his goods should bee carried away. Jury. The person presented fined for his Delinquency 40s & fees of Court 5s. Rebeccah Furbush (wife) presented for strikeing the Constable. Jury. The offender fined tenn shillings & Cost of Court 5s.[25]

Then, in 1681 we hear from him again. This time it sounds like he has got his own back on Richard Waldron – the court deputy who had issued the order against the Quaker women:

> On May 8th, 1681, William fforbes [Furbush] of Newichawannock [upper Kittery] testified that about two years since he being at the house of Joseph Hammond in the towne of Kittery in the province of Maine Major Waldern, now being of the Councill, took out of his pockett a paper which he read, being in derision of the government of England and after some discourse said these words, There was no more a king in England than thou, Richard Nason, unto whome he then spoke.[26]

Fred Pierce tells us that William was undeterred by fines or punishment, ever speaking his mind. In 1683 we are told he was fined for 'abuse of his majesty's authority, by – his opprobrious language in calling his officers devils and hellhounds'. In those days men had to be cautious with their speech, concludes Pierce. What is so likeable about William Furbush is that he was not.[27]

We were lucky enough to also correspond with another Furbush/ Forbes descendant, Alice Waters, regarding William's brother Daniel.

I am a descendant of Daniel Forbes (Forbush) who, along with presumed relatives (John, William and James), survived the death march to Durham and the subsequent ship transport to the American colonies. Daniel served an indentured servitude for a tavern owner in Cambridge, Massachusetts. He then married twice, the second marriage was after his first wife died. He had children from both marriages … I descend from the second marriage.

I have spent almost seven years researching my genealogy and have collected a huge file of documents establishing the father–son– father–son relationship down the genealogical line … all the way down to me and my siblings. My greatest find was Daniel's Last Will & Testament which really made him 'come to life' for me. The Scottish Clan name Forbes took quite a beating in America, morphing into numerous spelling variations which made research a challenge. Daniel was illiterate (established by his mark made on his will) so he would not have known how to spell his last name and would not have known if others had spelled it correctly. The Forbush spelling latched onto Daniel's children from his second marriage and survived to this day.

I am grateful for the seeds Daniel sowed here in America. And while none of my ancestors became rich or famous, they were hard working patriots, working the land and fighting our wars. I'm very proud of my heritage.[28]

Sometimes we find two groups of Cromwell's deportees meeting up. Alexander Innes was one of the men transported on the *Unity* who served his time at the Saugus works. He settled in Taunton, Massachusetts, where he married an Irish woman, Katherine Briggs.[29] Was she one of the Irish transported by Cromwell in the wake of his Irish expedition?

Massachusetts historian William Saxbe posits this theory, suggesting, she was sent with several hundred other Irish to Marblehead, near Lynn, in 1654.[30] Saxbe writes, 'an Irish woman named Katheren Aines [Innes]' was brought before the court at Plymouth in February, 1656/7, 'vpon suspision of comiting adultery'. We have translated the following text into modern English to make it easier to follow:

> At this Court, William Paule, Scotchman, for his unclean and filthy behaviour with the wife of Alexander Aines, is sentenced by the Court to be forthwith publicly whipped … which accordingly was performed … Katheren Aines, for her unclean and lacivious behaviour with the aforesaid William Paule, and for the blasphemous words that she hath spoken, is sentenced by the Court to be forthwith publicly whipped here at Plymouth, and afterwards at Taunton, on a public training day, and to wear a Roman B cut out of red cloth and sewed to her upper garment on her right arm; and if she shall be ever found without it so worn while she is in the government [i.e. in the boundaries of the area] to be forthwith publicly whipped … Alexander Anis, for his leaving his family, and exposing his wife to such temptations, and being as bawd to her therein, is sentenced by the Court for the present to sit in the stocks the time the said Paule and Katheren Ainis are whipped, which was performed....[31]

Abby Chandler provides more detail. We don't know if William Paule was another Dunbar man – he is listed as a 'probable' rather than a 'definite' on the Scottish Prisoners of War Society website. Alexander Innes was away at the time of the affair and was initially called as a witness at the trial rather than as a defendant. However, the law held the husband responsible for his wife's morals as well as her behaviour (women were viewed as naturally wicked, a result of Eve's original sin). Alexander was convicted for leaving his wife unsupervised (in fact, the sentence suggests he was effectively acting as her pimp by doing so since no woman could be trusted if left alone to her own devices). He was also ordered to pay his and Katherine's court fees, something he had to do in instalments of 12*d.* a week.[32] Abby suggests that the findings of the court reflected an English unease with Irish and Scots society dating back to the medieval period.

By publically punishing all three of them, the Plymouth authorities were trying to 'indoctrinate all three players in proper Anglicised behaviour'.[33]

Peter Grant was another *Unity* transportee who fell foul of the authorities' suspicions of libidinous behaviour. An article on the family history site tells us that Peter Grant was one of 140 men of Clan Grant who fought under the command of the Clan Chief's brother at Dunbar. He ended up working at Lynn. His brother James was also a transportee, having been captured at Worcester in 1651. By 1659, Peter was living in Kittery, Maine. It sounds as though both were married men – a Kittery court ordered them back to Scotland (to return to their wives) in 1661. There is no indication that they went. Both would marry in America, although it is interesting to note that Peter and his wife Johanna had no children for the first six years of their relationship. Perhaps they were waiting for Peter to be properly widowed or for the Scots spouse to remarry?[34]

On 6 January 1657 Peter and James Grant were among those who formed the Scots' Charitable Society for the relief of Scottish prisoners in the New World. James disappeared in 1663/4. It looks as though Peter had been living with his brother and his sister-in-law, Joanna Ingersoll, prior to this and he stayed on.

On 10 July 1664 Peter and Joanna were taken to court for living together while unmarried. Joanna was pregnant at this time and it was believed that Peter had a wife living in Scotland. Peter claimed that the child was not his, but promised to care for it, and Joanna claimed that the child was her husband's. The court decided otherwise and penalized Peter £10 or 10 lashes. Peter married his sister-in-law and her child was born and named Elizabeth. She [Elizabeth] was raised by Peter's kinsman, another James Grant and his wife Elizabeth Everell. The kinsman James left his foster daughter Elizabeth property in his will. Peter's will states that he has 7 children and he names them, excluding Elizabeth.[35]

Two of Peter's grandsons fought in the Revolutionary War. Landers and Samuel Grant both served in Massachusetts units. It is interesting to speculate to what extent their attitude to Britain was formed by their ancestors' experience and views. Sadly, we have no record of their thinking, only their actions. Unusually though, we do have a glimpse of one personality – Samuel Grant. 'Spoken of in the American Series of Popular biographies, (Maine Ed.) p. 167 as a quiet, reserved man, he spent his last days chiefly in Gardiner with his son Peter. He died in Clinton Aug. 13, 1805 and his grave is in the family lot in Gardiner Cemetery in the Episcopal Churchyard.'[36]

In 1679, a second James Grant (also a transportee) died, leaving Peter some clothes and tools. Peter's son, James, was willed his 'fyrelock muskett, sword & belt'. He will have needed the weapons.

Leola Grant Bushman, in a 1976 family history, notes that Peter's brother had disappeared and offers a very good reason for Peter to have remained with Joanna.

> It is not known whether he had been killed by Indians or what had happened to him. Peter agreed to look after Elizabeth, but both denied the child was his.
>
> It might be noted here that in that era danger from Indians, and the need for a provider of food and protection, probably was the necessity of Peter's remaining in the home were James, Peter and Joanna had been living prior to James' disappearance.[37]

The colonial period, 1540–1774, saw a succession of conflicts with Native Americans – usually referred to as the Indian Wars. A number of the Dunbar men were affected – one, David Hamilton, who came over on the *John and Sara*, was actually killed near Dover in 1691.[38]

The French became involved in a number of these conflicts, seeking to promote and maintain their economic interests by supporting and using tribes such as the Abernaci as proxies. That led to numerous instances of New Englanders being taken captive and transported to Canada. One of the most famous examples of this was the February 1704 raid on Deerfield when French and Native American forces attacked the Massachusetts frontier settlement, just before dawn. They burned part of the town and killed 47 villagers. The raiders left with 112 settlers as captives, whom they took overland the nearly 300 miles to Montreal. Some died along the way, and 60 were later redeemed (ransomed by family and community).

Others were adopted by Mohawk families and became assimilated into the tribe. There was no long-term certainty that a family member lost in this way would ever make it home, a fate researched by one of the Dunbar descendants.

Doreen Leahy is a descendant of George Gray (who may have come over on the *Unity*). George was sent to the sawmills in Berwick, Maine and settled in the area.

> My 8x great grandfather, was George Gray. He was one of the few survivors sent to the Colonies in 1650 from the battle of Dunbar. He was sent to the sawmills in Berwick Maine. He was later released from servitude, married and raised four sons and a daughter.
>
> His second son, George Jr., was captured during the Indian raids of King Philip. Jr. decided to stay in Canada and preach the gospel. He never returned.[39]

George's will (dated 31 March 1692) left half his land to his wife, Sarah, as long as she remained a widow. His son, Robert, was to receive the other half at the age of 21 and the missing George (in captivity) was to be given his mother's share if he returned. Two other sons, Alexander and James, were to get George's share if he did not return or on the death or remarriage of their mother. It's a peculiar mix of grief and practicality.

> Many who went on to serve in many wars, become politicians, businessmen, farmers, frontiersmen, and even sawmill owners. Full circle! I would love to share what I have researched these last six years in doing my family genealogy. I have been to Scotland twice, tracing what I believe to be my family roots.
>
> Needless to say, the journey has been difficult. Paper trails in the early 14th, 15th and 16th century are almost non-existent to the amateur genealogist. None the less, I am determine to find out what 'ole George was doing before Sept. 1650. Was he a nobleman, farmer, businessman, fisherman? His amazing will to survive, and ability to adapt and preserve is my inspiration to keep digging.[40]

Becky Richardson, descendant of Thomas Ranney, has another probable Scots ancestor, Thomas Miller, who was killed by Indians in 1675. It is unclear whether Thomas Ranney was one of the Dunbar men but the date of his first appearance and his association with a number of those we know are on the 'definites' list is suggestive. Thomas Ranney first appears in New England in Middletown, Connecticut on 10 January 1658 when a land lot was granted to him. It has not been proven when he arrived in New England and settled in an area known as Middletown Upper Houses, now Cromwell (interesting name), Connecticut. Another Scottish POW, Alexander Bow, settled in Middletown in 1659/60.[41]

Land records of this town show that a house lot was granted to one Thomas Rany in 1658. Where he came from is not known, but it is believed that he may have come from Scotland, where Rany and Renny are familiar names. It is believed that he was born in Scotland in 1616 from the information on his gravestone, for he died in 1713 at age 97. The Rany homestead in Middletown was in the main street, extending south from what is now Rapello Avenue, and reaching back to the Connecticut River. His house, which stood from 1660 to 1880, was a large, plain, three-story frame house with one large chimney in the center. On the 1670 census, Thomas Rany is rated as worth 105 pounds, the ninth in wealth in a list of 52 proprietors. His father-in-law, George Hubbard, headed the list.[42]

His granddaughter, Mary Mercy Savage, married an Alexander Stocking who was a Revolutionary War soldier – their son, Abner Stocking, also served. Again, one finds oneself wondering how far that reflected family history and attitudes passed down through the generations. It is something of which their descendant is proud: 'It is in Abner's record that I joined the D.A.R. [Daughters of the American Revolution].'[43]

Descendant Michelle Start brought Ninian Beall (pronounced 'Bell') to our attention. He may well have been one of the officers held at Tynemouth who were subsequently shipped to Barbados. We have a physical description of him from an unlikely source:

The following quotation is from Sally Somerwell Mackally, Early Days of Washington, p. 48: 'In 1783 there were no public burying grounds. Prominent families had private ones adjoining their homes. Ninian Beall's lot was on Gay [N] street [Georgetown]. In recent years this lot has been built upon, and when the foundations were being dug … the body of Ninian Beall was removed. His skeleton was found in perfect preservation, and measured six feet seven inches, and his hair which was very red had retained its natural color.[44]

He was born in 1625 at Largs and was married at the time of Dunbar (his son Thomas would join him in America in 1667). He was indentured for five years and, after a short stay in Ireland, was dispatched with 149 other Scotsmen to Barbados. In about 1652, he was transferred, still a prisoner, to the province of Maryland where he served five years with Richard Hall of Calvert County.[45]

In 1688, the government of the Maryland colony passed to the Crown, and the Church of England was made the established church. In 1699, as a member of the Assembly, Ninian Beall signed the petition to King William III for the establishment of the Church of England in Maryland, although Ninian was a Presbyterian Elder.

Maryland became a royal province in 1691. But after the colony became a royal province, he continued to rise and was appointed Chief Military Officer of Calvert County.[46]

Ninian did well in his new country, benefiting from the incentive offered to increase the size of the population: 1,000 acres for every five men brought to Maryland. The rent of the land grant was frozen at 20s. a year, which could be paid in kind. Tobacco, Maryland's main crop, was a valuable commodity. We are told he was responsible for the arrival of about 200 immigrants. His left substantial wealth to his numerous family when he died in 1717.

Item.
I give and bequeath unto my son-in-law, Joseph Belt, part of tract of Land called Good Luck, containing two hundred forty five acres, he allowing unto my heirs the sum of four thousand pounds of tobacco according to our former agreement, he deducting what I doe owe

him on his books for several wares and merchandizes to the said Joseph and unto his heirs forever.

Item. I give and bequeath unto my son Charles a thousand acres of land called Dunn Back lying on the South side of great Chaptank in a creek called Wattses creek, unto him and his heirs forever

Though the will also indicates great loss – his son, also Ninian, had predeceased him – he leaves half his personal estate to his lost son's daughter.

There is one striking point about the will: 'Item. I doe give and bequeath unto my son in law Andrew Hambleton my negro woman Alie unto him and his heirs forever.'[47] Slavery was to overtake indentured servitude in the years – here is one precursor of the process (though Ninian was not the only Scots transportee to become a slave owner in New England and elsewhere).

William Thompson is on the list of 'probables' for the *Unity*. He settled in Kittery, Maine.

In Charles Edward Banks' 'Scotch Prisoners Deported to New England by Cromwell, 1651–1652', William is listed as being from the Battle of Dunbar and working at the Great Works Saw Mill managed by Richard Leader, who fled to Barbados in 1656 after getting into a bit of trouble with ruling politics between Maine and Massachusetts. He left the Scots POWs destitute and it is unclear if he set them free at that time. However, grants of land for these men began appearing in court records at that time. William did not adapt to his new environment well and was always at the 'post' and being punished.[48]

A few years later William Thompson is in the town of South Berwick, where there are early indications of the impact of the Indian Wars on the Dunbar survivors. Like so many migrant communities, the Scots prisoners settle near each other.

In 1650 there were within the town Thomas and William Spencer, Tom Tinker, James Heard, Wm. Chadbourne, James Warren, Daniel

Hubbard, and Daniel Goodwin, Richard Abbott, John Taylor, Roger Plaisted, Daniel Ferguson, Wm. Thompson, and George Rogers bear names found a few years later in the Berwick records ...

Owing to dangerous incursions of the Indians, the hardships of a rigorous winter in an unbroken forest, and the prevalence of wolves and beasts of prey, there was but little advance on the frontier for many years. Humphrey Chadbourne, Sr., is known to have said when seventy-five years of age there was then no house between his own and Canada. He died in 1666.

The whole attention of the few inhabitants seems to have been given to lumbering, and the forests were stripped with astonishing rapidity. Shingles and pine boards were legal tender 'delivered at the landing, when the sloops ran,' or were discounted by the merchants for store orders payable in rum, molasses, and the less-pressing necessities of life.

The settlement gradually but steadily increased in numbers until the outbreak of Indian hostilities in 1675, the horrors of which are given in the history of the old town of Berwick.

There were times in which the settlers were suffering with hunger, cold, and the privations of frontier life, and a less courageous and hardy race would have abandoned their new homes for a safer and more populous district. Bears and wolves were continually destroying the growing corn or stealing from the sheepfold, and the settlers were compelled to hunt those marauders for their extermination and the protection of life, as well as for the meat furnished for the table. Wives and daughters shared in the hardships of out-of-doors life, and this developed that hardihood and bravery which made them able consorts of their brave husbands when war came, and stimulated them to deeds of daring which will never be forgotten.[49]

William's sons were very prosperous and descendants of his include Ebenezer Thompson, New Hampshire's first Secretary of State, and Benjamin Thompson, Jnr, who willed all of his land (several farms and other), his bank and railroad stocks and his cash to form a College of Agriculture and the Mechanical Arts which became the University of New Hampshire.

Sometimes, though, relationships between the Dunbar men and the local people were more cordial. One of Duncan Bohannon' descendants would marry into the Choctaw nation (who were to have their own trail of tears).

> I don't really know how my ancestor ended up in Barbados in 1650. However, he did marry and had a child before he came to Maryland and settled in Virginia at Mobjack Bay. One of his descendants made the Choctaw Trail of Tears after marrying a Choctaw maiden. He came to Eagleton, Indian Territory (Oklahoma) in 1833. The first Bohannon in Indian Territory![50]

Roger Spring, Duncan's descendant, tells the tale vividly:

> What I know really begins in Barbados, as I can find nothing on his parents that has credibility with me. We believe he arrived in 1650 at the age of 15. Possibly an indentured servant, as he appeared to be a free man some time around 1658.
>
> I don't know if it was poverty, the British or adventure which sent him to Barbados at age 15. The more I learn about the times then, the more brutal they become. I do know he found his true love, Cicely Collmore while in Barbados. They were married in July 1658 and had a child in January 1659, so she was pregnant with my direct ancestor John Bohannon, when they were married. Young Love.... my John was just a few years old when he came with his parents to America.
>
> There are church records on his marriage and the birth of their first son soon after. They finally settled at Mobjack Bay in the Colony of Virginia. One lasting legacy is a town called Bohannon, Virginia. I believe the Post Office is located on Duncan (Dunkin) Bohannon's original allotment.
>
> Duncan Bohannon descendants were all in the American Revolution. This I will have to do a bit of work on, as I know my direct line fought at the Battle of Guilford Courthouse. I had an uncle who spent the terrible winter at Valley Forge in 1777–78.
>
> Duncan (Dunkin) Bohannon (Buchanan) enters my imagination almost every morning while I drink coffee.[51]

It would seem that Bohannon was a version of Buchanan – another example of the difficulty some had with Gaelic pronunciation. As for 'Dunkin', that sounds like another misperception made permanent. You can just imagine somebody trying to write down the way he pronounced his name. If that was the case, we've got the sound of his voice.

> We have been researching our family history and it looks as if our however many great Grandfather James Mackall was one of the indentured servants that came to the US.
>
> He would eventually settle down in Calvert County Maryland where his/my family would become a prominent part of society owning lots of land and farming tobacco. The family has many Military officers and one daughter married a sitting US President. Many parts of Calvert County Maryland are named for the Mackall. Our branch ended up in Ohio and would be considered almost poor. My line lives in Texas.[52]

There is more information on the Scottish Prisoners of War Society website. There we learn that James and Robert MacKall were Protestant highlanders who moved to Ulster to escape persecution. Both were captains at Dunbar, serving with what sounds like exceptional gallantry.[53]

One of the fascinating things about the Scottish Prisoners of War Society website is the excitement expressed by descendants of one individual discovering each other and sharing information. It reflects the lasting legacy of these men as well as the work of the Durham Team in bringing their stories to life. We experienced a little of the same thing in researching this book – no fewer than five descendants of George Darling contacted us: Scott Fair, Marlene K. Lemmer Beeson, Eve Hiatt, Douglas Darling and Misty Scheidt.

George Darling was born in about 1620 in Lasswade, Midlothian, Scotland. At about 30 years old he was among the older of the Dunbar prisoners. As Eve Hiatt pointed out, his age also increases the likelihood of his having already established a family and profession prior to going to war. 'There is no doubt that George Darling was one of the lucky ones, as a survivor of war, the death march and confinement as a prisoner, or the sea voyage and of the term of indenture. He went on to become a successful member of the Salem community and owned a tavern.'[54] Scott Fair pointed out that George was number 8 on the 'Scots at Lynn in 1653' list. 'I became aware of this 5 years ago and have spent countless hours researching his story and his descendants that followed.'[55]

Marlene Lemmer Beeson is a genealogist and historian with a particular interest in George Darling who appears to have been one of her ancestors. She, quite rightly, notes that George Darling and the other men could well be defined as political prisoners. 'George Darling is, by my research and others but not proven, my 9th Great Grandfather. I have other Scot lines with later entries into the USA between the 1715 and Culloden. I have lots of materials and evidence but no "smoking" gun.'[56]

It is Misty Scheidt who really sums up why history matters: why the search for our origins and our attempts to understand them have such an impact on how we understand ourselves. The photograph she has so kindly allowed us to include encapsulates the generations of the Dunbar Scots in America. Her words speak for themselves:

> I have done some family research before, but I never dug deep until this past year and a half. My father, Larry Gene Schepker, passed in 2009 very unexpectedly and my mother, Genevieve Schepker, she passed December 26th, 2016 so it hasn't even been two years.
>
> Her death was very unexpected as well, a misdiagnosed heart attack, which hit our family extremely hard and we are still trying to find our way. This is what led me to digging deep into my roots, when I didn't know what else to do. It helped to feel closer to both of them.
>
> I did not know a lot about my parents' families. Neither spoke too much about their background having lived a very tough childhood. On my father's side, he was one of thirteen children. Most were placed in homes, some were lucky to be adopted out, others not so lucky to be adopted by the families that adopted them. Either way, none of them had it easy at all.
>
> My grandmother, Winifred (Darling) Schepker, just couldn't afford to feed them and my grandfather, Harold Schepker, had been in the Army in the 1940s so she was alone most of the time.

I believe I once counted the number of years my grandmother was pregnant. Since most children are only a year apart, some not even a full 12 months, you can imagine she was pregnant for the better part of 13 whole years.

After the eight years that George Darling served at the Ironwork's, he settled in and around Massachusetts as a yeoman farmer by occupation. He died in Salem and his estate inventory is listed September 13th, 1693, and his will was dated April 12th, 1693. It mentions himself and many of his children living at Marblehead Massachusetts.

There is a book 'The Pioneers of Massachusetts' regarding of his wife, Katherine Gridley, although there is some confusion regarding her background. He met her in Massachusetts (Ma) after becoming an indentured servant. However I have found some indications that he possibly left a wife and children back in Scotland before he was captured at Dunbar, only to never return when his sentence was completed. In 1672 George purchased two plots of land referred to as the Coy Pond Property in Lynn/Salem/Essex/Ma and became the owner of a tavern and inn on that property.

One of the Darlings, Benjamin Darling, who was born in 1687 in Mendon Ma, accumulated a considerable amount of property in which he lived and farmed at what is now the town of Blackstone Ma, three miles east of Millville – also known as the Blackstone Poor Farm (at least this is what it was when the article was written).

Somehow, the Darlings, my line anyway, made their way to Indiana, around Dearborn, then spread out across Nebraska. Most are still in Nebraska, my parents moving to Colorado in 1967 which is where I still reside. They purchased their home there in 1973 and lived in this home for 43 years until the home was sold in 2017 after my mother's passing.

Discovering one's family roots and history is so extremely important to future generations for many reasons but for me, every single bit of information holds a place in my heart no matter how minor. Recently, I found the Facebook page of the Scottish Prisoners of War Society. In my genealogy research, I've found that I am a descendent of George Darling, he is my 9th great grandfather and was transported from London to Boston on the Unity and was a servant at the Lynn Ironworks. My father's mother is Winifred Darling, this is how I am connected.

We had a family portrait taken after my mother passed and right before we sold her home, 43 years of memories in that house. We have a framed photo of my parents in the portrait.

Left to Right; Joe Schepker (my brother), Christine Sean (Joe's girlfriend), Johanna Schepker Emery (Joe's daughter holding her daughter, Genni Emery), Audrey Emery (Johanna's daughter) on the lap of Johanna's husband Joe Emery, behind in the maroon is Richard Schepker, Joe's son, Roberta Schepker (Joe's x wife), sitting in grey suit is my husband Alan Scheidt, standing is my sister Holly Schepker Hall, next to her is her husband Troy Hall, Tawny Hall and next Austin Hall, their two children, and seated is my daughter Lexi Scheidt (red hair) and then myself, Misty Schepker Scheidt. In the picture frame on the grass are our (Joe, Holly, and myself, Misty) parents, Larry and Genevieve Schepker, both passed.

When you asked how and why I started my journey on Ancestry, this basically is what led me to start digging. The mystery and stories I have heard, just about my father's family, immediately intrigued me, and it kept going from there, I couldn't stop. I am a bit sad knowing my father never even knew about his 8th Great Grandfather being a Scottish Prisoner of War, nor another ancestor being on the Mayflower. I can only hope that he now knows, and is still with me.[57]

The Dunbar men's story has an impact on everyone who encounters it. That includes the Durham Team who worked so well on their behalf. This is Professor Chris Gerrard, quoted in a local paper on the day they were re-buried:

It has been a privilege to research these soldiers. I have got to know these individuals quite well – almost every ache and pain they suffered during the course of their lives.

I have got to know them, but I don't know their names. They are anonymous to us. All of the ordinary soldiers were, except for those from the Battle of Dunbar who ended up in New England in the US.

I think we have humanised their story and given back their history, because some of these were only young guys, as young as 13-years-old.

We would have known nothing of them. But now they are probably the best understood group of individuals from Scotland in the first half of the 17th century. Their story will stay with us and will never be forgotten.[58]

Appendix 1

Scottish Order of Battle at Dunbar

This Order of Battle is based on the contemporary record, Harleian Manuscript No. 6844, folio 123 (British Museum), augmented by later study, particularly E. Furgol, *A Regimental History of the Covenanting Armies 1639–1651* (Edinburgh: John Donald, 2001) and P. Reese, *Cromwell's Masterstroke* (Barnsley: Pen & Sword, 2006), pp. 135–7 and S. Reid, *Crown, Covenant and Cromwell – the Civil Wars in Scotland 1639–1651* (London: Frontline, 2012), pp. 204–8. As all authorities agree, the overall picture is far from clear and all reconstructions are, in part, based on heroic assumptions.

Cavalry

1st Brigade – Major General Sir John Browne
2nd Brigade – Colonel Archibald Strachan
3rd Brigade – Colonel William Stewart
4th Brigade – Major General Sir Robert Montgomerie
5th Brigade – Lieutenant General David Leslie
6th Brigade – Alexander Leslie, Earl of Leven

Dragoons

Sir John Douglas of Mouswall's Regiment
William Menzies' Regiment
Colonel John of Kirkcudbright's Regiment

Infantry

1st Brigade – Lieutenant General Sir James Lumsden (his own Regiment, the Regiment of the General of the Artillery and Sir William Douglas of Kirkness' Regiment)

2nd Brigade – Major General Sir James Holborn (his own Regiment, Regiment of Sir George Buchanan of Buchannan and Colonel Alexander Stewart's Edinburgh Regiment)

3rd Brigade – Major General Colin Pitscottie (his own Regiment, the Regiment of Sir David Home of Wedderburn and Colonel John Lindsay of Edzell's Regiment)

4th Brigade – Colonel Sir James Campbell of Lawers (his own Regiment, the Regiment of Sir George Preston of Valleyfield and Sir John Haldane of Gleneagles' Regiment)

5th Brigade – Colonel John Innes (his own Regiment, the Regiment of Colonel John Forbes, the Master of Lovat's Regiment)

Artillery

This comprised 32 guns of mixed bores including lighter pieces, a total complement around 400 gunners/matrosses

Appendix 2

The List of Scottish Officers Taken at Dunbar

From *Original Memoirs written during the Great Civil War being the life of Sir Henry Slingsby and Memoirs of Captain Hodgson*, ed. Walter Scott (Edinburgh: Arch, Constable & Co., 1806), pp. 306–11 and P. Reese, *Cromwell's Masterstroke* (Barnsley: Pen & Sword, 2006), pp. 125–9.

General Officers

Lieutenant General Sir James Lumsden

Colonels

Lieutenant Colonels Wallis; Lesley; Murray; Henry Malvin; Arthur Forbes; Wanhap: Of Horse – Lieutenant Colonels Dunbarre; Hamilton; Crawford; Ingles; John Montgomery; James Bickerton (Adjutant General of Horse)

Majors

Henry Carmhill of Foot; James Cranster of Horse; George Moat of Foot; George Forbes, Reformado*; Moor; Oagle; Freesle

Captains of Foot

James Sterlyn; Francis Agnue; Sibbald; Alex Monpreff; George Hollibuton; Thomas Brown; William Murray; James Scott; William

---

* An officer who has lost his command due to amalgamation or disbandment but retains his status and stays on half pay.

Rudderford; James Macularoy; Hugh Montgomery; James Aken; George Smith; John Maclellan; Robert Mackellum; Hugh Madole; George Pringle; Robert Scot; Alexander Wood; Robert Hamilton; Thomas Grey; Robert Adamson; Beaton

Captains of Horse and Foot

Robert Duncan; Robert Maccaulla; Walter Scot; Matthew Creshton; James Steward; William Douglas; Walter Lesley; William Manhop: Of Horse – James Borthick; David Murray

Captains of Horse

John Murray; William Burton; James Camil; William Bresbon. Of Horse – William Daurlmple; Charles Kerkpatrick; Nicholas Lawson; Robert Rudderford; John Car; Dundas; Ogleby; Gourdon; Bonner; Lieutenant Bruse, Lieutenant of Horse

Cornets of Horse

William Cunningham; James Maxwell; James Denham; James Magil; Walter Steward; John Hay; Anthony Macdoer; John Brown; Alex Michel; John Collerwood; George Winderum

Captains Lieutenant of Horse and Foot

John Monnergain; William Emery; William Blayer; Robert Anderson; Roger Holden; Robert Wood

Lieutenants of Foot

James Cunningham; James Blackwood; Patrick Macknab; Henry Cunningham; Lancelot Car; John Macknight; John Heume; John Gourdon; George Cunningham; James Weare; Henry Eston; William Gun; Nicholas Coston; Alexander Steward; Arthur Steward; William Petre; Norman Lesley; William Bailey; William Gladston; Robert

Hamberton; Geo. Mackburney; Robert Straughan; Richard Allen; James Mackbey; George Bisset; James Nichols; Thomas Mennis; William Sionis; John Car, Alexander Car; James Twede; Philip Leich; James Armor; James Sayers; John Meer; Andrew Pennere; Patrick Bailey; John Camil; John Rich; John Steward; John Camil [double entry?]; Allen Osborne; William Knocks; John Wilson; Thomas Anderson; Walter Wanhap; Patrick Holliburton; Lancelot Car [double entry?]; William Engley; Thomas Car; Alexander Gourdon; Lancaster Forguson; Robert Rankin; Cha. Coleman; John Lawson; Andrew Guiler; George Patterson; Thomas Hutchen; John Ennis; John Sken; John Hunter; John Mackdoughal; Andrew Drummon; George Lesley; George Moat; Francis Scot; William Elliot; Alexander Ciff; John Denguit

Quartermasters of Horse

Tho. Richman; William Forbis

Ensigns

Kirkpatrick; Walter Macdoughel; William Sinclare; George Jack; Hartley Gadley; William Carnecuse; Thomas Wallis; James Rollston; Andrew Myn; James Bennet; John Linsey; Andrew Hanna; Thomas Pringle; Robert Hamilton; James Delop; John Gray; James Edward; Colin Camel; – Heatley; Robert Roy; Gilbert Harral; James Musket; William Sample; Robert Ogleby; Robert Williamson; William Lesley; Ersby Shields; Robert Haborn; William Scot; Ja. Edminston; Robert Lawson; James Neicen; Andrew Barthwick; George Elphenston; John Fairdise; Henry White; Andrew Dunalson; David Camide; John Camil; Cornelius Engles; Duncan Camil; Patrick Canburn; William Manord; Robert Craw; George calley; James Rudderford; Walter Scot; Walter Steward; Robert Heume; Jas. Forquer; James Macknath; Henry Ackman; John Wayer; John Brown; William Chapman; John Macuo; Alexander Spence; John Black; Thomas Thompson; Robert Fryer; John Thompson; John Dixon; Geo. Smith; Alexander Johnson; William Egger; David Grant; George Gayler; John Wallis; John Kemmen; Thomas Enderson; James Brewse; William Maclan; John Carmihil; Wiliam Watson; William Anderson; James Dunbar; James Elderwood; Henry Roy; Thomas Boyd; David Reed

A Letter From Sir Arthur Hesilrige

October 1650. A Letter From Sir Arthur Hesilrige, To the Honorable Committee Of The Councel Of State For Irish and Scotish Affairs at White Hall, Concerning the Scots Prisoners

Gentlemen, I Received your Letter dated the Twenty sixth of October, in that you desire me, That Two thousand three hundred of the Scotch Prisoners now at Durham or elswhere, able and fit for Foot Service, be selected, and marched thence to Chester and Liverpool, to be shipped for the South and West of Ireland, and that I should take special care not to send any Highlanders. I am necessitated upon the receipt of this, to give you a full accompt concerning the Prisoners: After the Battel at Dunbar in Scotland, my Lord General writ to me, That there was about Nine thousand Prisoners, and that of them he had set at liberty all those that were wounded, and, as he thought, disabled for future Service, and their Number was, as Mr Downing writ, Five thousand one hundred; the rest the general sent towards Newcastle, conducted to Berwick by Major Hobson, and from Berwick to Newcastle by some Foot out of that Garison, and the Troop of Horse; when they came to Morpeth, the Prisoners being put into a large walled Garden, they eat up raw Cabages, Leaves and Roots, so many, as the very seed and the labor, at Four pence a day, was valued by sufficient men at Nine pounds; which Cabage, as I conceive, they having fasted, as they themselves said, near eight days, poysoned their Bodies; for as they were coming from thence to Newcastle, some dyed by the way-side, and when they came to Newcastle, I put them into the greatest Church in the Town, and the next morning when I sent them to Durham, about Sevenscore were sick, and not able to march, and three dyed that night, and some fell down in their march from Newcastle to Durham, and dyed; and when they came to Durham, I having sent my Lieutenant Colonel and my Major, with a strong Guard both of Horse and Foot, and they being there told into the great Cathedral Church, they could not count them to more then three thousand; although Colonel Fenwick writ to me, That there were about Three thousand five hundred, but I believe they were not told at Berwick and most of those that were lost, it was in Scotland, for I heard, That the Officers that marched with them to Berwick, were necessitated to kill about Thirty, fearing the loss of them all, for they fell down in great Numbers, and said, They were not able to march; and they brought them far in the night, so that doubtless many ran away. When I sent them first to Durham, I writ to the Major, and desired him to take care, that they wanted not any thing that was fit for Prisoners, and what he should disburse for them, I would repay it. I also sent them a daily supply of bread from Newcastle, and an allowance equal to what had been given to former Prisoners: But their Bodies being infected, the Flux encreased amongst them. I sent many Officers to look to them, & appointed that those that were sick should be removed out the cathedral Church into the Bishops Castle, which belongs to Mistris Blakiston, and provided Cooks, and they had Pottage made with Oatmeal, and Beef and Cabages, a full Quart at a Meal for every Prisoner: They had also coals daily brought to them; as many as made about a hundred Fires both day and night, and Straw to lie upon; and I appointed the Marshal to see all these things orderly done, and he was allowed Eight men to help him to divide the coals, and their Meat, Bread and Pottage equally; They were so unruly, sluttish and nasty, that it is not to be believed; they acted rather like Beasts then Men, so that the Marshal was allowed Forty men to cleanse and sweep them every day: But those men were of the lustiest Prisoners, that had some small thing given them extraordinary: And these provisions were for those that were in health; and for those that were sick, and in the Castle, they had very good Mutton Broth, and sometimes Veal Broth, and Beef and Mutton boild together, and old Women appointed to look to them in the several Rooms: There was also a Physitian which let them Blood, and dressed such as were wounded, and gave the sick Physick and I dare confidently say, There was never the like care taken for any such Number of prisoners that ever were in England. Notwithstanding all this, many of them dyed, and few of any other Disease but the Flux; some were killed by themselves, for they were exceeding cruel one towards another. If a man was perceived to have any Money, it was two to one but he was killed before morning, and Robbed; and if any had good clothes, he that wanted, if he was able, would strangle him, and put on his clothes: And the Disease of the Flux still encreasing amongst them, I was then forced, for their preservation, if possible it might be, to send to all the next Towns to Durham, within four or five miles, to command them to bring in their Milk, for that was conceived to be the best Remedy for stopping of their Flux, and I promised them what Rates they usually sold it for at the Markets, which was accordingly performed by about Threescore Towns and places, and Twenty of the next Towns to Durham continue still to send daily in their Milk, which is boiled, some with Water, and some with Bean flower, the Physitians holding it exceeding good for recovery of their health.

Gentlemen, You cannot but think strange this long preamble, and to wonder what the matter will be; in short its this, Of the Three thousand prisoners that my Officers told into the Cathedral Church at Durham, Three hundred from thence, and Fifty from Newcastle of the Sevenscore left behinde, were delivered to Major Clerk by order from the Councel, and there are about Five hundred sick in the Castle, and about Six hundred yet in health in the Cathedral, the most of which are in probability Highlanders, they being hardier then the rest, and other means to distinguish them we have not, and about Sixteen hundred are dead and buried, and Officers about Sixty, that are at the Marshals in Newcastle. My Lord General having released the rest of the Officers, and the Councel having given me power to take out what I thought fit, I have granted to several well-affected persons that have Salt-works at Sheels, and want Servants, Forty, and they have engaged to keep them to work at their salt-pans; and I have taken out more about Twelve Weavers, to begin a Trade of Linnen cloth like unto the Scotch-cloth, and about Forty Laborers. I cannot give you on this sudden a more exact Accompt of the prisoners, neither can any Accompt hold true long, because they still dye daily, and doubtless so they will, so long as any remain in Prison. And for those that are well, if Major Clerk could have believed that they had been able to have marched on foot, he would have marched them by Land; for we perceive that divers that are seemingly healthy, and have not all been sick, suddenly dye, and we cannot give any reason of it, onely we apprehend they are all infected, and that the strength of some holds it out till it seize upon their very hearts. Now you fully understand the condition and the number of the Prisoners, what you please to direct, I shall observe, and intend not to proceed further upon this Letter, until I have your Answer upon what I have now written. I am, Gentlemen, Your affectionate Servant,

Art: Hesilrige Octob, 31, 1650

Glossary

Backsword	A form of weapon with one sharpened cutting edge and the other flattened and blunt, primarily a horseman's weapon designed for the cut
Bastion	Projection from the curtain wall of a fort usually at intersections to provide a wider firing platform and to allow defenders to enfilade (flanking fire) a section of the curtain
Buff coat	A leather coat, long skirted and frequently with sleeves, fashioned from thick but pliant hide, it replaced body armour for the cavalry
Caliver	A lighter form of musket, with greater barrel length than the cavalry carbine (see below)
Cannon	Heavy gun throwing a 47-pound ball; a demi-cannon fired 27-pound ball; cannon-royal shot a massive 63-pound ball
Carbine	A short-barrelled musket used primarily by cavalry
Clubmen	Groups of able-bodied local men who formed associations of militia to defend their localities against incursions by forces from either of the warring factions – armed neutrals
Committee of Both Kingdoms	This was brought into being as a consequence of two parliamentary measures (16 February and 22 May 1644) to ensure close cooperation between the English and Scots, Cromwell, Manchester and Essex were all members of the Committee which sat at Derby House
Cornet	A pennant or standard and thus also the junior officer who carried it
Corselet	This refers to a pikeman's typical harness of breast and back, with tassets for the thighs

Culverin	A gun throwing a 15-pound ball; mainly used in siege operations, the guns weighed an average of 4,000lb, the lighter demi-culverin threw a 9-pound ball and weighed some 3,600lb
Dragoon	Essentially mounted infantry, the name is likely derived from dragon, a form of carbine; their role was to act as scouts and skirmishers and they could fight either mounted (rare) or dismounted
Drake or saker	Gun firing a 5¼-pound ball
Enceinte	The circuit or whole of the defensive works
Ensign (or Ancient)	A junior commissioned officer of infantry who bears the flag from which the name derives
Flintlock or firelock	A more sophisticated ignition mechanism than match; the flint was held in a set of jaws, the cock which when released by the trigger, struck sparks from the steel frizzen and showered these into the pan which ignited the main charge
Foot	Infantry
Guns	Artillery
Horse	Cavalry
Magazine	Bomb-proof vault where powder and shot are stored
Matchlock	The standard infantry firearm, slow and cumbersome, prone to malfunction in wet or wind, it was nevertheless rugged and generally reliable. When the trigger was released the jaws lowered a length of lit cord match into the exposed and primed pan which flashed through to the main charge; when the charge failed to ignite this was referred to as a flash in the pan
Matross	A gunner's mate, doubled as a form of ad hoc infantry to protect the guns while on the march
Minion	Gun shooting a 4-pound ball
Musket	The term refers to any smooth-bored firearm, regardless of the form of lock, rifled barrels were extremely rare, though not unknown at this time

Pike	A polearm with a shaft likely to be between 12 and 18ft in length, finished with a diamond–shaped head
Sconce	A small detached fort with projecting corner bastions
Touch-hole	The small diameter hole drilled through the top section of a gun barrel through which the linstock ignites the charge, fine powder was poured in a quill inserted into the touch-hole
Train	A column of guns on the move, the army marches accompanied or followed by the train
Wheel lock	More reliable and far more expensive than match, this relied upon a circular metal spinning wheel wound up like a clock by key. When the trigger was released the wheel spun and the jaws lowered into contact and fitted with pyrites, showered sparks into the pan

Notes

Chapter 1

1. Andrew Marvell (1621–78).
2. The Extraordinary Lords of Session were lay members of the Court of Session in Scotland from 1532 to 1762.
3. Clarendon, XI, p. 239, quoted in P. Haythornthwaite, *The English Civil War 1642–1651* (London: Weidenfeld Military, 1994), pp. 10, 240.
4. George Villiers, 1st Duke of Buckingham (1592–1628).
5. Soteriological beliefs within Protestantism followed the teaching of the Dutch reformer Jacobus Arminius (1560–1609). Introduced first in 1563, the Thirty-Nine Articles were a set of definitions which clearly differentiated between Anglican and Roman Catholic practice.
6. The Covenant was first signed in Greyfriars Churchyard on 28 February then circulated for signing throughout Edinburgh and then the kingdom.
7. Ended by the Pacification of Berwick signed on 19 June 1639 – at best a temporary truce.
8. Archibald Campbell, 1st Marquess of Argyll (1607–61).
9. These were: (1) condemnation of religious innovation; (2) condemnation of illegal taxes, particularly those of tonnage and poundage; and (3) a further condemnation of those traders who paid such illegal taxes, making them complicit in the wrongdoing.
10. Ship Money was originally a medieval legitimate imposition intended to oblige coastal towns and ports to meet the cost of naval precautions in time of war only.
11. Puritans were wedded, inter alia, to the notion of predestination.
12. The MPs included Sir John Eliot who had been a particularly inflamed critic of Buckingham, his death in the Tower further fuelled prevailing outrage.
13. William Laud (1573–1645) was an ambitious and capable prelate of modest antecedents. His tenure from 1633 was marked by opposition to the Puritans exemplified by a stubborn upholding of the apostolic succession.
14. John Hampden (1595–1643), leading champion of Parliament and inspiration to many, was killed at the fight at Chalgrove Field.
15. Thomas Wentworth, 1st Earl of Strafford was steadfastly loyal to the King and a leading figure in his administration, and acted as Lord Deputy of Ireland from 1632–9, where he was noted for uncompromising harshness. The final reward for his adherence was impeachment and execution.

16. Pym (1584–1643) was the effective leader of parliamentary opposition until his death from stomach cancer.
17. An obvious example would be Sir Edmund Verney, Knight Marshal of the Household, killed defending the King's colours at Edgehill.
18. The Triennial or Dissolution Act, passed on 15 February 1641, provided that Parliament should meet for at least a fifty-day session in every three years.
19. What became the Irish Confederate Wars began in 1641 as an attempt by Catholic gentry to expel the encroaching Protestants and rapidly became a war between Catholics and Protestants in Ireland.
20. This is now more frequently and correctly labelled as 'the Wars of the Three Kingdoms'.
21. This excludes the Anglo-Scottish border wars, which saw major fights on the English side in 1513 at Flodden and then in 1542 at Solway Moss.
22. Estimates vary but it could be that 34,000 Parliamentarian soldiers died, perhaps 50,000 Royalists and up to 100,000 civilians; that doesn't include Ireland: https://www.history.com/topics/british-history/english-civil-wars, retrieved 20 August 2018.
23. S. Reid, *Crown, Covenant and Cromwell – the Civil Wars in Scotland 1639–1651* (London: Frontline, 2012), pp. 19–22.
24. Records of the Parliament of Scotland – 1641/8/206: Act regarding the king's majesty's rents uplifted by warrant of the committee of estates for the public use.
25. David Stevenson, *Revolution and Counter-Revolution in Scotland 1644–51* (London: The Royal Historical Society, 1977), cited in G. Seel, 'The Scots in England 1640–1651' (*History Review*; London, Issue 25, September 1996), https://www.historytoday.com/graham-seel/scots-england-1640-1651, retrieved May 2018.
26. Records of the Parliament of Scotland – 1649/1/262: Letter from the parliament of Scotland to William Lenthall, speaker of the house of commons of the parliament of England. Quoted in P. Reese, *Cromwell's Masterstroke* (Barnsley: Pen & Sword, 2006), p. 12.

Chapter 2

1. Reese, *Cromwell's Masterstroke*, p. 56.
2. The bridge still stands, though dwarfed by the more modern crossing constructed in the 1920s.
3. Captain Hodgson joined up for Parliament in 1642 and left a lively memoir, published by Arch, Constable & Co. in Edinburgh in 1806, Captain Hodgson, *Original Memoirs written during the Great Civil War being the life of Sir Henry Slingsby and Memoirs of Captain Hodgson*, ed. Walter Scott; see pp. 128–9, writing of Chillingham Castle.
4. Reese, *Cromwell's Masterstroke*, p. 55, incorrectly places Chillingham outside Berwick, but in fact it's 15 miles away.
5. Hodgson, *Original Memoirs*, p. 129.

6. Reese, *Cromwell's Masterstroke*, p. 56.
7. Ibid.
8. Ibid., p. 58.
9. Ibid., p. 55.
10. Ibid.
11. Ibid., p. 56.
12. Ibid., pp. 58–9.
13. Ibid., p. 59.
14. Hodgson, *Original Memoirs*, pp. 132–3.
15. Reese, *Cromwell's Masterstroke*, p. 59.
16. Reid, *Crown, Covenant and Cromwell*, p. 49.
17. Robert Lilburne (1613–65), less famously contentious than his younger brother, remained with the army and was one of the regicides.
18. Hodgson, *Original Memoirs*, p. 135.
19. Reese, *Cromwell's Masterstroke*, p. 61.
20. Ibid., pp. 60–1.
21. http://www.olivercromwell.org/Letters_and_speeches/letters/Letter _129.pdf, retrieved 20 March 2018.
22. Ibid.
23. Ibid.
24. Ibid.
25. Ibid.
26. Ibid.
27. Reid, *Crown, Covenant and Cromwell*, p. 51.
28. http://www.olivercromwell.org/Letters_and_speeches/letters/Letter _130.pdf, retrieved 20 March, 2018.
29. Ibid.
30. Reese, *Cromwell's Masterstroke*, p. 63.
31. Ibid.
32. Ibid., pp. 68–9.
33. Ibid., p. 71.
34. http://www.olivercromwell.org/Letters_and_speeches/letters/Letter _131.pdf, retrieved 20 March, 2018.
35. Ibid.
36. Ibid.
37. Ibid.
38. Hodgson, *Original Memoirs*, p. 144.
39. Ibid., p. 145.

Chapter 3

1. Cromwell's military secretary Rushworth, as quoted in J. Buchan, *Oliver Cromwell* (London: Hodder & Stoughton, 1934), p. 378.
2. Reese, *Cromwell's Masterstroke*, p. 73.
3. Ibid., pp. 73–4.
4. Reid, *Crown, Covenant and Cromwell*, p. 61.

5. Ibid.
6. In 1644, Charles I had outfought the Earl of Essex who abandoned his army at Lostwithiel and fled by boat, a disaster and an embarrassment for Parliament.
7. Reid, *Crown, Covenant and Cromwell*, p. 61.
8. Ibid., p. 62.
9. J. Morley, *Oliver Cromwell* (London: Macmillan, 1901), pp. 304–5.
10. http://www.olivercromwell.org/Letters_and_speeches/letters/Letter_132.pdf, retrieved 20 March, 2018.
11. Ibid.
12. Ibid
13. Shakespeare, *Henry V*, Act IV, prologue.
14. Reese, *Cromwell's Masterstroke*, p. 89.
15. Reid, *Crown, Covenant and Cromwell*, p. 68.
16. Reese, *Cromwell's Masterstroke*, p. 91.
17. Ibid., p. 77.
18. Hodgson, *Original Memoirs*, p. 146.
19. Reese, *Cromwell's Masterstroke*, p. 85.
20. Morley, *Oliver Cromwell*, p. 307.
21. Reese, *Cromwell's Masterstroke*, p. 85.
22. Ibid.
23. Reid, *Crown, Covenant and Cromwell*, p. 70.
24. Ibid., p. 72.
25. *Iliad*, Book XII, 290–328.
26. Reese, *Cromwell's Masterstroke*, p. 88.
27. Hodgson, *Original Memoirs*, p. 146.
28. Reid, *Crown, Covenant and Cromwell*, p. 73.
29. Reese, *Cromwell's Masterstroke*, p. 91.
30. Ibid., p. 101.
31. Reid, *Crown, Covenant and Cromwell*, p. 75.
32. Hodgson, *Original Memoirs*, p. 147.
33. Ibid., p. 149.
34. http://www.olivercromwell.org/Letters_and_speeches/letters/Letter_133.pdf, retrieved 20 March, 2018.
35. Ibid.
36. Ibid.
37. Ibid.
38. Ibid.
39. Ibid.
40. Ibid.
41. Ibid.
42. Ibid.
43. W.S. Douglas, *Cromwell's Scotch Campaigns 1650–1651* (London: N&M repr., 2010), p. 113.
44. Durham County Record Office (DCRO), 'Listen to the Soldiers' oral history archive.

Chapter 4

1. http://www.olivercromwell.org/Letters_and_speeches/letters/Letter_135.pdf, retrieved 8 August, 2018.
2. Ibid.
3. Ibid.
4. W. Seymour, *Battles in Britain*, Vol. 2 (London: Sidgwick & Jackson, 1975), p. 146.
5. OS Ref: NT 698 768.
6. http://www.eyewitnesstohistory.com/bataandeathmarch.htm, retrieved 7 August, 2018.
7. P. Gaunt, 'Cromwell Day, 2000; the Battle of Dunbar and Cromwell's Scottish Campaign', *Cromwelliana – the Journal of the Cromwell Association*, 2001, p. 2.
8. Ibid.
9. Ibid., p. 3.
10. Ibid., pp. 5–6.
11. Ibid., p. 7.
12. http://www.el4.org.uk/el4-cd/du_index.html, retrieved 15 August 2018.
13. Ibid.
14. The fort has been nicely restored and gives a fine view of the harbour. The castle itself was badly vandalised and is largely inaccessible. Most of the current harbour was developed in the nineteenth century.
15. C. Gerrard with P. Greaves, A. Millard, R. Annis and A. Caffell, *Lost Lives, New Voices – Unlocking the Stories of the Scottish Soldiers from the Battle of Dunbar 1650* (Oxford: Oxbow Books, 2018), p. 111. East Lothian Council Archives, under ref B18/39/1, holds Accounts of losses sustained by the inhabitants and burgh of Dunbar after the Cromwellian invasion of Scotland, including accounts of free quartering and of provisions supplied to the English garrisons, 1650–1.
16. R.J.M. Pugh, *Swords, Loaves and Fishes, A History of Dunbar* (Balerno: Harlaw Heritage, 2003 (2015 edn)), p. 182.
17. Records of the Parliament of Scotland, A1650/11/11, Act in favour of Dame Margaret Fraser, lady Gleneagles and John Haldane, her son, https://www.rps.ac.uk/, retrieved June 2018.
18. Gerrard et al., *Lost Lives*, p. 48.
19. See K.J. Cullen, *Famine in Scotland, the 'ill years' of the 1690s* (Edinburgh: Edinburgh University Press, 2010).
20. See J. Wormald, *Court, Kirk & Community 1470–1625* (Edinburgh: Edinburgh University Press, 1991).
21. Ibid.
22. https://www.brainyquote.com/quotes/oliver_cromwell_156532, retrieved 13 August 2018.
23. See Wormald, *Court, Kirk & Community*.
24. Ibid.
25. M. Lynch, *Scotland, A New History* (London: Pimlico, 1997), p. 247.

26. Quoted in S. Reid, *Scots Armies of the 17th Century (1) The Army of the Covenant 1639–51* (Newthorpe: Partizan Press, 2001), p. 10.
27. Ibid., p. 11.
28. Ibid.
29. Quoted in D. Purkiss, *The English Civil War* (London: HarperCollins, 2006), p. 367.
30. Old fourteenth-century doggerel from the era of the border wars.
31. 'A letter from Sir Arthur Hesilrige, to the honorable committee of the Councel of State for Irish and Scotish affairs at White-Hall, concerning the Scots prisoners. Die Veneris, 8 Novembr. 1650. Ordered by the Parliament, that this letter be forthwith printed and published. Hen: Scobell, Cleric. Parliamenti. London: Printed by Edward Husband and John Field, printers to the Parliament of England, 1650', https://quod.lib.umich.edu/cgi/t/text/text-idx?c=eebo;idno=A86092.0001.001, retrieved February 2018.
32. Featherstone from Featherstonehaugh; they had Featherstone castle near Haltwhistle and were active in border affairs.

Chapter 5

1. His defeat was brought about by one of those lamentable failures of scouting and reconnaissance which had so nearly done for him before.
2. D.J. Sadler, *Scottish Battles* (Edinburgh: Canongate, 1996), p. 182.
3. http://bcw-project.org/military/confederate-war/dungans-hill, retrieved 7 August 2018.
4. Cited in Gerrard et al., *Lost Voices*, p. 125.
5. http://www.oradour.info/, retrieved 7 August 2018.
6. Christopher Browning, *Ordinary Men: Reserve Police Battalion 101 and the Final Solution in Poland* (London: Penguin, new edn, 2001).
7. http://old.seattletimes.com/html/northwestvoices/2018361896_sirotalets06.html, retrieved 9 August 2018.
8. Hesilrige, letter of 8 November 1650.
9. Cromwell's dispatch, 4 September 1650.
10. Wilfred Owen, 'Dulce et Decorum Est'.
11. Gerrard et al., *Lost Voices*, p. 135.
12. Ibid.
13. A savage retribution where up to 7,000 Scottish civilians are said to have been murdered.
14. The castle was finally demolished to make way for the present station in the nineteenth century, and only fragments remain now.
15. Vanburgh's barrack piles (blocks) weren't thrown up until after a later Scottish emergency, the Jacobite Uprising of 1715.
16. 'A letter from Sir Arthur Hesilrige'.
17. A relic from the earlier Scottish Civil War, 1568–73.
18. Information kindly supplied by John Malden (from the burial register of 1650).
19. Sprung ambulance carts wouldn't be introduced till Marlborough's era, half a century later.

20. DCRO, 'Listen to the Soldiers'.
21. Ibid.
22. 'A letter from Sir Arthur Hesilrige'.
23. Sir Nikolaus Pevsner, *Northumberland*, in the 'Buildings of England' series (London: Penguin, rev. edn, 1992), pp. 295–7.
24. This took place between the years 1603 and 1610 and proved draconian.
25. Pevsner, *Northumberland*, p. 163.
26. The present memorial is later, dating from 1774.
27. Northumberland Archives (NRA), M877; Alnwick St Michael – no references.
28. 'Listen to the Soldiers' oral history archive (DCRO).
29. Ibid.
30. Pevsner, *Northumberland*, p. 396.
31. 'A letter from Sir Arthur Hesilrige'.
32. Northumberland Archives (NRA), M871; Morpeth St Mary.
33. Listen to the Soldiers – Oral Archive (DCRO).
34. J. Mabbitt, 'Archaeology, Revolution and the End of the Medieval English Town: Fortification and Discourse in Seventeenth Century Newcastle upon Tyne' (unpublished paper), p. 5.
35. Ibid.
36. Ibid., p. 6.
37. Ibid., p. 7.
38. Quoted in Ibid., p. 8.
39. Ibid., p. 9.
40. E. Mackenzie, *A Descriptive and Historical Account of the Town and County of Newcastle upon Tyne Including the Borough of Gateshead* (Newcastle: 1827), Vol. 1, p. 106.
41. Ibid.
42. Ibid.
43. Woodhorn Archives, Northumberland, M697; Newcastle St Nicholas.
44. 'A letter from Sir Arthur Hesilrige'.
45. Chamberlain's Accounts (1642–50), Tyne & Wear Archives, TW 543/18, p. 249.
46. Ibid., p. 251.
47. Ibid., p. 252.
48. Ibid., p. 257.
49. https://www.chroniclelive.co.uk/news/history/newcastle-witch-trials-1650-saw-10455524, retrieved 7 August 2018.

Chapter 6

1. Malcolm Canmore came once too often and was killed at Alnwick in 1093.
2. Most dramatically at the Battle of Neville's Cross in October 1346.
3. William waged ruthless war of the recalcitrant northerners from 1069–70; 'he created a desert and called it peace' (quote taken from Tacitus' history of his father-in-law, *On the life and character of Julius Agricola*.

4. Sir Nikolaus Pevsner and E. Williamson, *County Durham*, in 'the Buildings of England' series (Harmondsworth: Penguin, 1985), pp. 17–19.
5. https:llolivercromwell.net/English-civil-war-casualties/, retrieved 27 September 2018.
6. Gerrard et al., *Lost Lives*, p. 128.
7. Letter from Oliver Cromwell to the Honourable Sir Arthur Hesilrige at Newcastle or elsewhere, dated 5 September 1650, LRO: DG21/275/p, https://discovery.nationalarchives.gov.uk/browse/r/h/26746029-12ae-4e2e-bb23-e61f904d73f4, retrieved May 2018.
8. 29 March 1644 and 27 October 1644.
9. Henry (1618–48) was the brother of firebrand John.
10. Calendar of State Papers Domestic – Charles 1 (1631–44), 'A Continuance of Certain Special and Remarkable Passages', No. 2, 03–10. January 1644, https://www.british-history.ac.uk/search/series/cal-state-papers--domestic--chas1?page=1, retrieved May 2018.
11. 'Freeborn' John (1614–57) was an influential thinker and agitator whose works guided the later philosophers of the Enlightenment. In his own day he managed to quarrel with just about everybody.
12. *Dictionary of National Biography* and http://bcw-project.org/biography/sir-arthur-hesilrige, retrieved 27 September 2018.
13. Letter Oliver Cromwell to the Honourable Sir Arthur Hesilrige.
14. Ibid.
15. 'A Letter from Sir Arthur Hesilrige'.
16. Ibid.
17. Following the Restoration his estate was confiscated, in 1660, by the Sheriff of Durham. His widow was still living in Newcastle at that time; http://bcw-project.org/biography/john-blakiston, retrieved 27 September 2018; John Blakiston's sister Frances married John Cosin (1594–1672) who had been appointed Prebendary of Durham in 1624 and was later elected Bishop of Durham in December 1660 when he started extensive restoration of Durham Castle as his Palace (also woodwork in Sedgefield church).
18. Gerrard et al., *Lost Lives*, p. 132.
19. 'A letter from Sir Arthur Hesilrige'.
20. Ibid.
21. B. Shephard, *After Daybreak: the Liberation of Belsen 1945* (London: Pimlico, 2005), p. 34
22. Ibid., p. 37.
23. 'A letter from Sir Arthur Hesilrige'.
24. Gerrard et al., *Lost Lives*, p. 131.
25. Ibid.
26. Ibid.
27. Ibid.
28. Ibid., pp. 129–30.
29. Ibid., p. 131.
30. Ibid.
31. Research courtesy of John Malden.

32. Gerrard et al., *Lost Lives*, pp. 134–5.
33. Ibid.
34. Ibid.
35. Ibid.
36. Ibid.
37. Ibid.
38. Ibid.
39. Ibid.
38. 'A letter from Sir Arthur Hesilrige'.
39. Daniel Defoe, *Journal of the Plague Year: Dover Thrift Editions* (1722; London: Dover Publications Inc., 2003) whilst fictionalised is graphically realistic.
40. 'A letter from Sir Arthur Hesilrige'.
41. Ibid.

Chapter 7

1. D. Jordan and M. Walsh, *White Cargo* (Edinburgh: Mainstream Publishing Company, 2007), p. 12.
2. Robert Johnson, *The New Life of Virginea*, a broadsheet of 1612 dedicated to Smythe, cited in Jordan and Walsh, *White Cargo*, p. 57.
3. Cited in Jordan and Walsh, *White Cargo*, p. 13.
4. Walter Hart Blumenthal, *Brides from Bridewell: Female Felons Sent to Colonial America* (Rutland, VT: Charles E. Tuttle Co. Inc., 1962). https://archive.org/stream/bridesfrombridew00blum/bridcs frombridew00blum_djvu.txt, retrieved June 2018.
5. Ibid.
6. Richard P. Hallowell, *The Quaker invasion of Massachusetts* (Boston, MA: Houghton, Mifflin and Company, 1883), https://archive.org/details/quakerinvasionof00hal/page/100, retrieved July 2018, p. 24.
7. J.D. Butler, 'British Convicts Shipped to American Colonies', *American History Review*, 1896, Vol. 2, pp. 17–30, https://archive.org/details/jstor-1833611, retrieved May 2018.
8. 'The Number of Souls in the Province of Maryland in 1755', *Gentleman's Magazine*, 1764 (London: printed by F. Jeffries, etc., 1731–1907), https://babel.hathitrust.org/cgi/ssd?id=chi.19211453;seq=7, Hathi Trust, retrieved June 2018.
9. Blumenthal, *Brides from Bridewell*.
10. Linda A. Newson, 'The Demographic Collapse of Native Peoples of the Americas, 1492–1650', *Proceedings of the British Academy*, Vol. 81 (The British Academy, 1993), pp. 247–88.
11. Mary Draper, 'Timbering and Turtling: The Maritime Hinterlands of Early Modern British Caribbean Cities', *Early American Studies: An Interdisciplinary Journal*, 15 (4), pp. 769–800.
12. Jenny Shaw, *Everyday Life in the Early English Caribbean: Irish, Africans, and the Construction of Difference*, Early American Places series (Athens, GA: University of Georgia Press, 2013), pp. 30–45.

13. James Walvin, *Sugar: The world corrupted, from slavery to obesity* (New York: Robinson, 2017).
14. Ibid., p. 109.
15. Blumenthal, *Brides from Bridewell*.
16. Jordan and Walsh, *White Cargo*, p. 161 (citing Abbot Emerson Smith, *Colonists in Bondage: White Servitude and Convict Labour in America, 1607–1776* (Chapel Hill, NC: University of North Carolina Press for Institute of Early American History and Culture, 1947)).
17. Avihu Zakai, *Exile and Kingdom: History and Apocalypse in the Puritan Migration to America* (Cambridge: Cambridge University Press, 2002), p. 212.
18. Heather Yuill, 'Dunbar tales', presentation on Dunbar history and mythology, Durham, 10 August 2018.

Chapter 8
1. Gerrard et al., *Lost Lives*, pp. 49–80, 135–51.
2. Ibid., p. 44.
3. Ibid., p. 33.
4. Ibid., p. 94.
5. Ibid., p. 54.
6. Robert Jonking came from the Scottish town of Brechin where parish records list plague as a cause of death for many in 1647. Alan D. Junkins, 'The Parish of Brechin in the 17th Century' (Junkins Family Association Newsletter no. 7, Winter 1992), http://junkinsfamilyassociation.wikidot.com/robert-at-dunbar, retrieved May 2017.
7. Gerrard et al., *Lost Lives*, p. 104.
8. Ibid., p. 138.
9. Ibid., p. 140.
10. Cited in Lynch, *Scotland*, pp. 178–9.
11. Quoted in A. Herman, *The Scottish Enlightenment* (London: HarperCollins, 2001), p. 10.
12. Scottish Flag Trust, 'The Legend of the Saltire', https://scottishflagtrust.com/the-flag-heritage-centre/the-legend-of-the-saltire/, retrieved October 2018.

Chapter 9
1. Post-performance question-and-answer session with Chris Gerrard at showing of the play about the Scottish prisoners at the Alphabetti Theatre in Newcastle, 28 June 2018.
2. Dan Hamilton, 'You Can Go Home Again, A Guest Post by Dan Hamilton', https://johnhamiltonofcharlestown.com/2015/04/08/you-can-go-home-again-a-guest-post-by-dan-hamilton/, retrieved June 2018.
3. Teresa Rust, 'New York Governor is Scottish POW Descendant', http://scottishprisonersofwar.com/2013/05/15/new-york-governor-is-scottish-pow-descendant/, retrieved September 2018.

4. Walter Kendall Watkins, *The Ochterloney Family Of Scotland, And Boston, In New England: The Scotch Ancestry Of Maj.-Gen. Sir David Ochterloney, Bart., A Native Of Boston, In New England* (Boston, MA: printed for the author, 1902; repr. from New-Eng. Historical and Genealogical Register for April, 1902), https://archive.org/stream/ochterloneyfamil00watk/ochterloneyfamil00watk_djvu.txt, retrieved May 2018.

5. http://junkinsfamilyassociation.wikidot.com/unity-scotts, retrieved June 2018.

6. Peter Grant Generation Report, compiled by Sandi Lee Craig née Grant, using material provided by Edward Allen Cooper, http://petergrantthescot.com/peter-grant-generation-report/, retrieved November 2018.

7. Watkins, *The Ochterloney Family Of Scotland*.

8. Ibid.

9. Ibid.

10. Dennis Bell, 'The Battle of Dunbar', http://www.krystalrose.com/kim/BEALL/dunbar.html, retrieved June 2018.

11. Suffolk Deeds, Liber I (Boston, MA, Rockwell and Churchill, City Printers, 1880), https://archive.org/stream/suffolkdeedslib07hassgoog#page/n4/mode/1up, retrieved June 2018.

12. Everett Schermerhorn Stackpole, Lucien Thompson and Winthrop Smith Meserve, *History of the town of Durham, New Hampshire (Oyster River Plantation) with genealogical notes* (Durham, NH: pub. by vote of the town, 1913), https://archive.org/details/historyoftownofd01stac_0/page/n9, retrieved July 2018.

13. Jean Seeley's information on her ancestor James Warren, https://www.findagrave.com/memorial/180248757/james-warren, retrieved July 2018.

14. Michele Fuller, email June 2018.

15. Stackpole et al., *History of the town of Durham, New Hampshire*.

16. Robert E. Thomas, 'The English Civil Wars: How The First Macthomas Clansmen Came To America', https://www.genealogy.com/forum/surnames/topics/macthomas/44/, retrieved October 2018.

17. Suffolk Deeds, Liber I.

18. Ibid.

19. Ibid.

20. Article written using research by descendant, Bob Scott, 'Descendants of William Furbush', https://www.genealogy.com/ftm/h/u/n/Royce-M-Hunt/GENE10-0001.html, retrieved June 2018.

21. B. Craig Stinson, 'William Furbish (1631–1694), How a Scottish Prisoner of War became One of My first American Ancestors', ed. Teresa (Hamilton/Pepper) Rust (July 2016), https://scottishprisonersofwar.com/william-furbish-1631-1694-by-craig-stinson/, retrieved July 2019.

22. Hallowell, *The Quaker invasion of Massachusetts*, p. 100.

23. Ibid.

24. Stinson, 'William Furbish (1631–1694)'.

25. Article written using research by descendant, Scott, 'Descendants of William Furbush'.

26. Ibid.
27. Fred C. Pierce, *Forbes And Forbush Genealogy; The Descendants Of Daniel Forbush, Who Came from Scotland About the Year 1655, and Settled in Marlborough, Mass., in 1675* (Chicago, Il: 1892), p. 20, https://archive.org/details/forbesforbushgen92pier/page/20, retrieved June 2018.
28. Email from Alice Waters, June 2018.
29. Michelle Boyd, 'Alexander and Catherine Innes', http://oliveandeliza.com/ennis/ennis/alexanderandcatherine.html, retrieved June 2018.
30. William B. Saxbe, 'Four Fathers for William Ennis of Kingston: A Collective Review', *New York Genealogical and Biographical Record*, Vol. 129, No. 4, October 1998, pp. 227–38.
31. Nathaniel B. Shurtleff (ed.), *Record of the Colony of New Plymouth in New England*, 12 vols (Boston, MA: William White, 1855–61), Vol. 3, 110–12. Cited in Boyd, 'Alexander and Catherine Innes'.
32. Abby Chandler, 'At the Magistrate's Discretion: Sexual Crime and New England Law, 1636–1718', *Electronic Theses and Dissertations* (2008), http://digitalcommons.library.umaine.edu/etd/114, retrieved October 2018.
33. Ibid.
34. Sandi Lee Craig and Edward Allen Cooper (both descendants), 'Peter Grant Generation Report', http://petergrantthescot.com/peter-grant-generation-report/, retrieved June 2018.
35. Ibid.
36. Leola Grant Bushman, *Peter Grant, Scotch Exile, Kittery and Berwick, Maine: Genealogy* (privately published, 1976), cited in 'Peter Grant Generation Report'.
37. Ibid., pp. 1–2.
38. Jon Grant – descendant, https://scottishprisonersofwar.com/david-hamilton-on-the-john-and-sara-passenger-list/, retrieved June 2018.
39. Email from Doreen Leahy, July 2018.
40. Ibid.
41. Becky Richardson, descendant of Thomas Ranney, email, July 2018.
42. Charles Collard Adams, *Middletown Upper Houses: A History Of The North Society Of Middletown, Connecticut, From 1650 To 1800, With Genealogical And Biographical Chapters On Early Families And A Full Genealogy Of The Ranney Family* (New York: The Grafton Press, 1908), http://www.archive.org/stream/middletownupperh00adamo/middletownupperh00adamo_djvu.txt, retrieved July 2018.
43. Becky Richardson, email, July 2018.
44. Kim Bealls Beall History Pages, http://www.krystalrose.com/kim/BEALL/ninian1.html, retrieved July 2018.
45. Michelle Start, descendant of Ninian Beall, email July 2018.
46. Kim Bealls Beall History Pages.
47. Ibid.
48. Phil Swan, descendant of William Thompson, email, July 2018. Banks had delivered a paper on the subject in 1925, see, *Proceedings of the Massachusetts*

Historical Society, Third Series, Vol. 61 (Oct., 1927–Jun., 1928; published by Massachusetts Historical Society, 1929), pp. 1–30.

49. W.W. Clayton and W. Woodford, *History of York County, Maine. With illustrations and biographical sketches of its prominent men and pioneers* (Philadelphia, PA: Everts & Peck, 1880), p. 315, https://archive.org/details/historyofyorkcou00clay/page/n509, retrieved July 2018.

50. Roger Spring, descendant of Duncan Bohannon, email, June 2018.

51. Ibid.

52. Bob Guy, descendant of James MacKall, email, July 2018.

53. Ray Rolla McCall, Esq., Captain and Armiger of Clan McCall (Caithness), Project Admin of the McCall Caithness Geographic DNA Project and Suzanne Wood, https://scottishprisonersofwar.com/james-mccall/, retrieved July 2018.

54. Eve Hiatt and Douglas Darling, descendant of George Darling, email, June 2018.

55. Scott Fair, descendant of George Darling, email, July 2018.

56. Marlene Lemmer Beeson, descendant of George Darling, email, July 2018.

57. Misty Scheidt, descendant of George Darling, email, June 2018.

58. Professor Chris Gerrard speaking to the *Northern Echo* on the day of the reburial, 18 May 2018, https://www.dur.ac.uk/news/newsitem/?itemno=34665, retrieved 29 October 2018.

Bibliography and Sources

Primary Sources

British Museum
Harleian 6844, fol.123

Durham County Record Office (DCRO)
'Listen to the Soldiers' oral history archive

East Lothian Council Archives
Under ref. B18/39/1, holds Accounts of losses sustained by the inhabitants and
burgh of Dunbar after the Cromwellian invasion of Scotland, including accounts
of free quarterings and of provisions supplied to the English garrisons, 1650–1

Leicester Record Office (LRO)
Letter: Oliver Cromwell to the Honourable Sir Arthur Hesilridge at Newcastle
or elsewhere, dated 5 September 1650, DG21/275/p, https://discovery.
nationalarchives.gov.uk/browse/r/h/26746029-12ae-4e2e-bb23-e61f904d73f4,
retrieved May 2018

Northumberland Archives (NRA)
Blackett Family Records
Copies of Letters from Francis Anderson and Others (Richardson, Reprints)
Delaval Family Records, NRA/1DE/ NRA/ 2DE, estate, family and personal and
business papers of the Delaval family of Seaton Delaval, Northumberland

Records of the Parliament of Scotland
1641/8/206: Act regarding the king's majesty's rents uplifted by warrant of the
committee of estates for the public use
A1650/11/11, Act in favour of Dame Margaret Fraser, lady Gleneagles and John
Haldane, her son, https://www.rps.ac.uk/, retrieved June 2018.

Scottish National Archives
E28/49 H.M. Receivers: General payments 1660
E28/45 H.M. Receivers: Charge by Sheriffs' Roll 1660–1668
E28/50 H.M. Receivers: Fees, pensions etc. 1661
E28/57 H.M. Receivers: Miscellaneous payments 1661–1662
E28/44 H.M. Receivers: Accounts of compositions 1661–1667
E28/46 H.M. Receivers: Charge by property roll etc. 1661–1667
E28/48 H.M. Receivers: Lists of payments etc. 1661–1668

E28/43 H.M. Receivers: Accounts of charge and discharge 1661–1668
E28/51 H.M. Receivers: Fees, pensions etc. 1662
E28/47 H.M. Receivers: Charge by burgh roll 1662–1663
E28/52 H.M. Receivers: Fees, pensions etc. 1663
E28/58 H.M. Receivers: Miscellaneous payments 1663–1664
E28/53 H.M. Receivers: Fees, pensions etc. 1664
E28/54 H.M. Receivers: Fees, pensions etc. 1665
E28/59 H.M. Receivers: Miscellaneous payments 1665–1666
E28/55 H.M. Receivers: Fees, pensions etc. 1666

Tyne and Wear Archives
NCA Chamberlain's Accounts (1642–50), TW 543/27 and TW 543/18

Miscellaneous
Barriffe, W., *Military discipline: or, The young artillery man. Wherein is discoursed and showne the postures both of musket and pike: the exactest ways, & c. together with the motions which are to be used, in the exercising of a foot -company. With divers and severall formes and figures of battell* … (London: printed and are to be sould by Andrew Kembe at St Margarets Hill in Southwark, 6th edn, 1661)
Calendar of State Papers Domestic – Charles 1 (1631–44), 'A Continuance of Certain Special and Remarkable Passages', No. 2, 03–10. January 1644, https://www.british-history.ac.uk/search/series/cal-state-papers--domestic--chas1?page=1, retrieved May 2018
Canne, John, *Emanuel, or, God with us. [microform] Werein is set forth Englands late great victory over the Scots armie, in a battle at Dunbar, Septemb. 3. 1650. And by many particulars of Gods acting and appearing then for us, it is certaine (and so much is clearly proved) that our armies marching into Scotland, and the wars undertaken and prosecuted against that nation, to be upon grounds of justice and necessity, as the Parliament of England hath declared. Also here is shewed, how grosly the Covenant is abus'd, and what an idoll it is now made. With the fraud and falshood of the Scots, and their kings hypocrisie and dissimulation* (London: printed by Matthew Simmons next doore to the Golden Lyon in Aldersgate street, 1650), https://catalogue.nla.gov.au/Record/1288263, retrieved March 2018
Diary of Mr. Robert Douglas when with the Scots Army in England (Edinburgh: 1833)
'Favver', *The Siege and Storming of Newcastle* (Newcastle upon Tyne: 1889)
Fenwicke, Lieutenant Colonel John, *Christ ruling in midst of his enemies; or, Some first fruits of the Churches deliverance, budding forth out of the crosse and sufferings, [microform] and some remarkable deliverances of a twentie yeeres sufferer, and now a souldier of Jesus Christ; together, with Secretarie Windebanks letters to Sr. Jacob Ashley and the Maior of Newcastle, through which the violent prosecutions of the common adversaries to exile and banishment, are very transparent. Wherein also the reader shall find in severall passages, publike and particular, some notable encouragements to wade through difficulties for the advancing of the great designe of Christ, for setting up of His kingdome, and the ruine of Antichrist* (London: printed for Benjamin Allen in Pope's-head Alley, 1643)
Gray, William, *Chorographia or a survey of Newcastle upon Tine* (Newcastle: printed by S.B., 1649), https://archive.org/details/chorographiaora00graygoog/page/n4, retrieved March 2018

'His Majesties Passing Through the Scots Army', pamphlet (1644)

A History of Northumberland, issued under the direction of the Northumberland County History Committee, Vol. ix, *History of Northumberland*, http://www.archive.org/stream/historyofnorthum09nort/historyofnorthum09nort_djvu.txt, retrieved March 2018

Hodgson, Captain, *Original Memoirs written during the Great Civil War being the life of Sir Henry Slingsby and Memoirs of Captain Hodgson*, ed. Walter Scott (Edinburgh: Arch, Constable & Co., 1806)

'The Journal of Sir William Brererton 1635 in North Country Diaries', ed. J.C. Hodgeson, Surtees Society, Vol. 124 (1915)

'A letter from the Corporation of Newcastle upon Tyne to the Mayor and Aldermen of Berwick', J. Raine, *Archaeologia Aeliana*, 1.2

'A letter from Sir Arthur Hesilrige, to the honorable committee of the Councel of State for Irish and Scotish affairs at White-Hall, concerning the Scots prisoners. Die Veneris, 8 Novembr. 1650. Ordered by the Parliament, that this letter be forthwith printed and published. Hen: Scobell, Cleric. Parliamenti. London: Printed by Edward Husband and John Field, printers to the Parliament of England, 1650', https://quod.lib.umich.edu/cgi/t/text/text-idx?c=eebo;idno=A86092.0001.001, retrieved February 2018

Newcastle upon Tyne Record Series, Vol. 1, *Extracts from the Newcastle Council Minute Book 1639–1656*, ed. M.H. Dodds (Newcastle upon Tyne: printed for the Newcastle upon Tyne Records Committee by Northumberland Press, 1920)

Newcastle upon Tyne Record Series, Vol. 3, *The Register of Freemen of Newcastle upon Tyne from the Corporation, Guild and Admission Books chiefly of the Seventeenth Century*, ed. M.H. Dodds (Newcastle upon Tyne: 1923)

An Ordinance with Severall Propositions 1643: in Reprints of Rare Tracts & Imprints of Antient Manuscripts, &c: Chiefly Illustrative of the History of the Northern Counties; and Printed at the Press of M. A. Richardson, Newcastle, Volume 1 (Newcastle upon Tyne: Mr M. Richardson, 1847)

Pedigrees recorded at the heralds' visitations of the counties of Cumberland and Westmorland: made by Richard St. George, Norry, king of arms in 1615, and by William Dugdale, Norry, king of arms in 1666 ([1891?]), http://www.archive.org/details/pedigreesrecorde00sainrich, retrieved June 2018

Pedigrees Recorded at the Herald's Visitations of the County of Northumberland [1615 and 1666], R. St George (Newcastle upon Tyne: Browne and Browne, 1891), http://www.archive.org/details/pedigreesrecorde00sainrich, retrieved May 2018

'The Taking of Newcastle or Newes from the Army' (Edinburgh, 1644), Letter from Lord Leven to the Lord High Chancellor of Scotland describing the siege and seizure of Newcastle in 1655', in Henry Bourne, *The history of Newcastle upon Tyne: or, The ancient and present state of that town* (Newcastle upon Tyne: J. White, 1736), https://archive.org/details/historyofnewcast00bour/page/232, retrieved June 2018

A True experimentall and exact relation upon that famous and renowned Siege of Newcastle, William Lithgow (Edinburgh: printed by Robert Bryson, 1645)

The Visitation of Northumberland in 1615, R. St George and George W. Marshall (eds) (London: 1878)

Secondary Sources

Books

Adams, Charles Collard, *Middletown Upper Houses: A History Of The North Society Of Middletown, Connecticut, From 1650 To 1800, With Genealogical And Biographical Chapters On Early Families And A Full Genealogy Of The Ranney Family* (New York: The Grafton Press, 1908), http://www.archive.org/stream/middletownupperh00adamo/middletownupperh00adamo_djvu.txt, retrieved July 2018

Ashley, M., *The English Civil War* (London: Thames & Hudson, 1978)

Ashworth, N. and M. Pegg, *History of the British Coal Industry* (Oxford: Oxford University Press, 1986)

Blumenthal, Walter Hart, *Brides from Bridewell: Female Felons Sent to Colonial America* (Rutland, VT: Charles E. Tuttle Co. Inc., 1962), https://archive.org/details/bridesfrombridew00blum/page/n7, retrieved June 2018

Bourne, H., *The History of Newcastle u[pon] Tyne; or the ancient and present state of that town* (Newcastle upon Tyne: 1736)

Brand, J., *The History and Antiquities of the Town and County of Newcastle upon Tyne* (London: 1789)

Buchan, J., *Oliver Cromwell* (London: Hodder & Stoughton, 1934)

Burne, A.H. and P. Young, *The Great Civil War 1642–1646* (London: Eyre and Spottiswood, 1959)

Bushman, Leola Grant, *Peter Grant, Scotch Exile, Kittery and Berwick, Maine: Genealogy* (privately published, 1976)

Clarendon, Edward Hyde, Earl of, *History of the Rebellion and Civil Wars in England*, ed. W.D. Macray (Oxford: Clarendon Press, 1888)

Clayton, W.W. and W. Woodford, *History of York County, Maine. With illustrations and biographical sketches of its prominent men and pioneers* (Philadelphia, PA: Everts & Peck, 1880), https://archive.org/details/historyofyorkcou00clay/page/n509, retrieved July 2018

Craig, Sandi Lee and Edward Allen Cooper (both descendants), 'Peter Grant Generation Report', http://petergrantthescot.com/peter-grant-generation-report/, retrieved June 2018

Craster, H.H.E., *The Parochial Chapelries of Earsdon and Horton* (Newcastle upon Tyne: Andrew Reid & Co., 1909)

Cullen, K.J., *Famine in Scotland, the 'ill years' of the 1690s* (Edinburgh: Edinburgh University Press, 2010)

Cooke, D., *The Forgotten Battle; The Battle of Adwalton Moor* (Heckmondwike: Battlefield Press, 1996)

Defoe, Daniel, *Journal of the Plague Year: Dover Thrift Editions* (1722; London: Dover Publications Inc., 2003)

Daniel Defoe, *Journal of the Plague Year: Dover Thrift Editions* (1722; London: Dover Publications Inc., 2003)

Douglas, W.S., *Cromwell's Scotch Campaigns 1650–1651* (London: N&M repr., 2010)

Dunn, Richard S., *Sugar and Slaves: The Rise of the Planter Class in the English West Indies, 1624–1713* (published for the Omohundro Institute of Early American History and Culture, Williamsburg, VA: 2000)

Firth, C.H., *Cromwell's Army* (3rd edn, London: University Paperbacks/Methuen, 1921)

Firth, C.H. (ed.), *Life of William Cavendish, Duke of Newcastle by Margaret, Duchess of Newcastle* (London: George Routledge and Sons, 1890)

Forster, S., *The Long Argument: English Puritanism and the Shaping of New England Culture 1570–1700* (Chapel Hill: published for the Institute of Early American History and Culture, Williamsburg, VA, by the University of North Carolina Press, 1991)

Furgol, E., *A Regimental History of the Covenanting Armies 1639–1651* (Edinburgh: John Donald, 2001)

Gardiner, S.R., *History of the Great Civil War 1642–1649* (London: Longmans, Green, and Co., 1893)

Gaunt, P., *The Cromwellian Gazetteer* (Stroud: Sutton Publishing, 1987)

Gaunt, P., *The English Civil Wars 1642–1651*, Essential Histories series, 58 (Oxford: Osprey, 2003)

Gerrard, C. with P. Greaves, A. Millard, R. Annis and A. Caffell, *Lost Lives, New Voices – Unlocking the Stories of the Scottish Soldiers from the Battle of Dunbar 1650* (Oxford: Oxbow Books, 2018)

Graves, C.P., R. Annis, A.C. Caffell, C.M. Gerrard and A.R. Millard, *The Dunbar Diaspora: background to the Battle of Dunbar, and the aftermath of the battle*, Project Report (Durham: Durham University, 2016), http://dro.dur.ac.uk/20941/, retrieved December 2016

Hallowell, Richard P., *The Quaker invasion of Massachusetts* (Boston, MA: Houghton, Mifflin and Company, 1883), https://archive.org/details/quakerinvasionof00hal/page/100, retrieved July 2018

Harrington, P. and D. Spedatiere, *English Civil War Fortifications 1642–1651*, Fortress series, 9 (Oxford: Osprey, 2003)

Haythornthwaite, P., *The English Civil War 1642–1651* (London: Weidenfeld Military, 1994)

Henry, C., *English Civil War Artillery 1642–1651*, New Vanguard series, 108 (Oxford: Osprey, 2005)

Herman, A., *The Scottish Enlightenment* (London: HarperCollins, 2001)

Howell, R., *Newcastle upon Tyne and the Puritan Revolution: A Study of the Civil War in North England* (Oxford: Oxford University Press, 1967)

Hunter-Blair, P., *The Mayors and Lord Mayors of Newcastle upon Tyne 1216–1940 And the Sheriffs of the County of Newcastle upon Tyne 1399–1940* (Newcastle upon Tyne: Northumberland Press, 1940)

Jordan, D. and M. Walsh, *White Cargo* (Edinburgh: Mainstream Publishing Company, 2007)

Kishlanskey, M.A., *The Rise of the New Model Army* (Cambridge: Cambridge University Press, 1979)

Lawson, C.C.P., *History of the Uniforms of the British Army*, 5 vols (London: Peter Davies, Ltd, Kaye & Ward, and Norman Military Publications Ltd, 1940), Vol. 1

Lynch, M., *Scotland, A New History* (London: Pimlico, 1997)

Mackenzie, E., *A Descriptive and Historical Account of the Town and County of Newcastle upon Tyne* (Newcastle upon Tyne: 1827)

Middlebrook, S., *Newcastle upon Tyne its Growth and Achievement* (Newcastle upon Tyne: *Newcastle Journal*, 1950)

Morley, J., *Oliver Cromwell* (London: Macmillan, 1901)

Morrah, P., *Prince Rupert of the Rhine* (London: Constable, 1976)

Murray, W.H., *Rob Roy MacGregor* (Edinburgh: Canongate, 2000)

Pevsner, Sir Nikolaus, *Northumberland*, in the 'Buildings of England' series (London: Penguin, rev. edn, 1992)

Pevsner, Sir Nikolaus and E. Williamson, *County Durham*, in 'the Buildings of England' series (Harmondsworth: Penguin, 1985)

Pierce, Fred C., *Forbes And Forbush Genealogy; The Descendants Of Daniel Forbush, Who Came from Scotland About the Year 1655, and Settled in Marlborough, Mass., in 1675* (Chicago, Il: 1892), https://archive.org/details/forbesforbushgen92pier/page/20, retrieved June 2018

Potter, R. and G.A. Embleton, *The English Civil War 1642–1651* (London: Allmark Publishing, 1973)

Pugh, R.J.M., *Swords, Loaves and Fishes, A History of Dunbar* (Balerno: Harlaw Heritage, 2003 (2015 edn))

Purkiss, D., *The English Civil War* (London: HarperCollins, 2006)

Ranney Memorial and Historical Association, Cromwell, Conn. [from old catalog]., Founders, fathers and patriots of Middletown Upper Houses (The Stewart printing company, Middletown, Conneticut, 1903), https://archive.org/details/foundersfathersp00rann/page/n6, retrieved July 2018

Reese, P., *Cromwell's Masterstroke* (Barnsley: Pen & Sword, 2006)

Reid, S., *All the King's Armies – A Military History of the English Civil War 1642–1651* (Staplehurst: Howell Press Inc., 1998)

——, *Like Hungry Wolves* (Marlborough: Crowood Press, 1998)

——, *Scots Armies of the 17th Century (1) The Army of the Covenant 1639–51* (Newthorpe: Partizan Press, 2001)

——, *Crown, Covenant and Cromwell – the Civil Wars in Scotland 1639–1651* (London: Frontline, 2012)

Reid, S. and G. Turner, *Scots Armies of the English Civil Wars*, Men-at-Arms series, 33 (Oxford: Osprey, 1999)

Roberts, K. and A. McBride, *Soldiers of the English Civil War (1) Infantry*, Elite series, 25 (Oxford: Osprey, 1989)

Roots, I., *The Great Rebellion* (London: B.T. Batsford, 1966)

Rushworth, J., *Historical Collections of Private Passages of State, Weighty Matters in Law, Remarkable Proceedings in Five Parliaments. Beginning the Sixteenth Year of King James, Anno 1618, and Ending the Fifth Year of King Charls, Anno 1629, Volume 2 Collection of Private Passages of State 1629–1638*, 5 vols (London: J.A., printed for M. Wooten at the Three Pigeons against the Inner Temple Gate at Fleet Street and G. Conyers at the Golden Ring on Ludgate Hill, 1686), Vol. 2

Sadler, D.J., *Battle for Northumbria* (Newcastle: Bridge Studios, 1988)

——, *Scottish Battles* (Edinburgh: Canongate, 1996)

Seymour, W., *Battles in Britain*, Vol. 2 (London: Sidgwick & Jackson, 1975)

Shaw, Jenny, *Everyday Life in the Early English Caribbean: Irish, Africans, and the Construction of Difference*, Early American Places series (Athens, GA: University of Georgia Press, 2013)

Shephard, B., *After Daybreak: the Liberation of Belsen 1945* (London: Pimlico, 2005)

Shurtleff, Nathaniel B. (ed.), *Record of the Colony of New Plymouth in New England*, 12 vols (Boston, MA: William White, 1855–61)

Spencer, Charles, *To Catch a King: Charles II's Great Escape* (London: William Collins, 2007)

Stackpole, Everett Schermerhorn, Lucien Thompson and Winthrop Smith Meserve, *History of the town of Durham, New Hampshire (Oyster River Plantation) with genealogical notes* (Durham, NH: pub. by vote of the town, 1913), https://archive. org/details/historyoftownofd01stac_0/page/n9, retrieved July 2018

Stevenson, David, *Revolution and Counter-Revolution in Scotland 1644–51: Issue 4 of Royal Historical Society studies in history series* (London: The Royal Historical Society, 1977)

Suffolk Deeds, Liber I (Boston, MA: Rockwell and Churchill, City Printers, 1880), https://archive.org/stream/suffolkdeedslib07hassgoog#page/n4/mode/1up, retrieved June 2018

Terry, C.S., *The Life and Campaigns of Alexander Leslie* (London: Longman Green, 1899)

——, *The Army of the Covenant*, 2 vols (Edinburgh: printed by T. & A. Constable for the Scottish History Society, 1917)

Tincey, J. and A. McBride, *Soldiers of the English Civil War (2) Cavalry*, Elite series, 27 (Oxford: Osprey, 1990)

Tincey, J. and G. Turner, *Marston Moor 1644*, Campaign series, 119 (Oxford: Osprey, 2003)

Trevelyan, G.M., *English Social History a Review of Six Centuries – Chaucer to Queen Victoria* (London: Longmans, 1946)

Tucker, J. and L.S. Winstock (eds), *The English Civil War; A Military Handbook* (London: Stackpole, 1972)

Walvin, James, *Sugar: The world corrupted, from slavery to obesity* (New York: Robinson, 2017)

Warburton, E., *Memoirs of Prince Rupert and the Cavaliers* (London: R. Bentley, 1849)

Watkins, Walter Kendall, *The Ochterloney Family Of Scotland, And Boston, In New England: The Scotch Ancestry Of Maj.-Gen. Sir David Ochterloney, Bart., A Native Of Boston, In New England* (Boston, MA: printed for the author, 1902; repr. from New-Eng. Historical and Genealogical Register for April, 1902), https:// archive.org/stream/ochterloneyfamil00watk/ochterloneyfamil00watk_djvu. txt, retrieved May 2018

Wedgwood, C.V., *The King's Peace* (London: Collins, 1955)

——, *The King's War* (London: Collins, 1958)

——, *The Trial of Charles I* (London: Collins, 1964)

Wenham, P., *The Great and Close Siege of York, 1644* (Kineton: Roundwood Press, 1970)

Wilson, C.A., *Food and Drink in Britain* (London: Penguin (Peregrine Books), 1976)

Woolrych, A., *Battles of the English Civil War* (London: B.T. Batsford Ltd, 1961)

Wormald, J., *Court, Kirk & Community 1470–1625* (Edinburgh: Edinburgh University Press, 1991)

——, *Civil War England* (London: Osprey, 1981)

——, *Marston Moor 1644* (Kineton: Roundwood Press, 1970)

——, *The English Civil War Armies* (London: Osprey, 1973)

Young, Brigadier Peter and W. Emberton, *Sieges of the Great Civil War* (London: Bell & Hyman, 1978)

Young, P. and M. Rolfe, *The English Civil War Armies*, Men-at-Arms series, 14 (Oxford: Osprey, 1994)

Zakai, Avihu, *Exile and Kingdom: History and Apocalypse in the Puritan Migration to America* (Cambridge: Cambridge University Press, 2002)

Chapters, Articles and Theses

Andrews, G., 'Acts of the High Commission Court within the Diocese of Durham', Surtees Society, Vol. 34 (1858)

Butler, J.D., 'British Convicts Shipped to American Colonies', *American History Review*, 1896, Vol. 2, pp. 17–30, https://archive.org/details/jstor-1833611, retrieved May 2018

Chandler, Abby, 'At the Magistrate's Discretion: Sexual Crime and New England Law, 1636–1718', *Electronic Theses and Dissertations* (2008), http://digitalcommons.library.umaine.edu/etd/114, retrieved October 2018

Como, D.R.,'Women, Prophecy, and Authority in Early Stuart Puritanism', *The Huntington Library Quarterly*, Vol. 61, No. 2 (University of California Press, 1998), pp. 203–22, http://www.jstor.org/stable/3817798, retrieved June 2018

Draper, Mary, 'Timbering and Turtling: The Maritime Hinterlands of Early Modern British Caribbean Cities', *Early American Studies: An Interdisciplinary Journal*, 15 (4), pp. 769–800

Gaunt, P., 'Cromwell Day, 2000; the Battle of Dunbar and Cromwell's Scottish Campaign', *Cromwelliana – the Journal of the Cromwell Association*, 2001

'The Number of Souls in the Province of Maryland in 1755', *Gentleman's Magazine*, 1764 (London: printed by F. Jeffries, etc., 1731–1907), https://babel.hathitrust.org/cgi/ssd?id=chi.19211453;seq=7, Hathi Trust, retrieved June 2018

de Groot, Jerome, 'Chorographia: Newcastle and Royalist Identity in the late 1640's', in *The Seventeenth Century*, Vol. viii, issue 1 (Manchester University Press, April 2003), http://www.manchesteruniversitypress.co.uk/uploads/docs/180061.pdf, retrieved June 2018

Junkins, Alan D., 'The Parish of Brechin in the 17th Century' (Junkins Family Association Newsletter no. 7, Winter 1992), http://junkinsfamilyassociation.wikidot.com/robert-at-dunbar, retrieved May 2017

Langton, J., 'Residential Patterns in pre Industrial Cities Some Case Studies from Seventeenth Century Britain', in *The Tudor and Stuart Town, 1530–1688*, Readers in English Urban History, ed. J. Barry (London: Routledge, 1990)

Mabbit, J., 'Archaeology, Revolution and the End of the Medieval English Town: Fortification and Discourse in Seventeenth Century Newcastle upon Tyne' (unpublished paper)

Newson, Linda A., 'The Demographic Collapse of Native Peoples of the Americas, 1492–1650', *Proceedings of the British Academy*, Vol. 81 (The British Academy, 1993), pp. 247–88

Newton, D., 'Doleful Dumpes: Northumberland and the Borders 1580–1625', in *Northumberland, History and Identity*, ed. R. Colls (Bognor Regis: Phillimore & Co., 2007)

Saxbe, William B., 'Four Fathers for William Ennis of Kingston: A Collective Review', *New York Genealogical and Biographical Record*, Vol. 129, No. 4, October 1998, pp. 227–38

Seel, G., 'The Scots in England 1640–1651' (*History Review*, Issue 25, September 1996), https://www.historytoday.com/graham-seel/scots-england-1640–1651, retrieved May 2018

Terry, C.S., 'The Scottish Campaign in Northumberland and Durham Between January and June 1644, *Archaeologia Aeliana*, 2nd Series, Vol. 21, 1899

——, 'The Siege of Newcastle by the Scots in 1644', *Archaeologia Aeliana*, 2nd Series, Vol. 21, 1899

Yuill, Heather, 'Dunbar tales', presentation on Dunbar history and mythology, Durham, 10 August 2018

Internet Sources

Boyd, Michelle, 'Alexander and Catherine Innes', http://oliveandeliza.com/ennis/ennis/alexanderandcatherine.html, retrieved June 2018

Hamilton, Dan, 'You Can Go Home Again, A Guest Post by Dan Hamilton', https://johnhamiltonofcharlestown.com/2015/04/08/you-can-go-home-again-a-guest-post-by-dan-hamilton/, retrieved June 2018

Rust, Teresa, 'New York Governor is Scottish POW Descendant', http://scottishprisonersofwar.com/2013/05/15/new-york-governor-is-scottish-pow-descendant/, retrieved September 2018

Scott, Bob, 'Descendants of William Furbush', https://www.genealogy.com/ftm/h/u/n/Royce-M-Hunt/GENE10-0001.html, retrieved June 2018

Scottish Flag Trust, 'The Legend of the Saltire', https://scottishflagtrust.com/the-flag-heritage-centre/the-legend-of-the-saltire/, retrieved October 2018

Stinson, B. Craig, 'William Furbish (1631–1694), How a Scottish Prisoner of War became One of My first American Ancestors', ed. Teresa (Hamilton/Pepper) Rust (July 2016), https://scottishprisonersofwar.com/william-furbish-1631–1694-by-craig-stinson/, retrieved July 2019

Thomas, Robert E., 'The English Civil Wars: How The First Macthomas Clansmen Came To America', https://www.genealogy.com/forum/surnames/topics/macthomas/44/, retrieved October 2018

http://www.bbc.co.uk/news/uk-england-tyne-42311397, retrieved June 2018

http://bcw-project.org/military/confederate-war/dungans-hill, retrieved June 2018

https://archive.org/stream/bridesfrombridew00blum/bridesfrombridew00blum_djvu.txt https://www.chroniclelive.co.uk/news/history/newcastle-witch-trials-1650-saw-10455524, retrieved June 2018

https://www.dur.ac.uk/archaeology/research/projects/europe/pg-skeletons/history/, retrieved 2 September 2015

http://www.eyewitnesstohistory.com/bataandeathmarch.htm, retrieved June 2018

https://www.history.com/topics/british-history/english-civil-wars, retrieved June 2018

https://olivercromwell.net/English-civil-war-casualties/, retrieved June 2018

http://old.seattletimes.com/html/northwestvoices/2018361896_sirotalets06.html, retrieved June 2018

http://www.olivercromwell.org/Letters_and_speeches/letters, retrieved June 2018

https://scottishprisonersofwar.com/david-hamilton-on-the-john-and-sara-passenger-list/, retrieved June 2018

Index